Create the Perfect
Sales Piece

➤ ROBERT W. BLY

Create the Perfect Sales Piece

How to Produce Brochures, Catalogs, Fliers, and Pamphlets

A WILEY PRESS BOOK
JOHN WILEY & SONS, INC.
New York • Chichester • Brisbane • Toronto • Singapore

Publisher: Stephen Kippur
Editor: Elizabeth G. Perry
Managing Editor: Katherine Schowalter
Design, Composition & Make-Up: Ganis & Harris, Inc.

Library of Congress Cataloging-in-Publication Data

Bly, Robert W.
  Create the perfect sales piece.

  Includes index.
      1. Advertising. 2. Catalogs. 3. Advertising
fliers. 4. Pamphlets. I. Title.
HF5823.B635   1985   659.13′2   85-12457
ISBN 0-471-82525-5

Printed in the United States of America

92 91 90 10 9 8 7 6 5 4

To Sharon and Richard Armstrong

Acknowledgments

There are two groups of people who helped make this book a reality, and I'd like to thank both of them.

First, there are those advertising professionals who specialize in creating successful promotional literature: John Mongelli, Tom Quirk, Terry Smith, Mark Braga, Lansing Moore, Steve Brown, Ed Marson, Mark Handler, Steve Isaac, Joel Friedlander, Bruce Thaler, Bruce Bloom, Bill Flanagan, Carolyn Keelen, Joe Lane, Don Kaufman, Martin Siegal, Nancy Agababian, John Chrzanowski, Ted Babcock, Len Lavenda, Ilene Beckerman, Fyrth Reckseit, and Ken Weissman. Working with them has taught me a lot about design, copywriting, and production.

Second, I thank the people and organizations who have graciously permitted me to reproduce examples of their work in this book:

Apple Bank for Savings
Barrett, Haentjens & Co.
Steve Brown
Caterpillar Lift Truck
Crane Co., Chempump Division
Susi Dugaw
George Duncan
Emergy Printing Co.
English Heritage Antiques
W. L. Gore & Associates, Inc.
IBM
Kristin Johnson
Herschell Gordon Lewis
Mars Mineral Corporation
Polaroid Corp.
Prentice-Hall, Inc.
RCA Communications
Stanley J. Robens
Rosemont Inc.

Finally, thanks to my editor, Betsy Perry, for her usual fine job in making this book much better than it was when it first crossed her desk, and to Ruth Cavin, Elizabeth Morse-Cluley, and Alan Ross for their helpful comments and suggestions.

Contents

Preface

Just about every company in business today needs some type of printed literature to establish credibility and provide information on its products or services.

You bought this book because you want to produce promotional literature for your organization, but you're not quite sure how to go about it. *Create the Perfect Sales Piece* provides step-by-step instructions for every phase of the job—from evaluating what type of sales literature you need, to planning and outlining your brochure, writing and design, illustration, photography, paste-up, and printing.

Create the Perfect Sales Piece is written for everybody who has to produce printed literature, including:

- Entrepreneurs and small-business owners who have to produce their own sales literature on limited budgets, without help from advertising agencies or other professionals
- Advertising and marketing managers at small, medium, and large corporations, who are responsible for producing sales literature within set budgets and tight deadlines
- Advertising agencies, public relations firms, graphic design studios, photographers, writers, illustrators, printers, and typographers—specialists who want to expand their knowledge beyond their specialties and understand all the steps involved in producing printed material
- Nonprofit organizations, schools, government agencies, trade associations, church committees, and any other group that needs to produce printed booklets and fliers to inform, educate, or sell

Create the Perfect Sales Piece tells you how to create printed literature that fits your product, your company, your image, and your budget. It can guide you in producing anything from a $100,000, 32-page corporate capabilities brochure to a $10 offset flier to be posted on the local community bulletin board.

Sample illustrations of different types of promotional literature are included to show you what works in design and layout—and what doesn't. The book also contains many other visual aids: a selection of typefaces, illustrations of folding and binding techniques, sketches of rough layouts, sample artwork and photography, plus a number of work sheets and checklists to help you design, budget, schedule, plan, and supervise the writing and production of your literature. Numerous case histories illustrate the problems others have encountered in producing promotional literature and show you how to overcome such stumbling blocks.

At each step along the way, the book tells you both how to do the job yourself and how to find, hire, and work with a professional when you can't.

If this book has a philosophy, it is that the appropriate literature for your business isn't necessarily the glossiest or the most expensive. The book's emphasis is on creating promotional literature that fits your product, your sales approach, your customers, and your budget. I assume you want to do this as economically as possible, and my approach is to point out ways of saving money at every stage.

Over the years, I've created just about every type of brochure imaginable for clients ranging from mom-and-pop operations to multinational conglomerates. These clients have included businesses from a wide variety of fields—from accounting to agriculture, computers to construction, publishing to pollution-control, and more. I tell you this, not to brag, but to let you know that *Create the Perfect Sales Piece* is based on years of experience, not on guesswork or secondhand research. The book is long on sound, practical, proven advice and short on theory. If you want to know how to produce clear, distinctive, persuasive literature at reasonable cost and with a minimum of trouble, you've come to the right place.

CHAPTER ONE

So You Think You Need Printed Literature!

A world of paper

A stockbroker phones a prospect to explain a new investment opportunity. The prospect is mildly interested but isn't ready to take the plunge. "Send me some literature on the fund," says the would-be investor, "and I'll give you a call when I'm ready to spend."

An executive secretary walks into her local delicatessen. "I'm looking for someone to cater our company's sales meeting next month," she explains to the counterman. "Do you have a catering menu I can take with me to show my boss?"

A management consultant visits a major insurance company and is asked for a client list, schedule of fees, and business card.

A high school senior starting to think about college sends for catalogs from the schools he might be interested in attending. The tone, look, and content of the catalogs play a major role in helping the student decide which schools to apply to—and which to rule out.

We live in a world of documentation, of paper, of establishing credibility. A friendly smile and a handshake aren't enough. We like to feel that we are dealing with people who are established in business, in the same way we prefer a brand name over brand X.

Of course, no amount of fancy brochures, business cards, streamlined logos, or colorful catalogs can guarantee that a job will be done well or that a product won't stop working five minutes after it has been purchased. Still, promotional literature does go a long way toward setting a professional business tone, one that adds a sense of credibility and stability to a business enterprise. Today, almost every business requires some form of sales literature to keep its products and services in the customer's mind, distinguish itself from the competition, and answer a prospective buyer's questions.

A brochure can do many things for you

Most organizations discover the need for printed literature as they conduct their daily business. Frequent requests for brochures force the seller to produce a booklet or flier to satisfy the customers' thirst for information.

But a brochure can do more than take up space in a customer's shopping bag or desk drawer. When executed and used correctly, your brochure can become a powerful tool for promoting your business.

Specifically, a brochure can:

Inform
Educate
Build image
Establish credibility
Sell (or help sell)
Screen prospects
Add value

In its most basic role, a brochure is a vehicle for providing information to prospects, customers, and others who want to know more about your product, process, program, system, service, company, idea, or plan. The brochure can be used to provide a basic education for the uninformed or to answer the specific questions a more knowledgeable prospect is likely to ask.

A brochure can also build image and establish credibility. Anybody can have business cards printed for $35 and claim to be a company. But a sales brochure establishes immediate credibility and says to your prospects, "This is a *real* business, not a fly-by-night organization."

By making deliberate choices about the look, quality, and tone of your brochure, you can transmit an image to the reader. A slick, glossy brochure packed with attractive color photographs conveys an image of size, prosperity, and corporate professionalism. But a black-and-white flier on ordinary offset paper may be more appropriate for a company that exterminates roaches and rats.

A brochure can do more than give information and build image. With strong selling copy that stresses the benefits and advantages of a product or service, a brochure can be as effective a sales tool as an ad, television commercial, or direct-mail campaign.

In addition to pulling in the right prospects, promotional literature can weed out the wrong ones. Let's face it: Your product or service isn't for everyone. Some buyers can't afford your price; other buyers are better off with a different type of product. Literature that defines the applications and limitations of your product or service screens out those inquiries that don't represent real prospects. And screening leads with a brochure is a lot cheaper than making sales calls.

Finally, promotional literature can add value to the product or service itself. For example, a purchasing agent may buy one brand of ball bearings over another, not because the first product is any better, but because the first manufacturer's catalog makes it easier to specify and order the bearings. In the same way, a well-written instruction manual for software is often a more critical factor in the product's success than the software itself.

Case history: How to lose a $300,000 order

Some years ago, I was the advertising manager of a company that manufactured industrial process equipment. We had recently invented a new product, but when I suggested that we produce a technical bulletin on it, the product manager balked.

"The product's design is still in the development stage, so it's too early to commit to a brochure," he explained. "Besides, we're only selling to a small group of buyers, and they all know us."

Well, a few months later, my firm had a bid in for a $300,000 order, and it looked like a sure thing. But then the customer called and canceled! It turned out that the purchasing department had a firm policy: It would not place an order for a product unless it had a copy of a product brochure or technical bulletin in its purchasing files.

So we lost a $300,000 order—all because we hadn't spent a few hundred dollars to print a bulletin.

Later, I learned that our customer was not in the minority. According to Thomas Publishing Company, publisher of the country's largest industrial product directory, 90 percent of all buyers in industry say they must see some type of printed literature before they put a product's manufacturer on their approved vendor list. In today's highly competitive business world, producing printed literature has become a necessity, not just a promotional stunt.

And industrial manufacturers are not the only ones who need brochures. Practically every business and organization—service firms, retailers, consultants, free-lancers, educational institutions, trade associations, publishers—can benefit from describing their operations in printed form.

Five ways to put promotional literature to work for you

Smart business people just don't sit down and write a brochure. They first think about how they're going to use the brochure—who will read it, what it is designed to accomplish, how it fits into the buying process.

Not every brochure serves the same function. For example, let's say you sell furnaces. You might have two separate brochures. The first describes the general benefits and nontechnical features of your furnace and is used to generate interest in the product at the beginning of the buying process. The second brochure is filled with detailed technical specifications. It answers every question a contractor might have. It is used at the end of the buying process, when the homeowner has pretty much made a decision but wants to check with a trusted expert before shelling out $2,500 for your furnace. The first brochure starts the selling process; the second brochure helps to close it.

There are five ways in which you can put promotional literature to work for your firm: as a leave-behind, for inquiry fulfillment, as direct mail, as part of a point-of-sale display, and as a sales tool.

➤ **Leave-behind**

As its name implies, a *leave-behind* is a piece of literature that you leave with your prospect at the end of a sales call. For example, a door-to-door encyclopedia salesperson probably won't close the sale with one visit but will, instead, leave behind colorful folders describing the encyclopedia. The customer can study this material at his or her leisure and make a decision without the pressure created by the presence of a "live" salesperson.

Using a leave-behind ensures that the prospect knows where to reach you because the brochure includes your name, address, and phone number. Moreover, the leave-behind helps the prospect to recall the gist of your sales pitch.

➤ **Inquiry fulfillment**

When I was an advertising manager, our company's advertising and publicity campaign generated 19,000 inquiries a year. Obviously, we couldn't call all these people or visit them personally. So we mailed product brochures to give them the information they requested.

The brochure was only part of the inquiry fulfillment package. We also sent a sales letter encouraging the prospect to contact our local representative in his or her area. And we included an order form, reply card, or some other device the prospect could use to let us know his or her level of interest.

Mailing a brochure is the sensible first step in responding to advertising inquiries. Many people who inquire are only marginally interested, or maybe the product isn't right for them. The brochure lets you make contact with these folks for much less than the cost of a phone call or sales visit. Even the more serious prospects want a chance to read a brochure in private before deciding whether it's worthwhile to call you, see your salesperson, or visit your store.

One way to increase inquiries in response to your advertising is to highlight the offer of the free literature in the ad copy. Instead of just printing your logo and address, say, "The tax-saving benefits of this new bond offering are described in a free, informative pamphlet, *How to Invest*

Figure 1. The headline on RCA's brochure lures the reader into turning the page by offering a reward for reading the copy. What business manager does not want to cut the company's phone bill by 50 percent? (Reprinted with permission of RCA American Communications.)

Figure 2. A direct mail piece, such as this one for Polaroid, must sell from the first word to the last. The graphics on the front and back of this envelope are not simply an efficient use of space, but are warm and attractive as well. Thus, it serves as an inviting introduction to the "sales pitch" literature inside. (Copyright © Polaroid Corp., Cambridge, MA.)

Profitably in Municipal Bonds. To receive your copy without cost or obligation, write or call us today."

If a brochure is to be used in inquiry fulfillment, be sure to give it a title that will make people want to send for it. Instead of the title, *Telecommunications Equipment and Services,* call the brochure *How to Cut Your Long Distance Phone Bills by 50% or More.* More people will send for your literature if they think it contains useful information instead of just straight sales talk.

➢ **Direct mail**

Direct mail is a fast, efficient way of transmitting news to current customers and of prospecting for new ones.

A manufacturer of office equipment maintains a computerized mailing list of people who have purchased equipment from the company. The manufacturer mails a different sales flier to everyone on the list every month. Each month's flier announces a new product or a special sale on supplies and accessories for the old products.

An engineering firm wants to tell plant managers about its new inspection and maintenance service for wastewater treatment equipment. They send out a direct-mail package consisting of a letter, pamphlet, and reply

card. The letter introduces the service and highlights the cost savings it offers to industrial plants. The pamphlet gives detailed facts on how the service works and what type of equipment it covers.

There's an old saying among direct-mail marketers: "The letter sells; the brochure tells." In a mailing package, the letter makes the sales pitch, and the brochure gives complete details and illustrates the product with drawings and photos.

Not every mailing requires a brochure. If your mailing is designed to generate sales leads, you can send a letter only and offer the brochure to readers who respond to the letter. If you're selling a product by mail order, you want to give complete details and should include a circular or illustrated folder.

If the product is familiar and easily understood, a letter may be all you need. But if it is unfamiliar, complex, or needs to be shown, include literature with your mailing.

Many mailers go beyond one brochure or one letter and include multiple elements in their mailings—two letters, two or three pieces of literature, reply cards, order forms, reply envelopes. This puzzles a lot of people. They ask, "Why stuff the envelope with all this junk? Why not put everything in one letter or brochure?"

There is a reason. John Caples explains it in his book *Tested Advertising Methods* (Prentice-Hall):

Much direct mail advertising goes directly to the wastebasket. However, a prospect will rarely throw all of your mailing pieces into the wastebasket without at least glancing at them. If your entire advertising message is contained in a single circular or single booklet, the prospect will devote a few seconds to it and if it doesn't arouse his interest, he will throw it away. On the other hand, if your envelope is stuffed with half a dozen different mailing pieces, the prospect will probably glance at each piece before throwing it away. People hate to throw things away without at least glancing at them. They want to avoid disposing of anything valuable. Therefore, your six different inserts give you six opportunities to catch the interest of the prospect instead of only one.

Figure 3. This brochure from the same Polaroid direct mail piece further attracts the reader's attention with the notion that "firsts only happen once." Here, Polaroid is banking on parents not wanting to miss out on preserving such a special time in their lives. (Copyright © Polaroid Corp., Cambridge, MA.)

➤ **Point-of-sale display**

Many merchants display racks of sales literature at the place the product or service is sold. Visit a travel agent's office and you'll find dozens of colorful pamphlets describing faraway places. Stop in at the local bank and you can pick up informative folders on certificates of deposit, individual retirement accounts (IRAs), KEOGH plans, money market funds, and other profitable investments. Your insurance agent is likely to have a brochure about a new policy sitting in a wall rack.

Point-of-sale literature, more than any other type of promotional piece, must have an attractive, attention-grabbing cover that causes the brochure to stand out in the literature rack and compels the casual browser to pick it up and keep it. Colorful photos or illustrations help in this area; so do powerful headlines that tell a story.

➤ **Sales tool**

Salespeople depend on sales literature to do part of the selling job for them. Literature can educate the prospect in advance of the salesperson's visit. What's more, there are three ways in which it can help the salesperson give the presentation.

First, no salesperson can remember every fact about the product. So the literature can be used as an *aid to memory.* Some salespeople keep the brochure open during their presentation and use it to guide them through the pitch. Others turn to it for occasional reference or to look up answers to difficult questions.

Second, brochures with photos, charts, graphs, and drawings serve to *illustrate the sales pitch.* The salesperson can't bring the company's forklift to the prospective buyer in a warehouse but can bring a brochure with color photographs of it. If the buyer asks a question about the forklift's consumption of electric power, the salesperson can turn to page 5 and show a graph that compares battery charge vs. time in use.

Third, sales literature adds believability to sales presentations. Buyers who would question a salesperson's statements accept a printed sales argument as gospel. As publisher Edward Uhlan explains in his autobiography, *The Rogue of Publishers' Row,* "The reverence people have for the printed word is amazing. Simply because a man appears in print, the public assumes that he has something authoritative to say."

Uhlan was talking about newspaper articles and books, but the principle applies to promotional literature as well. Committing your sales arguments to print will hasten their acceptance by your customers and prospects.

The eleven basic types of promotional literature: Which one is right for you?

This book covers all types of promotional literature, from brochures and booklets to invoice stuffers and newsletters.

When the distinction between one type of literature and another is important, I use the specific term. But in some cases, what I'm talking about applies to all types of promotional literature. In these discussions, I use the terms *promotional literature, sales literature, printed literature,* and *brochure* interchangeably.

I don't want to get bogged down in advertising jargon. If you produce an effective piece of literature, it makes little difference whether you call it a brochure, a broadside, a booklet, or a folder.

On the other hand, some of these labels *do* connote important differences among types of promotional literature, and it helps to know your options. For this reason, I shall begin by describing the eleven basic types of promotional literature and offering advice on the appropriate applications of each.

➤ **Annual report**

The annual report is a once-a-year affair. It summarizes a company's performance for the past year and promises great things for the year ahead.

Annual reports are generally divided into two parts. The first tells the company's story in narrative form. For large firms, this narrative might consist of several separate subsections, with each subsection devoted to one of the firm's various operating companies, divisions, or subsidiaries. The second part consists mainly of numbers reported by the corporation's accounting firm. These numbers tell the story of the firm's financial fitness to those people who understand such things.

The annual report is aimed at a number of audiences, including stockholders, the financial community (especially analysts), vendors, customers, employees, and the business community in general. It also has a number of different purposes: to convince current stockholders to hold onto their shares; to induce potential investors to buy the company's stock; to present an overview of the firm's activities to journalists, employees, prospective employees, vendors, customers, and others who need to know; and to enhance the firm's image.

Most annual reports you see are fancifully produced—overproduced, in my opinion. Glossy paper stock, a large number of pages, commissions for original four-color photography, far-out graphics, and special printing requirements can push the cost of producing one of these pretty things up to six figures.

There's no law that says annual reports have to be so fancy; firms are just used to doing them that way. But I've seen sharp, crisp, exciting annual reports printed in 8 pages in two colors on attractive but inexpensive stock.

Too many companies rely on size and money as substitutes for imagination at annual report time. The result is reports that win design awards, not investors.

Do you need an annual report? Not if your business is small or privately held or if the scope of your product line and your organization chart are fairly simple.

When your company goes public, when your business activities are diverse and complex, when your company grows and spreads across the country or the world—then you might consider an annual report. (In fact, publicly held companies are required by the Securities and Exchange Commission to publish an annual report.)

> **Booklet**

The dictionary defines *booklet* as a small bound book. The difference between a booklet and a pamphlet is that the booklet is bound with staples, glue, or stitching, whereas the pamphlet is unbound (the pages are formed by folding a single large sheet into many smaller panels).

In a promotional sense, a booklet is printed matter that gives *useful information*. In this respect, it is different from the brochure, which is written to give *sales information*.

One moving firm publishes a sales brochure titled *Jenkins Movers— The Name You Can Trust*. The brochure contains a blatant sales pitch for Jenkins Movers. But few people pick up or send for the brochure because they realize it contains only sales talk. And for that same reason, those who do receive it don't hold on to it. When it comes time to move, Jenkins is forgotten.

Another company, Consolidated Movers, publishes a booklet titled *A Moving Checklist—What to Do Before the Van Arrives*. It contains useful tips on organizing, packing, and planning for a move. People thinking of a future move send for the informative booklet and keep it on file. When it comes time to move, they find it and refer to it. They call the publisher of this useful booklet, Consolidated Movers, and Consolidated gets the job.

As you can see, there are several advantages to publishing informative booklets. People are more likely to respond to your ad or pick literature from your rack if it contains useful information. They are also more likely to keep it around. Moreover, by providing free information, you are perceived as a friendly, helpful company representative rather than a pushy salesperson.

Just about every business can benefit by offering this type of literature. For some, an informative booklet is an alternative to sales brochures. For example, not many people would be interested in reading a brochure promoting the services of an executive recruiter. But most people would read a booklet titled *How to Get a Higher Position in Less Time—An Executive's Guide to Profitable Job-Hopping.*

For other businesses, a blend of informative booklets and hard-sell brochures is best. A manufacturer of pumps might get more response to its ad when it offers a booklet titled *Pump Performance Checklist.* But the checklist, while helpful to the engineer, does not sell the customer on the advantages of the manufacturer's pump. A separate sales brochure is needed for that job.

➤ Brochure

A brochure has two jobs: 1) to explain how a product or service works; and 2) to sell the product to the reader by highlighting its advantages, benefits, and applications. There are three basic types of brochures: *product, service,* and *capabilities.*

The product brochure can describe either a single product or a product line. The brochure tells what the product is, how it is put together, what it is made of, how it works, what it can do, why it is better than similar products, and what sizes, models, and accessories are available.

The service brochure describes a service offered, such as accounting services, legal services, consulting services, or inspection services. The brochure explains what the service is, why you need it, how it works, and the methods used to perform it.

The capabilities brochure, also known as the *corporate* or *company* brochure, gives an overview of a company and its capabilities. The brochure tells what the company does, how big it is, what resources it has, and how it is organized. A corporate brochure is like an annual report without the financial section, except that the corporate brochure is written to be applicable over a period of several years instead of just the current year.

Brochures come in all shapes and sizes, but two formats are most common: the *slim jim* and the *full-size* format.

The slim jim is designed to fit in a standard number 10 business envelope. It usually has between 4 and 8 pages and is formed by taking a large piece of paper and folding it into multiple panels. Slim jims are used when there is not a lot of information to be conveyed, when the company wants to save money on mailing costs, or when the brochure is to be displayed in a literature rack.

The pages of the full-size brochure measure approximately 8½ by 11 inches. These brochures typically have anywhere from 4 to 8 pages, although they can be longer if the product is unusually complex or detailed.

The 4-page brochure is formed by folding an 11-by-17-inch sheet of paper in half; the 8-page brochure is formed by stapling two 4-pagers together at the fold. (For illustrations of folding and binding techniques, see Chapter 9.)

Unlike the booklet, which is merely informative, the brochure must also be persuasive. It must sell the reader on the product by highlighting the product's benefits. A good brochure gives the reader many reasons to buy your product rather than another. These reasons can include quality, cost, service, maintenance, efficiency, energy savings, and product performance.

➤ **Case history**

A case history is a product success story. It tells how a customer saved money, solved problems, or improved his or her life by using a product or service. Each year, thousands of case histories are published as magazine articles, ads, brochures, and publicity releases. Experienced marketers know that case histories make powerful promotions for a number of reasons.

People believe in case histories more than they believe in the regular type of advertising. In a conventional brochure, the manufacturer has to beat its own drum in extolling the virtues of its product. In a case history bulletin, your customer does your selling for you. Furthermore, prospects are more likely to believe this third-party endorsement than your own self-serving claims.

Case histories also make interesting reading. They tell a story, and the story deals with problems similar to those the reader is facing. People relate to case histories because case histories speak directly to their own lives and business situations.

And by their very nature, case histories deal with specifics: who had the problem, what the problem was, how the person decided to deal with it, how the product or service solved it, and the results of buying the product or service. Such specifics are far more believable and persuasive than the vague generalities that pepper so much of today's lamentable advertising copy.

Detailed case histories can serve as the basis for separate pieces of product literature. And summaries of these case histories or specific facts or quotations from them can be woven into your other literature.

Case histories are ideal for promoting anything the public may be skeptical about, from a new invention to a worthy cause to a political issue. Let's say you are trying to get people to vote for a bill allowing an industrial park to be built in your county. You could do research to find out how having an industrial park has been beneficial to towns similar to yours. Your literature could highlight these case histories to show voters that others in their situation voted yes and are now quite happy with the results.

➤ **Catalog**

Whereas a brochure is usually restricted to a single product or product line, a catalog is a comprehensive directory of all of a company's products. There are two basic types of catalogs: *mail order* and *industrial.*

Mail-order catalogs offer merchandise the consumer can order directly by mail. They give complete information on each product, including size, weight, colors, materials available, and price. Photos are used to show the consumer what he or she is getting for the money. Mail-order catalogs also contain order forms and postage-paid reply envelopes to make ordering easy for the customer.

Industrial catalogs contain descriptions of products sold to business and industry. The readers of industrial catalogs include purchasing agents, plant managers, engineers, and others who buy such equipment. The catalog descriptions stress technical details such as safety factors, quality, precision, utility, maintenance and repair methods, weights, sizes, shapes, method of operation, packaging, and power, temperature, and pressure ratings.

A catalog is useful when you are selling a large number of products geared to one type of buyer. A software publisher with a library of sixty game cartridges would logically use a catalog aimed at buyers of computer and video games. On the other hand, a programmer who designs customized software for a specific industry, such as transportation, would be better off with a brochure outlining these unique services.

➤ **Circular**

A circular is a printed sheet used by retailers to announce sales and specials. It is usually printed in color, on newspaper stock, and in newspaper format. Circulars may be mailed, distributed door to door, inserted in newspapers, or made available at supermarket checkout counters, shopping malls, and other points of sale.

The focus of the circular is on generating immediate retail sales through price-off coupons, discounts, and other specials. The circular is a short-lived promotion piece whose value lasts only as long as the sale goes on. After the sale, it is discarded, and a new one is written for the next promotion.

Who uses circulars? Supermarkets, drugstores, stereo and video stores, department stores, and any other retailer with merchandise to move.

➤ **Data sheet**

A product data sheet (also called a *specification sheet* or *spec sheet*) contains detailed facts and specifications about a product.

The data sheet is used at the end of the sales cycle. The prospect has responded to your ad, and your sales brochure has piqued his or her interest. Now, your prospect is nearly ready to buy, but first there are some questions to be answered. The data sheet is designed to provide those answers.

"The data sheet should answer all of the customer's questions," writes Joe Lane, president of J. J. Lane, Inc., in an article in *Sales & Marketing Management* (5/14/84). "If the information the customer needs to make the buying decision isn't there, the data sheet is worthless."

Data sheets are usually $8\frac{1}{2}$ by 11 inches with copy on both sides. Longer data sheets can run 4 to 6 pages.

The data sheet is the place to put all your nuts-and-bolts information about the product, all the technical details you thought were too boring for your ad or general brochure. For example, a data sheet describing the Halleyscope (a new telescope) includes descriptive information on the lens system, power range, camera adaptor, material of construction, tripod, zoom focus, carrying case, display case, filters, and shipping specifications.

➤ **Flier**

A flier is an inexpensive piece of promotional literature with simple copy and line art printed on one side of an $8\frac{1}{2}$-by-11-inch sheet of paper.

Fliers can be posted on community bulletin boards or distributed by hand. They provide an inexpensive way for local businesses to get their message across to people in the neighborhood. Just about any business serving local residents can benefit from distributing a flier. The flier should state the name of the business, the product or service offered, plus store location, hours, and telephone number.

In the past six months, I've received fliers from such diverse businesses as a typing service, a pizza parlor, a Chinese restaurant, an exterminator, a locksmith, a music teacher, a handyman, a painter, a plumber, a limousine service, a taxi company, a computer dealer, and a hair salon.

Fliers are not appropriate for expensive products or systems, large national companies, or products sold to upscale (wealthy and sophisticated) buyers. The reason is that fliers are inexpensive to produce but also tend to have a cheap look about them. A company worried about projecting a dignified or successful image would not want to use them.

➤ Invoice stuffers

An invoice stuffer is a pamphlet or flier sent along with the consumer's monthly invoice. American Express is a heavy user of invoice stuffers; it offers collectibles, clocks, pen sets, and other fine products by mail. My local cable TV company uses invoice stuffers to promote subscriptions to new channels and program services.

The great advantage of invoice stuffers is that they get a free ride in the mail because they're sent with invoices, statements, and other regularly mailed routine correspondence.

Of course, if you don't mail out monthly statements or bills, you can't take advantage of invoice stuffers on a large scale. However, you can still print up a batch and send them out whenever you do write a letter or mail a bill. Even a small volume mailed can produce profitable returns.

➤ Newsletter

A newsletter is a short (2 to 12 pages), regularly published periodical sent to employees, customers, and prospects. Newsletters do not generate immediate sales. Instead, they build your image and keep your name in front of the select group of people who receive them over a long period of time.

Many organizations publish newsletters as promotional tools, but the reader expects a newsletter to contain real news. Therefore, yours should be a blend of industry and company news, useful information, and a sales pitch for your product or service.

If the product pitch is too blatant, or if it dominates the newsletter, readers will throw the newsletter away. The key to getting them to read and keep it is to publish information that is timely or helpful.

The length and frequency of publication are up to you, but you shouldn't publish if you don't have anything new to say. For a small or medium-size company, a 2-to-4-page newsletter published three to six times a year is just about right. Publish more if a lot is happening, less if it's not.

➤ **Poster**
Some companies take a full-page flier or ad, blow it up to poster size, and mail it in a cardboard tube to prospective customers.

Literature mailed this way almost always gets opened and read. After all, a 3-foot-long mailing tube is sure to stand out in a 9-by-13-inch "in" basket full of standard 4-by-9-inch white business envelopes. People are naturally curious, and so they will open the tube, unroll the poster, and read at least part of the copy.

Unfortunately, most people won't save your poster. People like to keep sales literature handy in a file folder, desk drawer, or three-ring binder, and a poster won't fit in any of these. It's far easier to throw the poster away than to try to find a place to keep it.

Most poster advertisers hope that the recipient will hang the poster on the office or study wall. The reality is that few people will consider your advertising literature a work of art, and it is the rare poster that is attractive or interesting enough to be hung in the prospect's home or office. (Of course, those that do make it act as daily reminders of the company and its sales pitch.)

One way to increase the poster's chances of getting taped to the wall is to enhance it with some useful information, such as a calendar, an inspirational message, a metric conversion table, or a product selection guide.

Do you need promotional literature?

Following is a checklist of some of the reasons why companies publish promotional literature. If any of these situations sounds somewhat like your own, it's a safe bet that there's a brochure in your future.

➤ **Your potential customers ask for it**
If people who walk into your office or call you on the phone are constantly asking to see a brochure, that's reason enough to have one. It means your prospects need more information before they're ready to buy. If you don't provide it, you can lose the sale. And if your competitors have literature and you don't, you're at a disadvantage.

➤ **Your salespeople ask for it**
Salespeople are in the best position to know what support they need from the home office in order to make a sale. Helping them make the sale is a

major function of promotional literature. So if your salespeople make repeated requests for you to supply them with printed materials, it will probably be profitable for you to do so.

➢ Your competitors have it

Without literature, you can't compete effectively against companies that *do* have marketing materials. What's more, prospects often choose one product or company over another largely on the basis of the literature they receive, so your brochure should be the best of the bunch.

➢ You sell to business and industry

As I mentioned earlier, Thomas Publishing Company reports that 90 percent of industrial buyers insist on seeing printed literature before they buy. So having a brochure is a must for anyone selling products and services to business, industry, and professionals.

➢ You sell by mail

In mail-order selling, your mailing package does the whole job; there is no salesperson to answer the reader's questions or explain the material enclosed. Therefore, the brochures you enclose with your mailing package must be persuasive, credible, and clear as a country creek.

➢ You sell through agents

Sales reps, distributors, and other agents who carry your product line expect you to support their selling efforts with first-class brochures, case history bulletins, data sheets, and other literature. It is just about impossible to convince a middleman to take on your line if you have no literature.

These distributors and reps rarely produce their own literature. They prefer to take your brochure and imprint it with their logo and address.

➢ You run advertisements or send out press releases

Even a modest advertising and publicity campaign can generate hundreds or thousands of mail and phone inquiries. It is impossible to answer all these inquiries with a personal phone call, visit, or letter.

Mass-produced sales literature is the answer. Mailing a brochure and form letter is the only way to efficiently and economically answer the queries generated by advertising and publicity.

➤ **You use direct mail to generate leads**
The most effective way to generate response to a sales letter is to offer a free sales brochure or informative booklet to readers who phone or mail in the reply card. Naturally, if you make such an offer, you must have literature on hand to fill the requests.

➤ **Your product is a considered purchase**
A *considered purchase* is a buying decision that the buyer has spent some time thinking about. Examples of considered purchases are the decisions to buy a car, home, refrigerator, microwave oven, stock, sprinkler system, computer, typewriter, telephone system, encyclopedia, photocopier, or college education.

When the customer takes time to make a decision, any information you can supply to help him or her make a wise choice will be eagerly accepted. A brochure provides this information and helps sway the customer by presenting the advantages and highlights of the product.

When customers buy on impulse, without taking the time to mull over the advantages and drawbacks of a product, they probably won't want to bother reading literature, and so a brochure is not required. Record albums, paperback novels, ice-cream cones, fast foods, greeting cards, ballpoint pens, and umbrellas (especially on a rainy day) are all impulse items. So is virtually every type of packaged good. (Packaged goods are items sold off the shelf at supermarkets and drugstores. They include toothpaste, shampoo, bathroom tissue, deodorant, coffee, and canned foods.)

➤ **Your product or service has tangible features and benefits**
Products whose function, construction, and benefits can be described in words and pictures are particularly well suited to be the subject of a sales brochure. For example, you could write thousands of words describing the virtues of a car, furnace, or home-study course.

There are many other products that don't have tangible features, and there is very little to say about them. Take soda pop, for example. You can say that it tastes good and is refreshing, but that's about it. Even worse, every other soda pop can make the same claims. So you'd have a hard time writing a brochure on the subject. What's more, most of the products in this category are impulse items, so there's really no need to produce a brochure.

> ### Your business is new, and you want people to know about it
A corporate brochure can go a long way in educating people about a new business venture. The more brochures you distribute, the more people there are who know of your existence.

Also, most new businesses have a credibility problem. People are reluctant to deal with a new business because they have never heard of it. They want proof that the company is real and not some fly-by-night operation. A corporate brochure can provide that proof.

> ### Your company is growing, and you want people to understand it
As companies grow, they become more complex. What was a simple business is now a multinational corporation with many products, offices, divisions, and different groups of customers. A company brochure helps give people a clear picture of the corporation and its mission.

The brochure can serve another purpose. It can help to clear up misconceptions or misunderstandings about a business. For example, I once worked at a firm that manufactured electronic defense systems for the U.S. government. A survey showed that although military buyers thought our products were excellent, they also thought we had a problem meeting production deadlines and supporting our systems after the sale.

Our track record showed this wasn't the case. So we created a corporate capabilities brochure that stressed our experience and success in all three areas: design, production, and support. Claims of superiority were backed up by case histories, track records, and other facts. The brochure went a long way toward correcting the buyers' misconceptions.

> ### You want to increase sales
Literature can be an effective promotional tool for generating leads, increasing sales, gaining new members, raising funds, bringing in votes, or getting support for your project or idea. Unlike print ads, where space is limited, or TV commercials, where time is short, brochures give you as much space as you need to make your sales pitch.

What's more, brochures allow you to get your message across to those people you can't contact by phone or personal visit. A friend of mine calls his brochures "silent salesmen" because every brochure sitting in a person's file

Figure 4. My local bank recently changed its name from the Harlem Savings Bank to Apple Bank for Savings℠. The cover of their brochure announces this change with words and the image of an apple. (This apple logo has been registered as a service mark of Apple Bank.)

or desk drawer may, at any time, be pulled from the file or drawer and turned into a sale. If you want to boost sales, create a persuasive piece of sales literature and get it into the hands of as many of your prospective customers as you can.

➤ **You want to build an image**
The look, feel, and tone of your promotional literature have much to do with the way the public perceives you. Do you want to be known as aggressive or laid back? Dynamic or dignified? Small and smart or large and established? Promotional literature can show the public the image you want to project.

➤ **You want it**
A perfectly valid reason for producing promotional literature is that you want it. I know many entrepreneurs who claim they didn't feel they were running real companies until they published their brochures. A brochure can be a boost to your own morale, as well as the morale of your partners and employees. A brochure can also solidify the direction and purpose of a company, perhaps because people take things more seriously when they see these things in print.

Where do we go from here?

The remaining nine chapters of this book provide a step-by-step guide for producing your promotional literature.

Chapters 2 to 4 show you how to set a production schedule and budget for the project and how to decide what information to include in the brochure. You'll also learn where to find and how to work with professional copywriters, photographers, illustrators, graphic artists, and printers.

Chapters 5 to 9 take you through the process of designing, writing, illustrating, and printing your brochure. We also take a look at a number of special problems that come up in the creation of promotional literature and suggest ways to solve them.

Chapter 10 is a guide to managing a *program* of successful promotional literature. It is for the person who is going to produce a whole series of brochures, not just one. You'll also learn how to gauge the success of your literature program and evaluate the results.

CHAPTER TWO

Getting Started:
Planning, Scheduling, Budgeting

You're not ready to start—yet

I know. You're in a hurry to hold that brochure in your hands. And maybe you're asking, "Why bother with all this planning? I'll just grab a piece of paper, write the brochure, and hand it over to my neighborhood printer. If he gets the job Monday, I'll have brochures by Friday!"

Some companies do produce their literature that quickly, but the results are seldom satisfactory. Poor planning usually produces second-rate literature: brochures that are sloppily designed and full of mistakes, poorly written, contain the wrong information, or are aimed at the wrong audience.

"The best-designed, most finely printed brochure will miss its goal if it is poorly planned," writes Nancy Edmonds Hanson in her book *How You Can Make $20,000 a Year Writing (No Matter Where You Live)*. The printing and production of brochures are expensive. Without proper planning, you may find yourself redoing your expensive folder or flier a lot sooner than you expected. For example, you might create a beautifully designed piece that fails because the copy is too technical for the intended audience. Or you could find yourself with a mail-order catalog that fails to generate even a single order because the designer forgot to include a reply envelope with the order form.

Although planning takes some extra work and time on your part, it pays off in a number of ways.

First, by helping you coordinate the many tasks involved in literature production, it can save time in the later stages. For example, without a production schedule, you might forget that you need a photo of an important subject. If you discover this in the design stage, you must then find and hire a photographer to shoot the picture, and that could delay publication by several weeks. Planning ensures that all the various elements of literature production are ready when they are needed.

Second, planning allows you to control costs. With a set budget, you know what you expect to pay and will be alerted if a specific item runs over budget. What's more, your planning schedule allows enough time for you to get competitive bids from independent contractors for printing, photography, artwork, and copy, rather than having to depend on one source only and not knowing whether the supplier might be overcharging you.

Third, planning produces better final results. You can allow time for reviews and to check and control the quality of the work every step of the way. When you plan, you allow enough time to do each task *right.*

This chapter addresses the ten considerations that are basic whether you're planning a single brochure or a whole series of pieces: (1) the objective, (2) the type of literature you need, (3) the subject of the literature, (4) the audience, (5) sales appeals, (6) image, (7) the environment, (8) the budget, (9) the format, and (10) the schedule.

What is your objective?

Your objective in producing promotional literature may be to do one or more of the following:

Provide product information to customers
Educate new prospects
Build corporate image
Establish credibility for your firm or product
Sell the product directly through the mail
Help salespeople get appointments
Help salespeople make presentations
Help close the sale
Support dealers, distributors, and sales reps
Add value to the product
Enhance the effectiveness of direct-mail packages
Leave something with customers as a reminder
Respond to inquiries
Hand out at trade shows, fairs, conventions
Display at point of purchase
Provide handy reference material for new employees, consultants, outside vendors, the trade press, and others who need to know about the organization and its products

Disseminate news about the company and its products
Announce new products and product improvements
Train and educate new managers, engineers, and salespeople
Recruit new employees
Provide useful information to the public
Generate new business leads
Qualify to be on a customer's approved-vendors list

Your brochure has a purpose: to cause the reader to take some action or at least change his or her understanding of or attitude toward you and your product. If the brochure leaves the reader unchanged, you've failed.

Know the objective of your brochure. Be able to state it in a brief sentence or two. If you can't think of a reason for publishing the brochure, maybe it doesn't need to be published.

What type of literature do you need?

The next step is to decide exactly what type of printed literature you need.

In Chapter 1, we looked at the basic formats. The table on the next two pages summarizes the eleven basic types of promotional literature and gives guidelines for selecting the one that best fits your requirements.

Nine out of ten times, you'll be producing some type of brochure describing a product or service. But some situations call for one of the other types of literature, and you should be familiar with them. For example, if you are having a garage sale, producing a brochure listing all the items would be too time-consuming and costly. A more effective promotion would be to post fliers around the neighborhood announcing the date and location of the sale.

Once you decide what type of literature you want to produce, you can begin to get an idea of how costly and involved the project will be. An annual report is likely to be an expensive project involving many levels of approval within your company, whereas an invoice stuffer can be as simple as printing a sentence or two on a slip of colored paper. The typical sales brochure falls somewhere between the two in cost and difficulty of execution.

➤ **Eleven types of literature you can use to promote your company, product, or service**

Use this	To do this
Annual report	Build your image Disclose financial information Communicate with shareholders, investors, and the financial community Tell your corporate story to customers, employees, and the business community Provide a quick overview of your business to potential customers, outside vendors, and the press Sell stock Impress vendors and other companies you deal with Recruit new employees
Booklet	Provide useful information Answer questions frequently asked by customers and prospects Generate more sales leads (by offering the booklet in advertising or direct mail) Teach customers to be informed consumers of your type of product
Brochure	Promote any product, service, or program Help salespeople get appointments Help salespeople close sales Answer inquiries Provide product information to customers and prospects Establish your product in the marketplace
Case history	Tell prospects and customers about the successful performance of your product or service Overcome skepticism Describe uses of the product in special applications Get testimonials for use in advertising, publicity, and other promotions Show a customer how to solve a specific problem
Catalog	Sell an entire product line instead of just a single product Sell products by mail Help buyers find and select the products they need Serve as a single source for all the customer's needs

Use this	To do this
Circular	Increase retail sales Promote Christmas sales and other special events Clear your warehouse of dead merchandise through discounts and other special deals Put coupons into the hands of shoppers
Data sheet	Answer buyer's questions Help salespeople close sales Satisfy the complete information needs of dealers, manufacturers' representatives, purchasing agents, and others
Flier	Promote your business on a local level Sell a product or service Get your name around Announce an event
Invoice Stuffer	Reinforce a sales message Provide useful information to customers Announce sales and specials Sell products and supplies by mail Communicate with employees and customers
Newsletter	Communicate with employees, customers, and prospects Keep your name before customers and prospects Build the buyer's trust in your organization over a long period of time Supplement your other promotional efforts Get more sales leads (by asking people to request a free subscription to your newsletter) Disseminate news and late-breaking product information and updates Advise your customers of new applications, new accessories, new policies, new products
Poster	Have your message stand out from the crowd Create some excitement about your product Get your name in front of the buyer Increase repeat business

What is the subject of the brochure?

Before you can write a brochure (or hire someone else to write it), you have to know what you want to write about. This means being able to specify the subject of the brochure, the scope of information you want to include, and the overall theme or story you want to tell. It also means knowing what shouldn't be included.

Determine the purpose, subject matter, content, and theme of your brochure before you call in your writers, designers, and photographers. These professionals can help evaluate the ideas you propose, but you are the final judge of what you want your brochure to say. The content is the most important factor in the brochure's success or failure, and it pays to take the time to figure out exactly what you want to say. Here are four things you should pay particular attention to.

The subject matter. What is the subject of the brochure? Is the brochure about a single product, two products, a product line, a particular application of a product?

The content. What information should be included? What should be excluded? Don't just guess. Have a reason for including or excluding a particular fact.

The theme. Does the brochure merely present a set of facts, or does it tell a story? If it tells a story, what should that story be? The theme dictates how you arrange and organize the copy.

The complete facts. Do you know all you need to about your product, your market, and your industry? Or is research required to fill in missing facts? If you're missing vital information, start collecting it now; otherwise, it may hold you up later on.

When you are sure of your subject, everything else falls neatly into place. When you don't know what you're selling, chaos and confusion plague the production process every step of the way.

Who is your audience?

A few years back, my mother and I went to see the New York City Ballet perform *The Nutcracker.* She loved it, but I was bored stiff. I was the wrong audience for the ballet; my mother was the right one. Now, the New York City Ballet knows it has a sellout audience for *The Nutcracker;* the occasional off-target, like me, doesn't matter. But with a promotion piece, you want to be sure of a receptive audience, and so you tailor your promotion to your audience. That way, you have a better chance of getting your message across. If you write in a vacuum, without thinking about who your reader is and what he or she wants to know, you're destined for failure.

"Your audience determines the design and diction of your piece," says Elizabeth Morse-Cluley, director of publications at Mercy College. "For example, a tour map for children should be 'bright' and simple in form and content; an annual report should be sophisticated and detailed in form and content."

Of course, you can't go out and interview every prospect to find out what they like or dislike, what they believe in, and what they're against. But you can learn much from the general characteristics of your target audience.

In particular, here are ten factors that will help you tailor your pitch to the needs and personalities of your customers.

Age. People's buying habits change as they grow older. Take financial products, for example. Senior citizens are usually conservative investors; they buy safe products such as IRAs, KEOGH plans, and money market funds so they can retire comfortably. Young people are more willing to take risks and gamble some money in the stock market.

Location. The place where your readers live and work has a lot of influence on their personalities, problems, and needs as consumers. For example, in New York City, convenience foods sell well because there are so many working, single people; but patio furniture does not sell well because few New Yorkers have houses, backyards, or patios.

Income level. People who earn $50,000 a year or more have the money to spend on luxury items such as videocassette recorders (VCRs), stereo equipment, cable TV, fine wine, luxury cars, designer clothes, and frequent dining out. Middle-class working families are more interested in the basics, such as solid furniture for the home, practical clothing, a station wagon, and saving for their children's education. People with more money spend more and also buy the more expensive brands.

Family status. Even if two people earn the same wage, the single person has more money to spend on leisure activities than the person who has a family. This is why so many companies are marketing products aimed at yuppies (young urban professionals): single, successful people who spend most of their money on themselves.

Industry. If you're selling products to business, the industry the buyer works in dictates his or her interest in and need for your product. Let's say your product is a word processing system. A mail-order house might be most concerned with how many letters it can print in an hour because the more letters the company mails, the more profit it makes. A newspaper editor, however, would be more interested in editing capabilities and whether text can be transferred from one terminal to another.

Job title and function. Within a company, there may be many people who have a say about whether your product is purchased. And each may have his or her own reasons for buying the product. Top management is interested in the reputation of your firm and your reliability. Engineering wants to know all about the technical specifications of your product. Middle managers want to know how the product can help them do business more profitably. The purchasing agent is worried about the cost. If you're selling to business and industry, your literature, which may be one piece or separate pieces aimed at each level, must sell the product to all these influential people.

Education. Is your customer a college graduate, a high school dropout, a Ph.D.? His or her level of education dictates the level of complexity of your language and the style of your copy. It's okay to use terms like *pilonidal cyst* and *septal reconstruction* in a brochure aimed at doctors, but these words would frighten and upset a patient. A brochure aimed at patients should speak in friendly, reassuring tones and use plain, simple English.

Politics. Is your reader a Democrat or a Republican, a conservative or a liberal, political or apolitical, patriotic or apathetic? Few attitudes are as strongly held as those surrounding the issues of the day: abortion, taxes, nuclear war, social security. If your product, service, or pitch touches on political issues or current events, you'd better know where your readers stand. If you don't, you'll end up angering people and turning them against you instead of persuading them to join your group, donate to your cause, or see your point of view.

Religion and ethnic group. In many areas, such as fashion, cuisine, music, entertainment, and fads, sales are concentrated among certain ethnic groups. You're asking for disaster if you make ethnic comments or use stereotypes in your literature. But you should be aware of what's hot (and what's not) among people of different cultural backgrounds. For example, breakdancing was popular among black and Hispanic young people long before it caught on as a national fad. That information would have been useful to you if you had sold breakdancing clothes, records, posters, and movies early in the game.

Concerns. The most important questions you can ask about your audience are: What do they really care about? What are their likes and dislikes? What's important to them—and what's not? What are the reasons why my product might appeal to them? Get inside the minds of your prospects. Talk to customers when they visit your store or when you call on them in the field. Visit industry trade shows. Find out what motivates your potential buyer, and you're on your way to a sale.

What are your product's benefits?

It is not enough simply to list all the facts and features of your product and hope that is what the reader is looking for. You have to find the *benefits* of the product, the reasons why the reader would want to buy it. And you've got to highlight these benefits in your brochure.

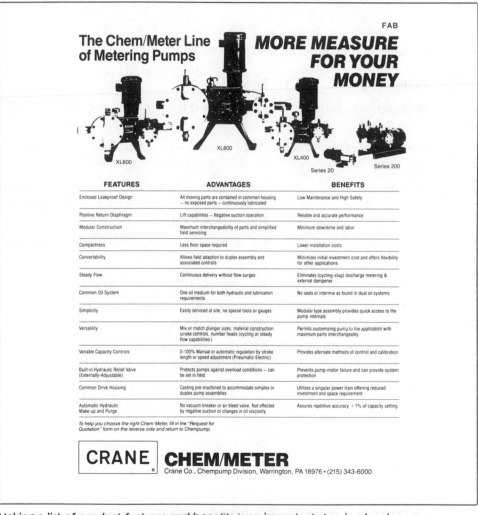

Figure 5. Making a list of product features and benefits is an important step in planning your literature. The Crane Company published their features and benefits list as a data sheet on their CHEM/METER line of pumps. (Credit: Crane Co., Pump Division.)

Discovering the sales appeals of your product is a two-step process.

First, translate the technical features into customer benefits. An easy way of doing this is to divide a sheet of paper into two columns. In the left-hand column, write down all the features of your product. In the right-hand, write down the benefits (how these features can help the user).

Try this exercise with an item around your house or office. I did it with my clock radio. Following are the results:

> **Features and Benefits of AM/FM Clock Radio**

Features	Benefits
Digital LED readout	Easy to read from a distance, even at night.
Push-button alarm set and time set	Wake up at the exact minute you want to—early on weekdays, later on weekends.
Snooze control	Reach over, hit the button, and get 10 extra minutes of sleep. The alarm will wake you when the 10 minutes are up.
Buzzer/radio alarm	Wake to soft music, hard rock, or alarm buzzer—the choice is yours.
AM/FM	Hear all your favorite stations.
Slide-tune dial	Pick your station with the twirl of a knob. Tuner illuminated for night listening.
Simulated wood-grain finish	Makes an attractive display on your dresser or nightstand.
Manufactured by Radio Shack	Warranty is backed by one of the country's leading suppliers of consumer electronics.
UL seal	Quality has been checked by independent testing organization.

Second, organize the benefits in order of importance. For the clock radio, the snooze control and push-button alarm would be the most important sales appeals. The UL seal and the name of the manufacturer would probably be at the bottom of the list.

You don't have to go through this exercise; your copywriter can do it for you. But remember: Nobody knows your product and your audience as well as you do. Generating a features/benefits list for each product will help your copywriter write a more effective brochure. And it will be a handy reference for many other promotions as well.

What is your image?

Like it or not, everything about you—the clothes you wear, what you order at lunch, the way you handle your fork, your manner of speaking, the length of your hair, the shine on your shoes—conveys an image to the people you're with. And regardless of whether image building is its primary goal, your brochure conveys an image, too—an image of your organization.

By consciously controlling the tone, look, and feel of your brochure, you can create the image you want to convey. But if you ignore this aspect of brochure production, your brochure could give people the wrong impression of your organization. And that could cost you goodwill, members, donations, and sales.

Here are some of the elements that dictate the image the brochure conveys to the customer. This list is just an overview; specific guidelines for controlling these elements are presented in later chapters.

Paper. There are three major factors to consider: weight, texture, and finish. Heavier paper gives an impression of solidity, of stability; thin paper has a cheaper look. Image is also conveyed by feel. Paper with body and texture can be warm, elegant, impressive. The finish is important, too. A glossy paper stock makes color photos look sharper and conveys a corporate, high-tech image. A flat finish is quieter, more subtle.

Color. Full-color brochures look expensive (and they are). People think, "They must have money if they can afford a brochure like this." But in the hands of a skilled designer, two-color printing (usually black and a second color, such as blue or red) can be attractive and effective. If the second color is used poorly, though, it can actually make a brochure look cheap and shlocky. A one-color brochure printed on colored stock—say, deep brown ink on light brown paper—can convey a warm, dignified, professional impression.

The choice of colors also dictates the image conveyed. Brown, as I've said, is quiet and dignified. Black is even more somber. Silver gives promotions a high-tech look.

Quality of photos. A poor-quality photo can ruin an otherwise fine brochure. If you can't get professional-quality photos within your budget, consider leaving the photos out. (Fortunately, there are a number of techniques that can enhance the look of so-so photos; these are discussed in Chapter 7.)

Size. An oversized brochure (larger than 8½ by 11 inches) can be a real attention-getter. But it will be hard to file. If you're trying to convey an image of corporate bigness and stability, a full-size brochure is usually better than a small pamphlet. But a small brochure can be very impressive if produced by a skilled designer.

Copy tone. The words you use have great effect on your image. You can come across as hard-sell or soft-sell, small and friendly or big and powerful, corporate or personal, firm and confident or helpful and supportive, product-oriented or people-oriented. For example, IBM writes its personal computer ads and brochures in a warm, friendly style in order to counteract the reader's fear of computers and technology. But most annual reports are written in a more businesslike tone to appeal to the business and financial communities.

How to Buy an Antique . . .

and Not Get Taken

The joy and pleasure of living with fine antique furniture is available to many people who hesitate to make that first purchase because they don't know how to go about it. Lack of knowledge, a previous bad experience with a dealer, or horror stories from friends are enough to deter many a potential buyer. Substantial sums of money can be involved, so caution is understandable and advisable.

However, there are 10 basic questions which should be answered before buying an antique, and these answers should be provided willingly by the dealer. If the dealer can not or will not provide explicit answers, don't buy from that dealer. These questions are designed to help in choosing a piece that will be enjoyed for years to come, and in purchasing it with the confidence that you have not been taken.

1. Does this antique fit my purpose?

When a buyer is considering a particular piece, he should be able to discuss with his dealer the appropriateness of the piece for his purpose. Antiques can be bought for investment, for daily family use, or for strictly decorative purposes. A piece which has had major restoration may not qualify as an investment. A set of museum-quality delicate Hepplewhite chairs might not be the best choice for a family with active elementary school-age children. If the piece is primarily decorative, then age will be less important than high style and finesse.

2. How does this antique rate in terms of quality of design, color, and finish?

The range of quality is limitless and will directly affect price. Your piece will fall somewhere on the broad spectrum between good Chippendale, for example, and bad Chippendale. The dealer should be able to point out to you how this aspect rates and why. The first thing you see when you look at an antique is its lines. Design is of great importance, because if the piece is not a beautiful thing in its own right, it really doesn't matter how old it is or in what condition. Stand back and look at the piece as a whole to evaluate the success of its design. Color is perhaps the next most obvious attribute, and any fine antique should have a lovely warm mellow color, a patina that only comes with two hundred years of natural aging. Stripping can ruin an antique, while refinishing may enhance it. A fine antique is generally French-polished, a procedure of applying shellac and alcohol with a pad which must be done by a professional. When done properly, with careful removal of old wax and dirt first, this procedure will not spoil the patina, which comes from the wood itself. Find out what kind of finish is on the piece you are considering.

3. How is the piece constructed and from what woods is it made?

Learn to recognize the basic woods, as identification is important in determining quality of construction and age. The open grain of oak has a very different look from the close grain of mahogany; knowing the difference will help you to spot a drawer, for example, made in 1900 from one made in 1800. English antiques with drawers typically have sides and bottoms of oak or pine and are constructed with small, even dovetails to join the four sides. The use of mahogany for drawer linings didn't come into common practice until late in the 19th century. Sometimes you will even see a drawer with a plywood bottom being passed off as 18th century! If the drawer has been stained inside, be wary (see Q. 5). American pieces generally have drawer linings of pine, a wood also used in England. But larger, cruder dovetails and chamfered drawer bottoms may help identify the piece as American and not English. Open the drawers of your piece, be sure all the drawers are made the same way, and ask the dealer to show you how they are put together.

4. What are the major periods?

English antique furniture is often referred to as "Georgian," after the three Georges who ruled for over a century, but the breakdown may be briefly described as follows (dates approximate):

William and Mary, last decade of the 17th century, characterized by the use of walnut and oak, spiral turned and "S" scroll legs, bun feet, elaborate veneers with the introduction to England of Dutch marquetry.

Queen Anne, 1700 to 1720, the Age of Walnut, characterized by simpler lines, chairs with solid shaped back splats, cabriole legs, pad or ball and claw feet, graceful curves.

Chippendale, 1735 to 1765, characterized by the predominant use of mahogany, with elaborate carving, rococo, Gothic, and Chinese elements, ball and claw feet, impressive proportions.

Hepplewhite, 1765 to 1790, characterized by elegant, refined lines and neoclassical elements such as carved swags of drapery, oval medallions, shield backs to chairs, square tapering legs, spade feet.

Sheraton, 1780 to 1800, with the wide use of satinwood for inlay and for whole pieces of furniture, chairs with straight lines, the full development of the sideboard, and the square, turned, or reeded leg.

Regency, 1800 to 1820, characterized by the use of classical and Egyptian elements, brass inlay, use of rosewood, gilding, saber legs, smaller proportions.

William IV, or *English Empire,* 1825 to 1840, with heavier treatment to turned legs, substantial bases for tables, beading, reeding and nulling for decoration—leading the way toward Victorian, which dominated the balance of the 19th century.

American furniture followed much the same course of development, though lagging a decade or more behind England. In both countries, during the last quarter of the 19th century, there was a revival of the furniture styles of the 18th century. These 'Centennial' reproductions were made in great numbers and are often passed off as 'Period' pieces. Some of them may be technically antiques now in that they are over 100 years old, but there is a vast difference in value between such a piece and the genuine article.

Figure 6. It's hard to prove that one antique store is better than another, and antique buyers would probably not respond to a hard sell. English Heritage Antiques of New Canaan, Connecticut, wins friends—and customers—by publishing an informative pamphlet called <u>How to Buy an Antique . . . and Not Get Taken.</u> (Credit: Cecily R. Collins of English Heritage Antiques, Inc., New Canaan, CT.)

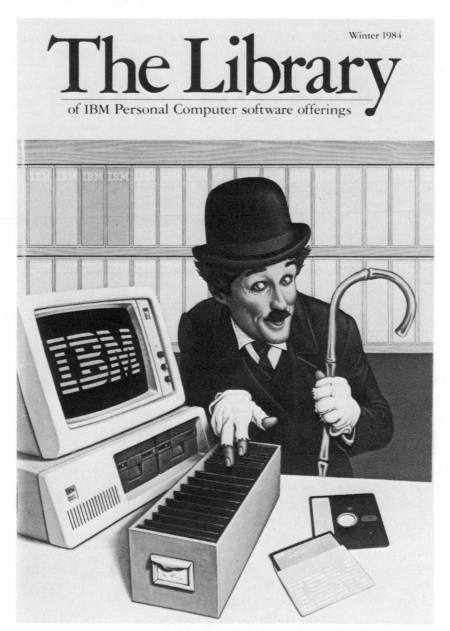

Figure 7. IBM's television commercials and print ads feature the "little tramp" character, and the theme is carried through in this software catalog and in other IBM product literature. (Courtesy of IBM.)

Design. The overall design and layout influence the image conveyed by the brochure in a hundred different ways. Take typography, for example. Most wedding invitations are printed with a flowing type resembling fine hand-writing. And that's no accident: this type has a personal, "nuptial" feeling. It would be inappropriate to set a wedding invitation in the same type as an insurance policy. A good designer is aware of all the nuances of design and layout and will use them to communicate the desired image.

In an understandable but misguided effort to save money, some large firms underspend when it's time to produce a new brochure. The result is a brochure that looks cheap and doesn't convey the image of wealth, stability, and class the corporation wants. On the other hand, many small companies make the opposite mistake. They overspend and produce brochures too gaudy for their audiences and too expensive for their budgets. I think the reason this happens is that some manager in the company gets envious of the fancy four-color brochures, gold-embossed mailers, and fat annual reports produced by Fortune 500 firms and says to the ad agency, "This stuff sure looks great. Why don't we do some brochures like this?"

That's a mistake. The look, tone, and image of your literature should be dictated by your product and your market, not by what other companies in other businesses put out.

Don't overpresent yourself. Producing literature that's too fancy for its purpose is a waste of money. And it can even hurt sales because your prospects will look at your overdone literature and wonder whether you really understand your market and its needs.

What is the sales environment?

When you walk into the lobbies of most ad agencies, you'll find samples of their work—ads, brochures, direct mail—preserved in metal-and-glass frames and mounted on the walls for all to admire. But brochures aren't museum pieces; they are sales tools, and they must operate in the real world. You need to be aware of this world before you can plan and produce effective literature.

There are three elements of the environment that have an effect on the design and writing of your brochure: the competition, your own sales cycle, and your other advertising and marketing efforts.

"The competition is probably already using a brochure and a variety of reports, newsletters and announcements," says Charles A. Moldenhauer, president of Lefkowith Inc., a marketing and design firm. "Such conditions make it difficult to gain attention or to differentiate an organization's services."

Differentiation is the key here. To get the buyer to use your product instead of a competitor's, you have to prove that your product is better than the competition's in some way. But you can't know how it's different unless you've studied competing businesses and brands.

I'd like you to start files on each of your competitors. Any intelligence you get on the competitor—a report, a product brochure, an annual report, a news clipping, a tear sheet of an ad—goes into the file. Getting this competitive material is easier than you think. You can find ads and news blurbs in industry magazines. And you can pick up their literature at their stores, outlets, or trade show exhibits. Often you can get a competitor's literature just by writing for it or calling up and asking.

In particular, pay close attention to the competitors' brochures. How do they present themselves and their products? Which sales appeals are highlighted? Which are omitted? Perhaps you can stress a benefit that your competitors haven't mentioned and win more customers by doing so.

Competitive literature is one element of the marketing environment. Your own literature is another. If your organization is typical, you have not one brochure but many, each with a different selling mission. Know where each brochure fits into your sales cycle. You might have a small pamphlet for answering initial inquiries, a more detailed sales brochure used by your salespeople, and data sheets to close the sale. Each brochure should move the reader one step closer to placing an order.

Finally, your brochures should complement your other promotional efforts (print advertising, direct mail, trade show displays, and publicity). There should be a common graphic look to all your marketing materials, and all the pieces should work in harmony to achieve a common sales goal. For example, a brochure used to answer inquiries should expand on the themes and answer the questions raised in the print ad. And the design of product manuals and instruction sheets should match the product's packaging.

What will it cost?

On the following page is a list of the expenses involved in producing promotional literature and the suppliers who handle each phase of the job.

Task	Vendor	Cost ($) for your job
Text	Writer	_____
Photography	Photographer	_____
Artwork	Graphic designer or illustrator	_____
Typography	Type house	_____
Design	Graphic designer or art studio	_____
Mechanical	Graphic designer, paste-up artist, or art studio	_____
Printing	Printer	_____
	Total cost	$_____

To ensure that you pay a fair price, you should get bids from three different suppliers for each phase of the job. To ensure that you get an accurate quotation, you must give each supplier complete specifications for the job.

The writer needs to know approximate word length, what source material you can supply, and whether any research or travel is involved.

The graphic designer or art studio needs to know, as precisely as possible, the format of the piece: number of words, number and size of pages, number and type of visuals, number of colors, and degree of design sophistication (plain, fancy, or in-between).

The photographer needs to know how many photos you want taken, the subject matter and setting of each photo, whether he or she has to travel to take the photos, and whether you want black and white or color (or both).

The illustrator needs to know the number and type of illustrations and the style and technique to be used for each (e.g., line art, technical diagrams, airbrush drawing).

The printer needs to know everything the graphic designer does plus the type of paper stock, the method of folding or binding, and the number of brochures you want printed.

And it helps all vendors if you give them a rough deadline for completion of the work along with any budget you may have in mind.

You may object, "But I don't know these things now! And I won't until the designer actually does a layout that I approve."

That's okay. The vendors know you haven't made all these decisions yet. But they do need to get at least a rough idea of what you want if they're to quote you a price. The more accurate and precise your specifications, the more accurate the price quotations will be. If you're vague, the vendors will have to make their best guess, and their uncertainty will be reflected in a higher price. In addition, the price can change substantially if you change the specifications once the job is under way.

When you add up price quotations from various vendors, you may be shocked to find that producing the brochure costs much more than you thought it would. This is likely to happen if you haven't had much recent experience hiring writers, photographers, artists, and other professionals. Their services can mean the difference between a successful brochure and a poor one, but these services are not cheap.

Does this mean you can't afford to produce a brochure? Of course not! You can cut corners and do away with some luxury items and still end up with a first-class piece. For example, maybe the cost of four-color printing and photography is putting the brochure of your dreams beyond your reach. But a talented designer skilled in using black-and-white photography and two-color design might be able to produce an equally impressive piece of literature that's far less expensive. Or it may be your choice of paper that's boosting the price. Perhaps you unintentionally selected a paper stock that's rare and expensive. There may be another paper that, although slightly different, looks just as good and costs far less.

The point is: Once you go through the exercise of determining your brochure specifications and putting together a budget, you can adjust different elements to fit your pocketbook without cramping your promotional style.

What is the format?

When I say *format*, I'm not talking about the subtle nuances of design or the complexities of the printing process. I am suggesting that you get a rough idea of the form your brochure will take so you can get a better handle on the cost of design, artwork, printing, and copywriting.

Basically, you should make educated guesses on four things: (1) the number of words of text, (2) the number and type of visuals, (3) the number and size of pages (and method of folding or binding), and (4) the use of color and paper stock.

Make your best guess on how many words of text (called *copy* in the advertising and publishing trades) your brochure will contain. This number helps estimate two expenses: the writer's fee and the cost of setting type.

You may object and say, "How do I know how long it will be until it is written?" But I'm asking for a rough guess, not an exact word count.

Make your rough estimate of word length as follows: When you type brochure copy, you'll use double spacing (for easy editing), and a double-spaced typewritten sheet contains about 250 words. Make a list of the topics you plan to cover in the brochure. Then guess how many pages you'll have to write to cover the topic adequately. If you're not sure, set a range (e.g., 3 to 4 pages). Add up the page count for the sections, multiply the total by 250 words per page, and you have your rough word count for estimating typography and writer's fees.

Estimating the number and type of visuals is a little easier. You simply make a list of all the subjects that you want to visualize and then assign the type of treatment most appropriate to each. For example, if you're doing a brochure on a car, you might want to feature the car interior, the exterior, the engine, and fuel efficiency information. Color photos are best for showing the interior and the exterior because people what to see exactly what they're buying. To explain the workings of the engine, you might prefer an exploded diagram that allows for more detail than a photo. And a graph of some sort is perfect for demonstrating fuel efficiency as a function of miles per hour.

However, assigning the number and type of visuals to be used is largely a matter of personal preference. You'll have to balance your ideas and personal preferences with what can actually be done within your budget guidelines. Knowing the number and type of visuals helps you estimate photography, illustration, and printing costs. (Chapter 7 covers visuals in great detail.)

The choice of page size depends on how you want to present the information and how the brochure is to be used. If your brochure consists of many short, separate sections, a smaller page may be most appropriate. If the brochure consists of a small number of lengthy sections illustrated with elaborate graphs and diagrams, the standard 8½-by-11-inch page is best.

For a brochure used in direct mail, the smaller size may be more economical in terms of envelopes and postage. But the small brochure can get lost in a file folder or binder, whereas the larger brochure won't. An oversized brochure (larger than 11 inches high) may grab attention when received but is likely to be discarded because it won't fit in a standard file folder or cabinet.

Once you've selected page size, the number of pages depends on the content and design. The more copy and visuals you have, the longer the brochure will be. However, a given brochure can have few pages if a lot of copy and artwork is crammed onto each page. Or it can be many pages long if the designer leaves a lot of "white space" and puts a minimum of art and copy on each page. The size of the type also helps determine number of pages.

Again, I don't expect you to design the brochure yourself. But if you have a rough idea of the look, size, and layout of your brochure, you'll have an easier time communicating your ideas to designers and printers.

If you set your brochure in the same size type that most newspapers and magazines do, you can fit a maximum of 1,200 words of solid text on an 8½-by-11-inch page. With white space, headlines, photos, and artwork, that number will probably drop to 500 words or so, depending on how tightly you want to pack each page. Keeping these constraints in mind, you can make an educated guess on the number of pages you'll need to accommodate all the copy you expect to write.

Whether to use color is another decision you'll make early on. The most inexpensive brochures are printed in one color. This is usually black on white, but it doesn't have to be. Sometimes, you can create an expensive-looking effect by printing a colored ink on a colored stock, such as maroon ink on gray paper or dark brown ink on off-white or beige stock.

Bob Bly Communications

INDUSTRIAL PUBLICITY AND SALES PROMOTION

Your Communication Needs
Bob Bly Communications is a company specializing in industrial publicity and sales promotion. It's our job to help you communicate with engineers, technical managers, purchasing agents, and other industrial buyers.

We can create:

- Brochures
- Technical bulletins
- Direct mail
- Catalogs
- Case histories
- Ads
- Journal articles
- Technical papers
- Speeches

- New product releases
- Publicity campaigns
- Slide presentations
- Films and videotapes
- Sales letters
- Newsletters
- Manuals
- Proposals
- Reports

We're in business to promote your business. Increasing your profits is our bottom line. We produce communications that can generate thousands of inquiries, build your image in the marketplace, and help increase your sales.

How We Work With You
Bob Bly Communications is here to help you in any way we can.

Here's how we work with our clients:

☐ Bob Bly Communications can create and manage your entire marketing communications program... including advertising, publicity, and sales promotion.

☐ We can also work with you by the project. Call us when you need an ad, brochure, catalog, or any other promotion.

☐ In addition, we can help you write and edit all your technical communications. Our editorial services include copywriting for bulletins and sales letters. Technical writing and editing for proposals, manuals, and reports. And ghostwriting for trade journal articles, technical papers, and speeches.

We do not charge a retainer or collect commissions for placing ads in magazines. You pay us only when you need us.

You can hire us by the job. By the hour. Or by the day.

Why We're Good At What We Do
Clear writing and an understanding of technology are the foundations of our work.

Our clients come from a wide variety of industries including computers, construction, chemical equipment, pollution control, plastics processing, defense, electronics, telecommunications, and many other areas. We strive to keep our technical knowledge of these industries thorough and up-to-date.

We combine technical know-how with the ability to write about industrial products and systems in plain, simple English. The promotions we produce are always interesting, helpful, and easy to read.

336 East 81st Street
New York, NY 10028
(212) 861 4717

Figure 8. This inexpensive service brochure consists of copy only. The type is printed in brown ink on fine, off-white paper stock. The brochure folds for mailing in a standard number 10 envelope.

A second color gives the designer another element to work with. It can highlight portions of text, headlines, and visuals. It also adds about 15 to 20 percent to the cost of printing.

Brochures with reproductions of color photos are called *full-color* brochures. Full-color printing is the most expensive, and each color photo you add can boost production costs by at least several hundred dollars.

The choice of paper stock also has a great effect on printing costs. You won't make the final selection until you're sitting down with printers to get bids, but now is the time to make some initial decisions. Do you want glossy or nonglossy stock? Heavy or lightweight paper? A smooth stock or a paper with body, feel, and texture? Do you want the cover printed on a heavier stock than the inside pages? Will you use white or colored paper?

If you find it hard to describe what you want in words or sketches, get some paper and tape and scissors and make a crude mock-up of the piece. Such a mock-up is known as a *dummy.* The dummy gives people an idea of the size, format, fold, look, and weight of the finished piece.

Another way of communicating your ideas on layout and format is to find a similar brochure published by another organization and show it to your artist or printer. I keep a thick file folder that contains any printed piece of literature that catches my eye. When I want to describe a particular look, style, typeface, paper stock, or graphic technique to someone, I can usually find a sample of what I want in this file. You should start your own sample file.

Don't worry about making the wrong choice or about whether you have bad taste. Remember, you're not locked into a particular format until the job goes to the printer, and your designer may suggest alternatives to what you originally selected. But you should try to decide on the basic format now so that you'll be better able to describe to others the look you want to achieve.

What is your schedule?

How long should it take to produce a brochure? That depends on many factors. You can write, design, and print a simple flier in a week. But an annual report can take three or four months to complete.

My feeling is: The more time, the better. I'd rather extend the deadline and get it right than do a rush job that is less than perfect. After all, producing literature is expensive, and you'll have to live with most pieces a long time.

Jane Maas, a senior officer at the Wells, Rich, Greene advertising agency, says that you should allow 120 days from the start of the writing and design to delivery of the finished literature from the printer. And my experience has proven that to be a good guideline for scheduling.

Each phase of each project is different and will take a different amount of time to complete. Sketching a few simple line drawings for a small pamphlet may take an artist only a few hours; illustrating a large brochure on a complicated medical procedure might involve several weeks of work.

To help you plan, I've listed the stages of brochure production in the left-hand column below. The middle column indicates how many days the task normally takes to complete on a typical project. Right now, use this as a guide; later, you can fill in the blanks in the third column. To do that, you'll have to get estimates from the writer, artist, typesetter, and printer to find out the time each phase of your project will take.

Task	Days to complete (typical project)	Days to complete (your project)
Research and writing	10	_____
Copy review	5	_____
Copy rewrite	5	_____
Design	10	_____
Design review	5	_____
Design revision	5	_____
Typesetting	3	_____
Photography	10	_____
Illustration	10	_____
Mechanicals (paste-up)	5	_____
Printing (add 15 days for four-color job)	10	_____
Delays, mistakes	5	_____
Total Days	83	_____

On some projects, you'll be uncertain about the exact content and appearance of the finished piece, and you will have to finish one phase of the project before you go on to the next (e.g., you can't take photos until the design is approved and you know what visuals you want). If that's the case, you can follow the sequence of steps as I have listed them: copy, design, typesetting, photography and art, paste-up, and printing.

According to my schedule, that takes 83 days. If your suppliers work fast, you can cut the time down. But if there are problems—the photos don't come out, there are mistakes in the type, the copywriter does a bad job— they can easily add a month to the job. That's why Jane Maas's 120-day rule of thumb is a good one.

However, if you've carefully followed and analyzed the first nine key planning points presented in this chapter, you may have a clear-enough description of the finished piece to combine steps and save time. If, for example, you know the format and the visuals you want, you can do the copy, design, illustration, and photography all at once. Then you would set type, paste up the mechanical, and print the brochure. By combining steps, you can cut the time required to 43 days—an example of how planning can save you time.

To sum it all up

I know we've covered a lot of ground in this chapter. To help you put it all together, I've included a literature specification sheet, which follows. This form provides a handy way of collecting the information.

Make copies of the form. When you're contemplating your next project, fill out a specification sheet as completely as possible. Then circulate copies of the completed sheet to vendors and company personnel involved in the project. Vendors can use the information to provide accurate price quotations, and your people can see at a glance the project you've planned.

Literature Specification Sheet

1. **Objectives of the literature** (check all that are appropriate):

   - ☐ Provide product information to customers
   - ☐ Educate new prospects
   - ☐ Build corporate image
   - ☐ Establish credibility of your organization or product
   - ☐ Sell the product directly through the mail
   - ☐ Help salespeople get appointments
   - ☐ Help salespeople make presentations
   - ☐ Help close the sale
   - ☐ Support dealers, distributors, and sales representatives
   - ☐ Add value to the product
   - ☐ Enhance the effectiveness of direct mail promotions
   - ☐ Leave with customers as a reminder
   - ☐ Respond to inquiries
   - ☐ Hand out at trade shows, fairs, conventions
   - ☐ Display at point of purchase
   - ☐ Serve as reference material for employees, vendors, the press
   - ☐ Disseminate news
   - ☐ Announce new products and product improvements
   - ☐ Highlight new applications for existing products
   - ☐ Train and educate new employees
   - ☐ Recruit new employees
   - ☐ Provide useful information to the public
   - ☐ Generate new business leads
   - ☐ Qualify your company to be on a customer's approved-vendor list
   - ☐ Other (describe): _____

2. **The type of literature needed** (check one):

   - ☐ annual report   ☐ booklet   ☐ brochure
   - ☐ case history   ☐ catalog   ☐ circular
   - ☐ data sheet   ☐ flier   ☐ invoice stuffer
   - ☐ newsletter   ☐ poster
   - ☐ other (describe): _____

3. **The subject**

   a. What is the subject matter of the literature (describe the product, service, program, organization, and so on)?

   b. What is the theme, the central message (if any)?

   c. What supporting information is to be included (price, reliability, efficiency, performance, quality, test results, testimonials, technical specifications, and so on)?

   d. What is the source of this information (where can the writer get the necessary background material)?

   e. What facts are missing? What research is required (if any)?

4. **Who is the audience?**

   a. Geographic location _____
   b. Income level _____
   c. Family status (married/single) _____
   d. Industry _____
   e. Job title/function _____
   f. Education _____
   g. Politics _____
   h. Religion/ethnic background _____
   i. Age _____
   j. Concerns (reasons why they might be interested in the subject matter of the literature): _____
       _____
       _____

   k. General description of the target audience (in your own words):

5. **Sales appeals**

    a. What is the key sales appeal of the product?

    b. What are the supporting or secondary sales points?

6. **What image do you want the literature to convey to the reader?**

7. **Environment**

    a. What images and sales appeals do competitors' brochures stress?

Competitor	Image	Key sales appeal
_____	_____	_____
_____	_____	_____
_____	_____	_____
_____	_____	_____
_____	_____	_____

    b. How does the brochure fit into your sales cycle? (check all that apply)

    ☐ Generate leads
    ☐ Answer initial inquiries
    ☐ Provide more detailed information to qualified buyers
    ☐ Establish confidence in company and its products
    ☐ Provide detailed product information
    ☐ Answer questions frequently asked by prospects
    ☐ Support for salespeople during presentations
    ☐ Reinforce sales message for prospects ready to buy
    ☐ Close the sale
    ☐ Other (describe): _____
    _____

8. **Budget** (What will it cost to produce?)

Task	Cost ($)
Copywriting	_____
Photography	_____
Artwork	_____
Typography	_____
Design	_____
Mechanicals	_____
Printing	_____
Total	$_____

Number of copies to be printed: _____

9. **Format**

a. Approximate number of words _____
b. Number of color photos _____
c. Number of black-and-white photos _____
d. Number and type of illustrations and other visuals (describe):

e. Number of pages _____
f. Page size _____
g. Method of folding or binding (describe): _____

_____

h. Number of colors used in printing _____
i. Color scheme of brochure (describe): _____

_____

j. Type of paper (weight, finish, texture, color) _____

_____

10. **Schedule** (How long will it take to complete?)

Task	Number of days to complete
Copy	_____
Copy review	_____
Copy rewrite	_____
Design	_____
Design review	_____
Design revision	_____
Typesetting	_____
Photography	_____
Illustration	_____
Mechanicals	_____
Printing	_____
Delays, mistakes	_____
Total	_____

Note: Total days can be reduced if steps are combined and done simultaneously.

CHAPTER THREE

People Who Can Help You (And Where to Find Them)

Do you need help?

Can you do the brochure yourself? Or do you need help? It is possible to handle the job yourself (except for the printing, of course). You can write the copy, take the photos, use *clip art* (stock illustrations) or create your own visuals, make headlines and subheads out of rub-on *press-type* lettering, type the body copy on your typewriter, and cut and paste the whole thing together. If it's a simple flier, you can even run it off on your office copier and avoid going to an outside printer.

Why, then, would you want to hire a writer, photographer, artist, or illustrator? Quality. These folks are professionals, just as you are. But whereas your area of expertise is management, engineering, retailing, fund raising, administration, or whatever, theirs is creating promotional material.

Most people wouldn't dream of defending themselves in court or removing their own appendix. They'd rely on a professional, a lawyer or doctor, to do the job successfully. But in business, these same people don't make use of advertising and graphic design professionals. Instead, they try to save money by writing their own copy, taking their own photos, pasting up their own mechanicals.

That's a mistake, one of the worst you can make. Unless you're a skilled writer, you'll weaken your brochure and obscure its message with poorly written, off-the-mark copy. Unless you're a gifted shutterbug, your amateur photos will look just that way—amateur and cheap—when published in your catalog or annual report.

I'm not saying that you should never tackle brochure work. If you simply can't afford professional help, or if you have the artistic and mechanical skills, you may be able to save money by doing much of the job yourself. Unfortunately, most of us aren't writers, artists, photographers, illustrators, and designers all rolled into one. We don't have the ability to pull off even a passable job on copy, art, or photography. And if we attempt to do the work ourselves, we'll botch it.

What should you do? Above all, you want to avoid poor quality and amateurish work. If you don't have the money to hire a professional photographer, and if neither you nor anyone you know can take professional-quality photos, try to get the photos you need from another source, such as a stock photo house or other organization. For example, many manufacturers provide free product photos to their distributors for use in circulars, local advertising, and other promotions. Another ready source of photos is books and magazines. If you're reading a book or magazine and see a photo you'd like to use in your own printed materials, write to the publisher for permission to reproduce it. You will receive a form you must sign and will usually have to pay a fee ranging from $50 to several hundred dollars.

If there isn't an inexpensive source for the photo you need, it's better to omit photos than to use the fuzzy shots taken by Uncle Joe. Perhaps simpler, less expensive spot drawings will do just as well. Or maybe the copy says it all, and you don't even need a visual. Often you'll find that the fancy photography, artwork, design, or typography you want but can't afford wasn't really necessary in the first place.

Many projects require more sophisticated design and production, and that's where the services of professionals are needed. This chapter will teach you how to find, choose, and work with various advertising professionals, as well as how to evaluate the work they've done for you.

Let's start by meeting all the people and organizations you might call on for help: advertising agencies, public relations firms, creative boutiques, art and copy services, design studios, copywriters, graphic artists, photographers, illustrators, typographers, and printers.

Advertising agencies

The main advantage of using an advertising agency is that it will handle the entire job for you, from strategy and concept to copywriting and design to paste-up and printing. The ad agency will assign an *account executive* to act as liaison between you and the various departments of the agency. You'll be spared having to coordinate the work of the writer, artist, photographer, printer, and other outside suppliers; the agency will do it all.

The disadvantage is that you'll pay a premium for this extra service. So you have to decide: Are you willing to pay to have someone else take over much of the burden of the job? Or do you want to save money by hiring free-lancers and outside suppliers and supervising the job yourself?

Another advantage of advertising agencies is that they're set up to handle coordinated campaigns of literature, advertising, publicity, and promotion. They can also act as advertising consultants, helping you to formulate a marketing plan and set your advertising strategy. So, if you're planning a program with many pieces of sales literature and other promotions, an ad agency can orchestrate it for you to increase its effectiveness.

Most advertising agencies shy away from one-shot projects. They prefer to work with clients on an ongoing basis. So if you're planning to produce only a single brochure or catalog, you'll have a hard time finding an ad agency willing to take on such a small amount of work. Even a small advertising agency expects a client to spend a minimum of about $50,000 a year on advertising and promotion. If your budget is less, an ad agency probably isn't for you. But don't despair. There are other suppliers who can help.

Public relations firms

Public relations (PR) firms are specialists at getting free coverage for their clients in newspapers and magazines and on radio and TV. For example, a PR firm representing a bank might arrange to have the bank president interviewed on the evening news or get the press to cover the grand opening of a new branch.

Today, many PR firms produce promotional literature as an added service for their clients. The literature is used as handouts at press conferences and other special events or to answer inquiries generated by press coverage of an organization or its products.

Like advertising agencies, PR firms handle the entire job for you from initial idea to finished printed piece. However, most require a monthly retainer from their clients, whereas most ad agencies do not. The minimum monthly retainer is usually $1,000, which comes to $12,000 a year. This means a small organization without the budget to hire an ad agency can still afford the services of a PR firm. However, you must pay the retainer fee even if you have no work for your PR firm that month.

Also, although many PR firms are quite skilled in literature production, their primary business is publicity, not brochures. If you hire a PR firm to handle your publicity, chances are they're a good choice to do your literature as well. But if you need literature only and have no ongoing public relations campaign, you'll be better off using another supplier.

Creative boutiques

A *creative boutique* is a limited-service advertising agency that offers only *creative services*—copywriting, design, illustration, photography, mechanical preparation, and production for commercials, advertisements, and literature. It does not get involved with ad placement, media planning, market research, marketing, mailing list selection, or any of the administrative or business services provided by full-service ad agencies.

The advantage of using a creative boutique instead of a full-service agency is that you don't end up paying for services you don't need. It costs the full-service agency money to maintain marketing, account management, and media departments. All clients end up paying for that overhead, either directly or indirectly. If you want just sales literature production, you don't need an agency with a television production department or a market research director. So why pay for it? A creative boutique can handle all your requirements and will probably cost you less.

Unfortunately, there are no listings for creative boutiques in the phone book or industry directories. Creative boutiques are lumped together with the full-service agencies. The way to find out what services an agency offers is by word of mouth or direct inquiry. Call the agency and ask. They'll tell you whether they offer full service or creative only.

Because their operations are more limited, creative boutiques are generally smaller than full-service agencies and are therefore more willing to take on smaller accounts. However, one or two small booklets may not be enough of an assignment to get a boutique to handle your business. The creative boutique is probably looking for a client who will give it work on a regular basis. So if you're a one-shot client, you might be better off looking elsewhere.

Design studios

A design studio provides design and paste-up services for printed material. It designs the layout and look of the piece, then prepares a camera-ready mechanical for reproduction by the printer. Unlike an advertising agency, which handles all phases of the job and supervises every activity from start to finish, most design studios provide design services only. The majority do not write copy, shoot photographs, or handle the printing for you (although some do).

Let's say you already have good photos on file, can write the brochure yourself, and want to save money by going to the printer directly and eliminating the middleman. All you need is someone to do the layout and paste-up. A design studio may be the perfect solution for you.

These days, many design studios are expanding their services to include copy, market research, and photography. But they rarely have writers, photographers, and researchers on staff. Instead, if they offer to handle the copy for you, it's likely they will go out and hire a free-lancer, the same free-lancer you could hire directly if you wanted to.

Art-and-copy services

An art-and-copy service is a scaled-down version of a creative boutique. Although some are large, most art-and-copy services consist of a free-lance artist and a free-lance copywriter working together to provide art and copy in a single package.

Is an art-and-copy service better than an agency, boutique, or studio? An art-and-copy service will probably cost less (because you're dealing with two people instead of a large organization) and give you a closer working relationship with the people who actually write and design your brochure (because you aren't working through an account executive or some other intermediary). However, art-and-copy services lack the resources of larger companies: comfortable offices, a large staff, money, and volume discounts with printers, typographers, and other vendors.

Is using an art-and-copy service better than hiring individual free-lancers? With an art-and-copy service, you get design and text from a single source. Some people feel that an artist and a writer working together produce work that is superior to the efforts of an artist and a writer working separately. Others disagree. In most cases, art-and-copy services are more expensive than individual free-lancers of comparable quality.

Free-lancers

Ad agencies, PR firms, and creative boutiques offer a completely integrated service, a single source for all phases of brochure production. Design studios and art-and-copy services are an intermediate step, offering some services but not all. At the other end are free-lancers, self-employed advertising and graphics professionals. Each free-lancer handles one specific task: copywriting, illustration, photography, layout, paste-up.

There are many arguments for and against going with an agency or using free-lancers. Here are some of the arguments in favor of free-lancers.

- The best writers, artists, and photographers are often free-lancers, because they can earn more money on their own than with a company or an agency.
- Free-lancers are available for small projects and one-time assignments. They work and get paid only when you need them. Agencies look for a long-term commitment and shy away from one-shot projects.
- Free-lancers don't require a lot of management or supervision. They often work at a remote location and have minimum contact with you, the client. You save time as a result.
- Using free-lancers gives you access to a diverse pool of talent and, hence, to a broader range of skills and ideas. An in-house advertising department or medium-size ad agency might have only two or three writers on staff. But if you use free-lance writers, you can choose from among several hundred.
- Free-lancers save you money. When you hire a free-lancer, you pay only for his or her time. When you hire an ad agency, you pay for the corporate overhead as well as for the many supervisory and intermediary people who coordinate the work between you and the writers and artists.

Of course, there are also disadvantages to using free-lancers.

- Your agency is available at your beck and call, but a free-lancer has no such commitment to you. Successful free-lancers are often booked up months in advance, and the free-lancer you want to use may not be able to take on a job when you need it.
- Agencies and staff employees gain a more in-depth knowledge about your product and your business than the free-lancer who is called in only occasionally. Every time you work with a new free-lancer, you have to brief him or her from scratch, and that can be time-consuming.
- When you use free-lancers, someone in your company must take on the responsibility of coordinating the activities of a half dozen or more different outside people. When you deal with an ad agency, an account executive handles the project coordination for you.
- Free-lancers are an independent lot. They may not develop the kind of team spirit and enthusiasm for your company that your in-house staff or agency has.
- Not all free-lancers are of equal caliber. Most are good at what they do, but I've heard horror stories from advertisers who have gotten burned by incompetents. You must check out free-lancers thoroughly before you hire them.

Despite these drawbacks, free-lancers are in heavy demand. *Adweek* magazine reports that in a recent survey of Connecticut and New York firms, 62 percent said they use free-lance writers and photographers. Alfred W. Brown, director of the September Days travel club, explains the logic behind using free-lancers:

> The main idea is to utilize the talents and skills of individuals who are uniquely suited to a particular project. It's like shopping at 10 specialty stores rather than writing one check to Sears.

If you need help producing a brochure, you'll probably deal with free-lance copywriters, artists, and photographers.

➤ Copywriters

A *copywriter* is a person who writes the text of advertising and promotional materials. Copywriters specialize. Some concentrate on TV commercials and print ads. Others ghostwrite feature articles and churn out press releases. Some of the highest-paid copywriters are those who handle direct mail.

It's important to select a copywriter who is experienced in writing brochures, catalogs, and other printed literature. Many copywriters who specialize in consumer ad campaigns or TV and radio commercials are accustomed to working with a limited number of words and cannot write the kind of lengthy, sustained informational copy that is effective in promotional literature. They are used to writing sixty words for a thirty-second commercial for soda pop or fast foods and simply cannot dig into the level of detail required to produce an 8-page brochure on a mobile home or a minicomputer.

There are several ways to locate free-lance copywriters. One is word of mouth; ask business associates to recommend a writer. Another method is to run a help-wanted ad in your local paper. You can also find free-lance copywriters listed in the Yellow Pages (under "writer," "copywriter," or "advertising services") and in the industry directories listed at the end of this chapter. Many copywriters also advertise their services in such trade journals as *Adweek, Advertising Age,* and *Direct Marketing.*

What will you pay for copy? As free-lance copywriter Sig Rosenblum observes, "Fees are all over the lot." Of course, the more experienced the writer, the higher the charge.

At the bottom of the scale, some junior writers in rural locations charge as little as $20 to $35 an hour. Such a person can write competently enough to handle simple fliers and announcements but may lack the copywriting skill and product knowledge needed to tackle more complex tasks.

In the middle are generalists, copywriters who take on any assignment and have no particular specialty. These writers can produce good copy. But because they have minimal background in your industry, they probably need a lot of help understanding your product and your marketing strategy. A generalist's fee ranges from $40 to $60 an hour.

At the top are specialists, copywriters who work exclusively in a certain industry or on a special type of copy. Some of the highest-paid copywriting specialties are financial, medical, industrial, high-tech, annual reports, and direct mail. Top copywriters charge from $100 to $400 or more an hour and earn anywhere from $125,000 to $250,000 or more a year.

I've given fees in hourly rates so you can make comparisons. But free-lance copywriters usually charge in one of three ways: by the hour, by the day, or by the project. I'm a free-lance copywriter, and I charge by the project. I think that method is fairest to the client. With an hourly or per-diem rate, the client and copywriter are never quite sure what the final bill will be. With a fixed project price agreed to in advance, there are no surprises.

What will copywriting cost by the project? Again, it varies, but I can give you a rough idea. For a small booklet or folded brochure designed to fit in a standard business envelope, expect to pay anywhere from $500 to $1,500. For a more complete brochure, with between 4 and 8 full-size (8½-by-11 inch) pages, the cost could range from $800 to $5,000, depending on the amount of copy. For a catalog, expect to pay anywhere from $25 to $200 per item. Annual reports are the most ambitious projects and can run from $5,000 to $10,000.

When you receive the copy, you may want to make changes. If your writer is working on an hourly or per-diem rate, you simply pay for the time it takes to make the revisions. But if you negotiate a project price, find out how much revision it includes (or whether it includes revisions at all). Otherwise, you could be stuck.

➤ **Artists**

Graphic artists perform three basic services: design, paste-up, and illustration. Some artists do all three; others, just one or two. That's something you will want to find out before you hire anyone.

Design involves determining what the printed page should look like: where the photos, type, and headlines are positioned; the size and style of the typography; the cropping and size of photos and illustrations; the number of columns of text and the size of the page; and the use of color.

The final product of the design stage is a sketch of what the pages of the finished printed piece will look like. This sketch is known as a *comprehensive* or *comp*. For design services, artists charge from $40 to $75 or more an hour.

The next step is to produce a *mechanical*, a paste-up of typeset body copy, headlines, and visuals, ready to be reproduced on a printing press. Some designers prefer to do their own mechanicals; some subcontract the work to other artists; others will turn the comp over to you and let you worry about finding someone to paste up the type. Because making mechanicals from someone else's comp requires a little less artistic creativity than designing a brochure from scratch, mechanical artists command a lesser fee, anywhere from $10 to $25 an hour.

If your brochure has drawings, you'll also need an illustrator. Hourly fees vary widely, from $10 to $100 and up, depending on the type of illustration required. Someone who produces elaborate full-color oil paintings is likely to get a higher fee than an artist who draws simple black-and-white line sketches.

Most illustrations are commissioned by the project, however, not by the hour. Again, price is a function of complexity and of your ability to define precisely what it is you want the artist to produce. A simple line graph can be bought for $75 to $125. A color portrait of your company's board of directors can run over $1,000.

When selecting an illustrator or designer, take a look at his or her portfolio (sample case of work). Pick someone whose style matches what you have in mind for your own brochure. If you like simple, dignified, straightforward, all-text pamphlets, you probably don't want Avante-garde Abie, whose latest annual report for Safebuy Supermarkets won many artistic awards but was considered unreadable because it was printed on the inside of a brown-paper shopping bag.

For mechanicals, the choice of artist is less critical. You want someone whose work is neat and clean, someone who knows the mechanical requirements of professional printers. Although some small businesses have gambled and won by hiring student artists from local art schools, I don't recommend this for mechanicals. Most students simply don't have enough experience working with real projects to produce a mechanical a printer can live with.

➤ **Photographers**

"Why should I hire a photographer to take photos for my slide show?" one product manager recently asked me. "Anyone can take a picture!"

"Very few people can take a good picture," I replied, "but most people think they can."

Don't fool yourself into thinking you can save $500 by setting a velvet cloth on your dining room table, taking out the 35-millimeter self-focusing camera you got for your birthday, and shooting a photo of your new widget for your brochure. The photo may look passable when it comes back from the developer. But when it's printed in the brochure, you'll know why you should have gone to a pro in the first place.

Photographers charge by the hour, the day, or the project. Day rates range from $125 to $2,000 and up; $500 is about average. When a photographer quotes you a fee, ask whether it includes film, processing, props, and other materials. These incidentals can add a hefty amount to the final bill, so if they're not included, try to get a rough estimate of what they'll cost.

If you need one or two shots at a single location, the job can probably be done in a day. Travel from one faraway location to the next is the most common cause of inflated photographer's bills, so if you can arrange to have all your photos shot in a single location, you'll save a lot of money.

As with artists and writers, choose a photographer whose specialty, style, and level of experience meet your needs—and your budget. A photographer specializing in food or fashion may charge as much as $2,500 for a single color photo. But an industrial photographer can take a competent photo of your submersible pump and charge you only $250 for it.

Whatever your needs, be sure to pick a photographer with experience shooting for advertising and promotion. Wedding photographers and those who take family portraits for a living aren't the ones you want for your brochure.

Typographers

Typographers use special machines to produce *type.* Type is lettering printed on photographic paper. This lettering can be pasted up on a board and reproduced on a printing press for use in books, catalogs, magazines, newspapers, advertisements, brochures, and other printed matter.

Type is much more flexible than the lettering produced by word processors or typewriters, which is why most brochures are typeset rather than typed on office typewriters. There are perhaps a dozen or so different styles of typewriter lettering, but there are thousands of different typefaces to choose from. What's more, typesetting machines let you alter the size, thickness, spacing, and height of the letters, as well as the width of columns and the spacing between lines. Typeset type also reproduces more cleanly and reliably than typewriter lettering, which can often smudge or form an incomplete character.

How much do you need to know about typesetting? Not much. The person designing your brochure will pick the typeface and show you a sample before the entire text of the brochure is set. (To be on the safe side, ask your designer whether he or she plans on doing this. If your designer doesn't, insist on it. Changing typefaces after the type is set is extremely expensive.)

If you're unhappy with the type, you can always choose another, but the designer takes the responsibility for selecting and *specifying* type (picking its size and style) and ordering it from the type house.

At least, that's how it works most of the time. The exception is if you're operating on a shoestring budget. A designer usually puts a small markup on the type he or she buys for you, so if you want to save money, you can buy the type directly. The designer writes the specifications, but *you* go to the typographer, place the order, pay them directly, pick up the type, and deliver it to your artist. I don't think the saving is worth the trouble, but if every dollar is a hardship, buying your own type is one way of stretching your brochure budget.

Type costs vary with the amount of type being set and with the style you choose. Some simple typefaces are *standard,* meaning every typesetter has them and they cost less to set. Other typefaces are available only at typographers with the special equipment needed to produce them, and these typographers charge a premium for such hard-to-get styles.

You can get a firm price quotation by taking your copy to the typesetter and picking the type you want to set it in. But I can give you a rough idea of type costs here. To set my name, address, and phone number in type for stationery and business cards has cost me as little as $7 at a neighborhood printshop (some printers also set type) and as much as $50 in a custom type shop. For a single page of solid text, typesetting can range from $50 to $300 or more—again, depending on the type style and where you buy. You can save money over the long run by shopping around; the cost of a specific job can vary by as much as 30 percent from one typographer to the next.

Even if you don't buy your own type, you might enjoy owning the *type books* from several local typographers. These books, given to potential customers free of charge, contain samples of the various typefaces the typographer can produce. Get some type books and thumb through them. You may spot a type that's perfect for your next project.

Printers

With a typewritten technical manual or a 1-page black-and-white flier, you may be able to get away with reproducing it on the office photocopier. But any piece of literature used to promote your organization or your product should be reproduced by a professional printer.

Selecting a printer is a two-step process. The first step takes place at the beginning of the brochure production cycle; the second step, when the mechanical is finished and the brochure is ready for printing.

In the first step, you call up half a dozen printers in your area. Explain the type of project you have in mind. The printers interested in handling the job will either stop by your office to show you samples of their work or have you come to their shops to see their operations firsthand.

Ask the printers to give you a rough idea of what your proposed brochure will cost to print. They can't give you a firm quotation because price depends on a number of factors that haven't been decided yet—use of visuals, use of colors, selection of paper stock. But they should be able to give a rough estimate based on your preliminary plans.

In the second stage, choose three printers whose work you like and whose rough estimates were reasonable. Go to these printers with the finished mechanical and complete specifications for paper stock, colors, and number of copies to be printed. Ask them to give you a firm price for the job.

You'll usually pick the lowest estimate, but not always. If the price difference is small, another factor—quality of work, speed of delivery, even the personality of the printer—may make you decide in favor of someone who is slightly more expensive.

What will printing cost? It depends on the quantity and quality desired and on the complexity of the job. You can print a thousand 1-page fliers for $60 on a simple *offset* press (the kind used by résumé shops). The printing bill on a fancy annual report can run well over $100,000. The way you know that you're paying a fair price for printing is to get three estimates on every job from sources you can trust.

How to select an outside vendor

How do you pick the right writer, photographer, artist, typographer, printer? Here are nine tips to help you make the proper selection.

➤ **Look around**

Collect brochures, catalogs, and other printed pieces that strike your fancy. Then call the organizations that published these pieces and ask for the names of the people who did the design, writing, and production. This will give you a list of suppliers whose work you are already familiar with and enthusiastic about.

➤ **Ask around**

Another way to find a service you need is to go to a colleague or competitor and say, "I'm putting together a brochure, and I need a good designer and photographer. Is there anyone you can recommend?"

Organizations in your community that produce printed literature already know who the best writers, artists, photographers, printers, and typesetters are. When you find a supplier through referral, you have the advantage of knowing that the supplier has at least one satisfied customer.

If no one can recommend a good supplier to you, you can go to outside sources, such as the Yellow Pages, trade magazines, and the industry directories listed at the end of this chapter.

➤ **Look for quality**

Your literature doesn't have to be complex, expensive, or elegant. But it should be crisp, sharp, and professional. Shoddy work in graphics, writing, photography, or printing can ruin an otherwise fine piece.

copy:

George Duncan

Copywriter/Consultant

Direct Mail, Mail Order and Direct Response Marketing

(617) 547-5638

29 Concord Avenue Cambridge, MA 02138

Concepts, copy and creative direction for direct response marketing including complete direct mail packages, self-mailer brochures, catalogs and space advertisements.

Consultant to direct marketers, publishers, advertising agencies, organizations and individuals.

Experience encompasses more than 16 years as senior copywriter, copy chief and promotion manager for such leading direct marketers as Ziff-Davis Publishing Co., Columbia House, Grolier Enterprises and Xerox Education Publications, plus full time freelance since 1976 serving a wide variety of publishers, manufacturers, distributors and others.

Awards include the prestigious John Caples Copy Prize and Boston Art Directors Merit Award.

Fees estimated in advance for concepts and copy with copywriter's rough layout and design recommendations. Artist's comprehensive layouts and camera-ready mechanicals quoted separately on request.

Author of monographs, how-to guides and articles in leading trade and professional journals including Direct Marketing, Folio, SRDS List Bulletin, Creative Forum and more. Author of "Copy and Creative" monthly column, Copley Mail Order Advisor.

Speaker and seminar/workshop leader for Direct Marketing Day, Folio Magazine's "Face-to-Face" Publisher's Conference, Paul Butterworth Copy Seminar, Newsletter Association of America plus other direct marketing groups and organizations.

Special attention to magazine and newsletter start-ups; launch promotions; spin-off products and application of direct marketing techniques to both new and existing products and services.

Figure 9. One way to judge advertising professionals is by the quality of their own promotional literature. Here's a sampling of self-promotional brochures produced by some of the country's top free-lancers.

When you're evaluating an outside supplier, check his or her work. If he's a writer, read his sample brochures and catalogs. If she's a photographer, carefully examine her photo portfolio. You'll be amazed at how quality varies from supplier to supplier.

➤ Find someone with experience in your business

Advertising professionals specialize in different areas and industries: fund raising, politics, direct mail, industry, fashion, retail, publishing, finance.

There are three reasons why it pays to pick a vendor with experience in your area.

First, you will be secure in the knowledge that the vendor can handle the assignment. After all, this person knows your business and your products and has handled dozens of assignments like this one.

Second, you will save the time you'd have to spend briefing a writer, designer, or ad agency that didn't already know the basics, and you will only need to supply the specific facts about the particular promotion at hand. Someone who doesn't know your industry would have to be educated from scratch.

Third, a supplier with in-depth knowledge of your industry can do more than write copy or design logos or set type. Often, such a person can provide advice and ideas on a whole range of topics, from sales training to market research to advertising strategy. This knowledge, gained from years of exposure to a particular field, is usually dispensed free to the client along with the professional service actually contracted for. In contrast, an indus-

try outsider can't really give advice, act as a consultant, or prevent you from making marketing mistakes. For the most part, he or she can only follow your lead.

➤ Look for a style that fits your corporate identity

Your organization, no matter how small, has an identity, a style all its own. If it is a big organization, this corporate identity is shaped by the structure and direction of the company as a whole. If it's a smaller, entrepreneurial firm, the style may be dictated entirely by the personality of the owner.

Short of a complete overhaul of your corporate identity (and there are high-priced firms and consultants that specialize in giving such overhauls), you usually want your printed literature to enhance your image, not distort it. That's why you should choose advertising professionals whose style in graphics and writing meshes with your own. If you like dignified, tasteful sales literature, pick a designer whose portfolio is full of dignified, tasteful sales literature. If you want your literature to communicate an image of corporate bigness, choose a designer who specializes in creating annual reports and capabilities brochures for Fortune 500 corporations.

➤ Don't overbook outside talent

Hire free-lancers, vendors, and consultants whose credentials, talents, and fees fit your job and your budget. For example, top advertising photographers get $1,000 a day or more. This may be worth the fee for a corporate ad running in *Forbes* or *Business Week*, but it's overkill for putting a picture of the company picnic in the employee newsletter. A competent publicity photographer can take a few informal shots of the company baseball team for a tenth of what the advertising photographer would charge.

➤ Examine the supplier's client list

Ask to see a list of clients the supplier has worked for recently. A good supplier has an active list of many clients. If a professional is unable to give you a list of clients, it may mean he or she is just starting out and too inexperienced to handle your assignment.

To make sure you're hiring a reliable supplier, you can call a couple of the companies on the client list. If the list doesn't include the names and phone numbers of the people the supplier worked with, ask for a couple of references to call. Then call and ask the references if they were satisfied with the supplier's work. Did the supplier do a top-quality job? Was he or she an easy person to work with or a prima donna? Were deadlines met? Did the final bill match the original estimate? And the most important question: "Would you hire this person again?" If the answer is no, or if it's yes but with some hesitation, you might want to check out a few more suppliers before making your choice.

➤ **Provide complete information**

The two most common questions advertisers ask advertising professionals are "Can you do it?" and "What will it cost?" (The third most common is "How long will it take?") The more information you can give the professional, the more accurate the estimate will be.

Estimating the cost and amount of work involved in writing or designing a brochure is a difficult thing. When you call on, say, a plumber, the plumber can take a look at your leaky toilet and see precisely how much work is involved. But the brochure producer *can't* know exactly what is involved because you don't yet know exactly how you want the finished piece to look and read.

You can help suppliers estimate the job by being as specific and complete as possible. For example, the printer doesn't expect you to name the brand of paper stock you want to use, but you could bring along samples of brochures you've collected to give him an idea of the approximate weight, finish, and appearance of the paper you want for your brochure.

At the end of Chapter 2, I gave you a literature specification sheet to help you plan your sales literature. Fill in this sheet as completely as possible, make copies, and distribute them to vendors you're thinking of hiring. The sheet gives them most of the information they'll need to quote a price on the job; and what they don't know, they'll ask for.

➤ **Talk about price up front**

As you've guessed, I think it's wise to talk about money *before* you hire an outside professional. That's the way I do business, whether I'm writing copy for a software company or hiring a mechanic to fix my car. Find out the supplier's fee and get a written estimate. If the fee is firm, the agreement between the two of you should say so. It should also spell out the terms and conditions of the deal—when the money is to be paid, whether there are additional charges for changes, what happens if you aren't satisfied with the work.

If the estimate is just that, an estimate, find out how much it can vary. If the supplier is working by the day or by the hour, ask for an estimate of how many days or hours it will take to complete the job.

When you come to terms, put them in writing. You can either send a purchase order or letter of authorization to the supplier or ask the supplier to send you a letter or contract that both of you sign. A written agreement clearly spells out what is expected from both parties and helps avoid misunderstandings that can lead to arguments, ill will, collection agencies, and court later on.

How to get the best results

Hiring the right people for the job is the tough part—and the scary part. After all, you've probably never dealt with writers and artists and printers and advertising people before, and their world may be a bit strange to you. But by following my advice and your own common sense, you'll end up with a production team that can do the job—a team you're comfortable with, a team you can trust with the important task of producing your organization's promotional literature.

However, your job doesn't end with hiring these people; that's when it begins. If you're using free-lancers, you will be coordinating the work of half a dozen or more outside suppliers and making sure everything meshes and is completed on schedule. If you're using a full-service source such as an ad agency or PR firm, you will still want to check their progress at each step (outline, copy, layout, illustration, mechanicals, printing) to make sure the job is being done the way you want it. This section offers some tips for getting the best work out of your free-lancers, agencies, and other outside resources.

➤ **Provide thorough and specific guidelines and instructions**

The more precisely you communicate what you're looking for, the closer the finished brochure will be to the vision you had in your head when you started out.

The biggest problem in advertising is that advertisers don't tell their suppliers what they expect from them, and the suppliers don't ask the questions they should ask to find out what the clients want. The result is dissatisfied clients, aggravation, and time and money lost in redoing work that doesn't meet specifications.

As the client, you can avoid this by giving specific and complete briefings to all your suppliers. For example, the artist needs to know any preferences you have concerning the design. You may hate brown, but the artist won't know to stay away from brown unless you make it clear. That's why it helps to sit down with the artist and explain what you have in mind before he or she starts designing the piece.

The writer also requires a thorough briefing. Ideally, you should collect all previously published material on the product and give it to your writer as background information. This material can include ads, brochures, catalogs, annual reports, press releases, articles, product manuals, marketing plans, package labels, diagrams, manufacturer's specification sheets, charts, presentations, speeches, and slide show and film scripts. Once the writer studies this material, he or she will have 80 percent of the information needed to write your piece. And the writer can get the other 20 percent by asking a few well-directed questions.

Printers, typesetters, account executives, consultants, and illustrators will also appreciate a thorough briefing on the project. The more they know, the better the job they'll do.

➤ Be available

Although your suppliers will probably work without direct supervision, they'll need to confer with you from time to time. Be available when they want to discuss an idea, show you a layout, or ask questions about the project. And if they submit work for you to review, approve it (or hand it back for revision) as soon as you can. There are many stages in a project where an outside vendor can't proceed without your input or authorization. If you're not available to review material or provide guidance, the project will be delayed until your supplier hears from you.

One person from your company, either you or your representative, should be the coordinator for the project and act as liaison between your organization and any outside suppliers. To ensure speedy completion of the job, the coordinator should make it his or her business to be available to outside vendors at all times. If the coordinator has to go out of town, he or she should leave a number where he or she can be reached and an address where layouts, copy, and other materials can be sent by overnight express courier.

An ad agency I know of once took on a rush project for an entrepreneur in the seminar business. Despite the tight deadline, the agency presented a schedule and explained that the deadline could be met if both sides, agency and client, adhered to the schedule to the day. The entrepreneur agreed, and the agency started the project. Unfortunately, the entrepreneur ran his business like a one-man band. He was always traveling overseas when the agency needed his input or approval, and he refused to delegate the project to any of his employees. As a result, the agency would work around the clock to produce layouts and copy, only to have it sit unopened for weeks at a time on the entrepreneur's seldom-visited desk. Somehow, the project was completed on time, and the promotion was successful. But the agency was so disgusted that it refused to continue handling the entrepreneur's account.

➤ Don't meddle

There's a difference between being available and being a meddler, and it's the difference between a good client and a bad one. The good client helps the agency or free-lancers when they need help and provides guidance when they ask for it. The bad client, the meddler, *tells* the agency or free-lancers how to do the job or, worse, tries to do it for them. Martin Gross, creative director of Doremus Direct, a direct-response ad agency, wrote about this in an article in *DM News* (Nov. 15, 1983):

> If you meddle with the judgments and the execution of the freelancer, you're not getting what you've paid for. Rewriting, redesigning, and second-guessing are wasteful practices. If you're unhappy with the job, speak up early.

If you don't like the copy, don't rewrite it; instead, tell the writer what's wrong with the copy and have him or her fix it. Don't go out and buy a sketch pad because you think the artist's layout is organized the wrong way. Instead, tell the artist how you want it organized and let the artist redo it.

➤ Be open to new ideas

As the person paying the bills, you're entitled to "have it your way," as the Burger King commercials point out. The final decisions on copy, art, design, layout, and printing are yours.

However, keep in mind that you've hired a team of experts whose only business is the production of advertising materials. If they suggest new ideas or want to handle the project in a somewhat different way, don't instantly reject these new ideas. Instead, listen carefully and think about the ideas and suggestions. Maybe they'll work better than your version; maybe not. But, remember, you're paying these people for their ideas, so why not get your money's worth? Their advice is based on years of experience in an area that is new to you; often, the agency or free-lancer has encountered your type of problem before and already knows how to solve it.

➤ **Make your criticism constructive**

I've never been involved in a brochure project where the client didn't want some changes made somewhere along the way. Sometimes the changes are minor and inconsequential. Sometimes they amount to a major overhaul and drastically change the nature of the finished piece. More often, the revisions lie somewhere between these two extremes.

When you want changes made, be as specific as possible. If you say, "I don't like it," "It doesn't send me," or something equally vague, the writer or artist will have nothing to go on. He or she will know that you're displeased but won't know how to make things right.

If the copy needs revision, go through the manuscript with a red pencil and write in corrections and suggestions. This doesn't mean rewriting copy; it does mean you should supply missing facts and correct wrong ones. Be specific with changes. If the writer has described the function of your product incorrectly, it means he or she doesn't understand how the product works. Don't just write in the margin, "System operation section WRONG!" The writer will have no way of knowing how to correct the error. Instead, attach a brief description of the operation to the manuscript, or tell the writer where to find the missing facts ("See page 3 of old brochure for correct explanation of operations").

Writers and artists are people, too. And creative types often have more fragile egos than the general population. They are, in a sense, putting themselves on the line in their work. So it pays to be tactful when you ask for revisions. Instead of being brusque and negative in your criticisms, be warm, supportive, and positive.

Don't say to your artist, "I can't accept a layout like this! The type is too small, there's too much text on the pages, and the whole thing looks cluttered. Don't you know how to use white space?" Instead, say, "First, let me thank you for getting this done so quickly. Basically, it looks good, and there are only a few changes we need to make. Let's take a look. . . ."

If you are a manager, you know that your employees perform well when they're treated decently. Apply this principle to outside agencies and freelancers, too, and you'll get their best efforts on your brochure.

➤ **Don't change your mind**

The time to agonize over the style and type of literature you want is before your hired help goes to work on it, not after. If you change your mind in midstream, you'll have to pay the price of redoing the work. Also, your indecisiveness will frustrate the people working on your account and cause them to put less than their best effort forward on your behalf.

If you have to make changes, make them early in the production cycle. As the brochure nears completion, even minor changes become extremely costly. For example, if you change the text while it's in manuscript form, the only cost is the writer's revision time. But to change text once the type is set means setting new type, pulling up the old type, and redoing page layouts— at a cost of hundreds or possibly thousands of dollars, depending on the size of the project and the extent of the revisions.

To avoid these extra charges, make sure everyone in your organization has approved the work submitted by your vendor before you authorize the vendor to go on to the next step. Once you approve something, stick with that decision; don't change your mind unless it's absolutely necessary.

➤ Simplify the review process

Most organizations put their promotional literature through an approval cycle before it can be published. The fewer people involved in the review process, the better. If the brochure is rewritten and redesigned by a corporate committee, it will lose its vitality, originality, and selling power; the result will be a bland piece of paper that pleases your management but fails to stir the buying public.

I've seen situations where fifteen people were required to sign off on a document before it could be published. For the best results, you should limit the number of reviewers to three: one person who knows the product from a technical point of view (an engineer, scientist, or researcher), the person responsible for the marketing of the product (a product manager, marketing manager, brand manager, or sales manager), and the person in charge of the company's literature program (an advertising manager, communications manager, or perhaps the division or company president). Any more than that is just excess baggage.

➤ Don't nitpick

If it is your responsibility to review a brochure manuscript and layout, concentrate your criticisms on the important issues: technical accuracy, completeness of content, organization, persuasiveness, readability, format, use of visuals, and overall appearance. Don't fuss about little things that are largely matters of subjective judgment—whether the writer should have used a comma instead of a semicolon, or whether the chairman of the board should be shown wearing a striped tie or a polka-dot tie. When you make changes, make changes of substance. Don't nitpick the copy and layout to death.

➤ **Don't waste time**

Avoid unnecessary meetings, paperwork, correspondence, and conferences. Limit contact with outside vendors to necessary communication. These folks are in business to make a profit. The more of their time you waste, the less profitable your business will be to them. And if your business is not profitable, they will not devote their best efforts to it.

Some clients have the bad habit of calling up their agency or free-lancer half a dozen times a day to ask, "How's it going?" Others expect the agency account executive or free-lancer to come in for a conference every time they want to change a word of copy or replace a photo. You should do neither. Leave your vendors alone, let them do their job, and don't pester. They'll be grateful, and that gratitude will translate into more time spent on your account.

➤ **Pay your bills on time**

Few things make ad agencies and free-lancers as unhappy as not being paid on time. Unpaid invoices put a strain on the supplier/client relationship, and this strain can affect the quality of the work. So pay your bills on time; your vendors will love you for it.

Where to find the help you need

Here is a list of some sources to help you locate the suppliers you need.

- *Standard Directory of Advertising Agencies: The Agency Red Book*, published by the National Register Publishing Company, Inc., 5201 Old Orchard Road, Skokie, IL 60077, (312) 256-6067. This directory lists 4,400 advertising agencies. For each agency, the *Red Book* reports income, number of employees, key accounts, personnel, and the addresses and phone numbers of its offices. The *Red Book* is available in most libraries.
- *O'Dwyer's Directory of Public Relations Firms*, 271 Madison Avenue, New York, NY 10016, (212) 679-2471. This book lists 1,200 public relations firms. It is available in most libraries.
- *The Creative Black Book*, published by Friendly Publications, Inc., 401 Park Avenue South, New York, NY 10016, (212) 684-4255. The *Black Book* lists thousands of photographers, illustrators, graphic designers, TV producers, ad agencies, typographers, audiovisual services, retouchers, and printers. It is available by mail order through the publisher and can also be found in major bookstores.

- *Adweek/Art Directors' Index,* copublished by RotoVision S.A. and Adweek, 820 Second Avenue, New York, NY 10017, (212) 661-8080. The *Index* lists illustrators, graphic designers, photographers, stock photography houses, artist's representatives, TV producers and directors, printers, art directors, audiovisual services, typographers, and copywriters. You can order it from the publisher.
- *Adweek,* 820 Second Avenue, New York, NY 10017, (212) 661-8080. This weekly advertising magazine has a special advertising section for creative services (including free-lance copywriters and graphic designers). It is available by subscription and at some newsstands.
- Also check your local Yellow Pages for listings under "advertising agencies," "public relations firms," "graphic design studios," "artists," "illustrators," "writers," "copywriters," "photographers," "phototypesetters," "typographers," and "printers."

CHAPTER FOUR

Telling Your Story:
The Outline

Why an outline?

Okay, you know you need a brochure. Now tell me what you want to put in it. Not sure? Then join the crowd.

An amazing number of clients come to me claiming an urgent need to produce a brochure as soon as possible. I ask them, "What's the brochure going to be about?" And they answer with a blank stare. They know they need something, but they're not sure exactly what that something is.

That's where an outline can help. An outline is an informal written description of the contents of a planned piece of writing—a brochure, catalog, booklet, article, book, manual, or any other document you want to produce.

I know the word *outline* gives you a twinge of anxiety. It dredges up memories of your schoolrooms, where teachers had you make endless outlines as academic exercises. But to the brochure writer, an outline is no academic exercise; it's a tool that helps the writer—and the client—determine what they want the brochure to say.

Outlines as taught in elementary schools were rigid, useless lists of facts locked into a system of roman and arabic numerals and uppercase and lowercase letters. Remember how you couldn't have a II-A unless you had a II-B? Such restrictions make people shy away from academic outlines, and rightly so.

But a brochure outline need not follow any particular format. It can be as formal or informal, as simple or complex as you like. A numbered list, a series of bulleted items, doodles, rough notes, a stack of index cards—use whatever format suits you. On the following page, for example, is the rough outline for a folder I recently published on my free-lance copywriting services:

Short Outline for Copywriting Folder
1. Introduction to services
2. Qualifications
3. Background
4. How service works
5. Costs, deadlines, revisions
6. How to order

For a short document, this type of simple outline may be more than enough to give your project the direction it needs. If not, you can always expand the outline by describing the contents of each section in detail.

Detailed Outline for Copywriting Folder
1. Introduction to services
   - Thank prospect for requesting brochure
   - Explain that my service is unique—combines copywriting skill with technical background
   - Explain how this service can fulfill prospect's needs
2. Qualifications
   - Number of clients
   - Work for both agencies and advertisers
   - Books published
   - Refer reader to enclosures for more information
3. Background
   - Degree in engineering
   - 95 percent of clients in industrial/technical fields
   - List industries in which I have experience
   - Mention computer books
   - Dedication to business/industrial copy versus consumer accounts
4. How the service works
   - Explain "copy by mail" concept
   - Describe advantages of working by mail—time and money saved, less work for client, ease of ordering copy
5. Costs, deadlines, revisions
   - Give cost of ad and sales letter
   - Firm estimates for other projects given with no obligation or charge
   - Refer reader to enclosed price sheet for more complete details
   - Normal deadline: two weeks

- Will complete job faster if requested
- Copy guaranteed to be completed on time
- No charge for revisions
- Will revise until client is satisfied
6. How to order copy
   - Instruct reader to mail background information on specific projects
   - Refer reader to optional order form (enclosed)
   - Explain policy of half the fee in advance
   - Assignment begins when background, advance check, and purchase order or order form are received
   - Finished assignment delivered by mail
   - Delivery guaranteed by deadline date or sooner
   - Customer satisfaction guaranteed or will rewrite at no cost
   - Ask reader to try my service for a small assignment and see how he or she likes it

An outline helps you divide a writing project into many small, easy-to-handle pieces and parts. For example, the writing of a 200-page technical manual seems a frighteningly complex task. But when you divide the manual into twenty 10-page chapters, it seems a lot less formidable.

Don't think dividing a brochure into separate sections is cheating; professional writers use this technique all the time. Did you ever notice that many magazine articles are written in a list format, such as "Nine Easy Steps," "Ten Tips," "Six Ways"? This is not an accident; articles with short sections are easier for the writer to write and for readers to read.

The level of detail included in the outline depends on what you're comfortable with. Some people like to work from a short list of the general topics to be included in the brochure. Others make a point-by-point outline covering every fact. An intermediate step is a rough outline with some notes describing in brief the contents of each section.

The danger of outlines is getting locked into one that doesn't work. That's why an outline should be treated as a tool, *not* as a commandment etched in stone. For example, your outline may include a product specification under one section, but during the writing you discover that this specification would fit better in a different section. Go ahead and make the change. Use the outline as a guide, but don't get trapped in it.

I tackled the task of writing this book by starting with a list of the chapters in the order they would appear. Because of the book's length, I felt I needed a more detailed guideline; and so under each chapter, I added a list of sections and their headings. When I began to write, I discovered that some new sections needed to be added and that other sections could be combined or cut altogether. I made these changes, and so the finished book doesn't follow my original outline to the letter. But it's pretty close, and without that outline, the book would have been much more difficult to organize and to write.

You might be wondering, "Who writes the outline?" Is it the writer, or is it you? I think the best way of approaching the project is for you, the advertiser, to come up with some idea of what you'd like to put in your brochure. After all, you've lived with the product or service or idea for a long time now. No one knows better than you what needs to be said about it. Your outline doesn't have to be long or formal or typed in any "proper" outline format. Just make a short list of the topics you think should be covered by the literature.

Give the writer this rough outline along with the other background material on the project (the previous ads, brochures, catalog descriptions, specification sheets, and other published material we discussed in Chapter 3). After looking over the background, the writer might decide that the outline needs a little revision. Perhaps some key facts were left out, or maybe the presentation is in the wrong order. The two of you can discuss it and see what changes (if any) you want to make. Or the writer might say that your original outline is right on the mark and follow it accordingly.

If everybody is comfortable with the outline, and if the project isn't terribly complex, the writer can proceed directly to the writing of the brochure text without formally submitting a new outline for your approval. But if the project is complex, if people in your organization can't seem to agree on an outline, or if you're still not entirely sure of the direction the project should take, the writer can create a more formal, more complete outline and submit it for review. Read it, make any changes, and return the corrected outline to the writer, who can then proceed with the first draft of the brochure.

This chapter presents generic or model outlines for some of the most common types of sales literature: product brochures, service brochures, corporate capabilities brochures, case histories, annual reports, and several others. They can serve as guides to shaping the content of your own promotional literature. Of course, don't feel obligated to follow my outlines. If you find a better way of organizing your material, use it. Each project is different, and you shouldn't force your own ideas into an overly simplistic formula. My samples should be used as rough guidelines only.

Product brochure

The most common type of promotional literature is the brochure describing a product. Years ago, product brochures were used mainly by industrial manufacturers for answering inquiries. But today's consumer has a great hunger for product information, and so many more brochures are being written about consumer products—telephones, space heaters, venetian blinds, microwave ovens, VCRs, personal computers, software, automobiles, home improvement products, even perfume and health care products.

The size of the brochure depends on the level of detail. For simpler products, you can use a small pamphlet made by folding an 8½-by-11-inch (or smaller) sheet two or three times into 4 or 6 panels. For complex products or lengthier sales pitches, product brochures use full-size (8½-by-11-inch) pages and usually range from 2 to 8 pages, with 4 being the average. Some very detailed brochures can be 12, 16, or even 20 pages or longer.

The content varies with the product, the audience, and the sales goal of the piece. The outline shown here is fairly comprehensive, the kind you might use for a larger product brochure. If you're doing a smaller piece, you can delete some of these topics or treat them in brief.

Here is my outline of the sections that can be included in a product brochure.

- Introduction—A capsule description of what the product is and why the reader should be interested in it.
- Benefits—A list of reasons why the customer should buy the product.
- Features—Highlights of important features that set the product apart from the competition.
- "How it works"—A description of how the product works and what it can do. This section can include the results of any tests that demonstrate the product's superiority.
- Types of users (markets)—This section describes the special markets the product is designed for. For example, a wastewater treatment plant might be sold to municipalities, utilities, and industrial manufacturers—three distinct markets, each with its own special set of requirements. This section can also include a list of the names of well-known people or organizations that use and endorse your product.
- Applications—Descriptions of the various applications in which the product can be used.
- Product availability—Lists models, sizes, materials of construction, col-

ors, finishes, options, accessories, and all the variations in which the product can be ordered. This section can also include charts, graphs, formulas, tables, or other guidelines to aid the reader in product selection.

- Pricing—Information on what the product costs, including prices for accessories, various models and sizes, quantity discounts, and shipping and handling.
- Technical specifications—Electrical requirements, power consumption, resistance to moisture, temperature range, operating conditions, cleaning methods, storage conditions, chemical properties, product life, and other characteristics and limitations of the product.
- "Q and A"—Frequently asked questions about the product and their answers. Includes information not found in other sections.
- Company description—A brief biography of the manufacturer, written to show the reader that the product is backed by a solid, reputable organization that won't go out of business.
- Product support—Information on delivery, installation, training, maintenance, service, and guarantees.
- "The next step"—Instructions on how to order the product (or on how to get more information about it).

Use this outline as a guide, but don't feel obligated to include all the sections or stick with this sequence. A brochure on an automobile, for example, probably shouldn't include the price because car dealers love to make deals and don't want to be locked into a fixed price.

Service brochure

In many ways, writing a service brochure is harder than writing a product brochure. The reason is that the product brochure describes an existing object with tangible features and benefits.

But selling a service involves selling intangibles—the reputation of the service organization, the expertise of its people, the benefits of using the service, the quality of your service versus competing services. You have to get the reader to trust you because you can't point to a package and say, "There's what we're selling." You have to write copy on a somewhat more personal level because you're really selling people and their talents.

Following are the sections to include in a service brochure.

- Introduction—A listing of the services offered, types of clients handled, and the reasons why the reader should be interested in the service.
- Services offered—Detailed descriptions of the various services offered by the firm and how they satisfy client needs.
- Benefits—Describes what the reader will gain from the service and why he or she should engage your firm instead of the competition.
- Background information—A discussion of the problems the service is designed to solve. This section can offer free advice on how to evaluate the problem and how to select professional help. Such free information, although not a direct sales pitch, adds to the value of the brochure and causes readers to keep your literature.
- Methodology—An outline of the service firm's method of doing business with clients.
- Client list—A list of well-known people or organizations who have used the firm's services.
- Testimonials—Statements of endorsement from select clients. Testimonials are usually written in the client's own words and attributed to a specific person or organization.
- Fees and terms—Describes the fees for each service and the terms and method of payment required. This section includes whatever guarantee the service firm offers its clients.
- Biographical information—Capsule biographies highlighting the credentials of the key employees plus an overall capsule biography of the firm.
- "The next step"—Instructions on what the customer should do next if he or she is interested in hiring the firm or learning more about its services.

Corporate brochure

Opinions about whether corporate brochures are useful are mixed. Some people claim that the corporate brochure is an exercise in self-flattery and that no one reads such literature except the company that publishes it. Others see the corporate brochure as a useful tool for quickly communicating the message of "who you are" to customers, prospects, distributors, new employees, vendors, the press, and the financial community.

In no other piece of literature (except annual reports) do you have to be as image-conscious as in the corporate brochure, simply because it is a statement of who you are, what you do, and what you're like. An image-conscious brochure doesn't necessarily have to be lavish or expensive, but the look of the design and the tone of the copy should mirror and enhance the image you want to project.

Here are topics you can cover in your corporate brochure, as listed in *Business-to-Business Advertising,* by Howard G. Sawyer (Crain Books).

The business (or businesses) the company is engaged in

The corporate structure (parent company, other members of the family, subsidiaries)

Addresses and phone numbers of all offices, branches, and representatives

Names and titles of major corporate officers

History

Plants and other facilities

Geographical coverage

Major markets

Distribution systems

Sales

Ranking in its field relative to competition

Extent of stock distribution

Earnings record

Dividends record

Number of employees

Employee benefits

Noteworthy employees (e.g., scientists, inventors)

Inventions

Significant achievements

Research and development

Quality control practices

Actions with respect to the environment

Contributions (to art, public welfare, etc.)

Awards

Policies

Plans

Catalog

A catalog is a comprehensive directory describing all the products a company sells. "Resting on the table in farm, suburban or city home, the . . . catalog functions like a one-stop shopping center," writes Julien Elfenbein in his book *Business Letters and Communications.*

A catalog contains numerous product descriptions and illustrations. The two key issues in organizing a catalog are (1) the information to include in each product description and (2) the order in which to organize the descriptions. A catalog may also include a letter from the manufacturer, an introduction, a table of contents, an index, a page describing conditions and terms, and if it's a mail-order catalog, an order form and reply envelope for the customer to use.

In each product description you should include as much of the following information as is applicable to the particular item.

Name of the product
Physical description
Features and benefits
Explanation of how it works
Weight
Dimensions, including choice of sizes available
Price, including quantity discounts
Quantitics available
Colors available
Shape
Styles
Applications
Tips on selection
Tips on usage
Packaging
Shipping information
Safety precautions
Quality
Materials of construction
Efficiency
Maintenance and repair methods
Cost savings
Service available
Nearest distributors

The amount of information to be included depends on the space available. Most catalog listings are limited to a quarter page or less, so you have to be extra concise, boiling copy down to a few essential sales points. Other catalog marketers find that by putting fewer items in their catalog or by printing a bigger catalog, they can devote more copy to each product and increase sales as a result.

The product descriptions can be arranged according to one of eleven organization principles. The choice depends on your product line, the size of the catalog, and your audience's buying habits.

➤ By catalog hot spots

Mail-order catalog marketers can measure the sales generated by every page and every item in their catalogs. They've discovered that certain pages generate more sales than others; these are the *hot spots*. According to the Performance Seminar Group, a company that gives seminars in advertising and marketing, the hot spots are the outside front cover, the outside back cover, the 2-page spread inside the front cover, the 2-page center spread, the 2-page spread inside the back cover, the pages around the order form, and the pages around ordering instructions. Other marketers have found that product descriptions printed directly *on* the order form generate a higher rate of response than the average page. On the basis of this information, mail-order catalog marketers can generate more sales by putting their best-selling items on these hot pages.

➤ By product demand

You can organize your catalog by the sales each product generates. Put your best sellers up front, and give each a full or half page. Slower-moving merchandise appears at the back of the book and occupies a quarter page or less. Dead items are dropped altogether.

This organizational technique takes advantage of a principle first articulated by David Ogilvy: "Back your winners, and abandon your losers." It puts your promotional dollars where they'll do the most good. However, in large or highly technical product catalogs, it may create some confusion.

➤ By applications

Organizing according to application makes it easy for your customer to find the product that fits his or her needs. For example, the Faultless Division of Axia Incorporated organized its caster catalog by application: general duty, light duty, light-to-medium duty, heavy duty, textiles, scaffolds, floor trucks, and furniture. The disadvantage of this scheme is redundancy: Many products handle multiple applications and must be listed or cross-referenced in more than one section.

➤ **By function**
A software catalog can be organized by the function each program performs: word processing, accounting, spread sheet, data base management, inventory, graphics, communications. Obviously, this scheme won't work in a catalog of products that all perform the same task (e.g., a catalog of pollution control equipment, light switches, or safety valves).

➤ **By type of product**
Radio Shack's consumer electronics catalogs are organized by product group: stereos on one page, car radios on the next, then VCRs, computers, tape recorders, and phone answering machines. This scheme is a natural for companies that carry multiple product lines.

➤ **By system hierarchy**
This technique organizes products by the level at which each component fits into the overall system. For example, if you manufacture computer hardware, your catalog can begin with the overall system you offer. Next come the major components: terminals, printers, plotters, disk drives, keyboards, processors. Then you get to the board level, showing various optional circuit boards you offer for memory expansion, interfaces, communications, instrument control, and other functions. Finally, you could even get down to the chip level (if you sell chips as separate items). Supplies—paper, printer ribbons, diskettes, instruction manuals—could go in a separate section at the end of the catalog. This unit-subunit-subsubunit approach is ideal for manufacturers who sell both complete systems and their component parts.

➤ **By price**
If you sell similar products that vary mainly in quality and price, you can organize your catalog by price categories. If your customers are concerned with savings, start with the cheapest items and work up. If you're selling to an upscale group willing to pay extra for top quality, start with the deluxe models and work your way down. This technique is excellent for organizing a catalog of premiums and incentives. After all, a company searching for gifts and giveaways has a price range in mind, not necessarily a specific item.

➤ **By scarcity**

If your catalog features hard-to-get items, consider putting them up front, even on the cover. This makes your catalog more valuable by offering buyers products they need but can't get elsewhere. Don't worry that these hard-to-find items aren't big sellers. Customers who know that you offer a stock of rare merchandise and pull out your catalog to order it will be more inclined to do their other buying from you, too.

➤ **By size**

If you make one product and the basic selection criterion is size, it's only natural to organize your catalog according to dimensions, weight, horse-power, British thermal units (BTUs), diameter, or some other unit of measure. This is handy for catalogs selling such things as boilers, motors, hoses, shipping drums, envelopes, light bulbs, and air conditioners.

➤ **By model number**

If you've worked out a sensible numbering system for your product line, organize your catalog by model number. If there's a simple meaning to your product coding, explain it at the start of the catalog. Don't rely solely on the numbers to describe your products; include headings and descriptive text as well.

➤ **By alphabetical order**

If no other organizational scheme works for you, you can always organize alphabetically. A tool catalog can start with adjustable strap clamps and angle plates and end with wing nuts and wrenches. A vitamin catalog can begin with vitamin A and end with zinc.

Annual reports

Annual reports are big documents. According to a 1984 survey conducted by the Graphic Arts Center, an Oregon printing firm, the average annual report is 44 pages long. Most annual reports are divided into two major sections: descriptive and financial. The descriptive section reviews the company's activities for the year; the financial section provides the account-ing information that the Securities and Exchange Commission requires publicly owned companies to disclose.

Here's an outline you can use for the descriptive portion of your annual report.

- Financial highlights—A table summarizing a few key financial figures (sales, net income, earnings per share of stock, cash dividend paid per share). If business was good, you can compare this year's figures with previous years' results to show a growth pattern.
- Capsule corporate biography—Three or four paragraphs that sum up the nature and mission of the corporation and touch on its key areas of business.
- Table of contents—Necessary to guide the reader through a lengthy document.
- President's letter to shareholders—Used to communicate key messages to shareholders, investors, and the business and financial communities. The president's letter typically highlights company successes and earnings and stock performance, acknowledges problems and tells how they are being solved, sums up the year's major triumphs, and talks about plans for the coming year.
- Corporate overview—A more detailed look at the structure, workings, and business functions of the corporation.
- Year in review—The bulk of the report's narrative and pictures reviews the year's business activities. Topics to be covered include products, markets, market share, revenues, expenses, sales, distribution, mergers, acquisitions, joint ventures, new areas of business, new technology, new facilities, plant improvements, state of the industry, and strategic goals. This information is given for each of the corporation's divisions, subsidiaries, and operating units.
- Photos—Photos with captions create visual interest and highlight people, products, projects, and other developments. They can be scattered throughout the report as well as placed in specific sections.
- List of board of directors, corporate officers, and top management.

As for the financial side, the Securities and Exchange Commission requires annual reports to satisfy certain guidelines, and your accounting firm can produce this information for you. Here's an outline of what is typically included in the financial report.

- Management discussion—Your management's interpretation of the data in the financial report.
- Accountant's report—Signed statement made by your accountants verifying the accuracy of the financial report.

- Statements of consolidated earnings—Table showing the year's revenues, expenses, net earnings, and earnings per share.
- Statements of consolidated retained earnings—Beginning-of-year and year-end balances, net earnings, retained earnings, and cash dividends on common stock for the current year and previous years.
- Consolidated balance sheets—Assets, liabilities, and stockholders' equity.
- Statements of changes in consolidated financial position—Sources and uses of funds and increase or decrease in working capital.
- Notes on accounting methods—Explains accounting procedures used in preparing the report.
- Supplementary information on changing prices—Explains the effect of inflation on the firm's earnings and financial position.
- Business segments—Breakdown of revenue, earnings, assets, capital expenditures, and depreciation and amortization by corporate subunit.
- Selected financial data—A concise table summarizing key data (e.g., revenue, net earnings, dividends) for current and previous years.
- Quarterly financial summaries—Key financial data for current and previous years broken down by quarter.
- Miscellaneous corporate information—Date of shareholders' meeting, name of accounting firm, banks, stock exchange listing.

Case history

A case history is a product success story. It tells how a product or service was used to solve a problem, improve an operation, or save time and money. All case histories follow the same basic outline.

- Problem—What was the problem? How and why did it come about? What were the unfortunate consequences of the problem?
- Solution—What solutions were considered and tried? What were the results? What solution finally worked? How was this solution arrived at? How was it implemented?
- Results—Was the problem cleared up? How are things now compared with the way they were before the solution was implemented? How have things improved since the product or service was used?
- Conclusions and recommendations—Why did the product or service work so well? Under what circumstances would it have worked better or worse? What guidelines can be used to determine when the product or service should be applied to a similar problem in a different situation? What was learned about the performance and reliability of the product or service?

Newsletters

In his book *Mastering Graphics*, Jan White defines the newsletter as "a publication of limited circulation that is essentially informative in nature." He goes on to say that "a true newsletter is simple, informal, relaxed. Its effectiveness lies in the illusion it creates of being a person-to-person letter."

Newsletters deal with specialized subjects of interest to narrow groups of readers. A typical newsletter has anywhere from 2 to 8 letter-size pages (8½ by 11 inches) and is simply produced, usually typed on a typewriter, with a minimum of photos or illustrations. Fancier newsletters, often produced by large organizations, may be typeset and elaborately designed, but these are closer to being magazines than traditional newsletters.

There are two basic types of newsletters: *subscription* and *promotional*. Subscription newsletters are newsletters people pay to receive. Publishing a successful newsletter can be a profitable venture, with annual subscription fees ranging from $65 to more than $600. Promotional newsletters (the kind discussed in this chapter) are produced by organizations and distributed free to customers, members, donors, sponsors, and prospects in order to promote the organization's product, service, idea, or cause.

But the newsletter promotes in a subtle way: Instead of making a straight sales pitch, as a product brochure or TV commercial would, the newsletter's sell is somewhat softer. The reader receives a blend of useful information, ideas, and advice that is helpful in daily life or on the job. Some advertising messages may be woven into the newsletter, but only in moderation. Rather than seek an order directly, the newsletter builds credibility with its audience over the long haul.

Stories in a newsletter can range from a few paragraphs to a page, but most are shorter rather than longer. Unlike a brochure, in which each section builds on the previous section, each article in the newsletter is self-contained. Consequently, the order is not particularly important. Common sense dictates that you put the most important and interesting stories on page 1 and other copy on the inside pages.

What type of articles can you include in your newsletter? Anything goes—anything that is interesting to your reader and relevant to your organization's goals. Here's a partial list of the topics you can cover in your newsletter.

Company news
Industry news
New products
Product improvements
New models

New accessories
New applications
Tips on product selection
Installation tips
Maintenance and repair tips
Troubleshooting guides
Application notes (how to use the product)
Explanatory articles (how the product works)
Recent innovations in research and development
Manufacturing success stories
Quality-control stories
Case histories (product success stories)
Technical information and tips
Industry roundups
Technology roundups
New employees, transfers, promotions, other employee news
Employee profiles
Customer profiles
Customer news
Community relations activities
Interviews
Financial report
Announcements and write-ups of conferences, seminars, meetings, trade shows
Photos (of people, facilities, and products) with captions
Announcements of newly published literature
President's letter
Sales roundup
"Q and A" column
Quizzes
Contests

All stories should be concise, lively, and interesting, and all should have news or informational value.

The newsletter does not have to be written from scratch. You can use it to recycle press releases, excerpts from executive speeches, published articles, and papers. Lengthy material that the reader might not normally finish can be condensed and rewritten to make it more readable.

The newsletter can be published as often as you like—every month, every other month, twice a year. But don't publish an issue if you have nothing new to say; it is better to postpone the issue until there is real news to report. The reader will forgive a late issue but will not continue to read a newsletter that contains nothing of real value.

Typing your newsletter on a typewriter is the simplest and least expensive method of production. It has the added advantage of making the newsletter look like news because typewriter type communicates a sense of timeliness. A typeset document, although more attractive, looks like your other promotions, not like a piece of hot-off-the-typewriter news.

Informational booklets

Producing a piece of literature that is wholly or partly informational rather than promotional is an effective tool for building a good relationship with your established and prospective customers. People hunger for information—about being a better consumer, managing money, health, career, family, love, home, technology. You can win people over by providing some of this much-needed information in your literature.

One tactic is to include some useful information in literature that otherwise makes a direct sales pitch. For example, a product brochure on a line of cosmetics can contain a 1-page feature "How to Apply Makeup." This single page of beauty tips can compel many people to keep a brochure they might otherwise throw away.

Another approach is to publish purely informational literature as part of your total literature program. For example, a seed company could publish a series of informational pamphlets on gardening as a supplement to its seed catalog. Each pamphlet tells the reader how to grow a certain type of plant. The pamphlets contain no direct sales pitch or production information. But to grow the plant, you need seeds—seeds that you can order from the company's catalog.

Let's say you want to publish an informational pamphlet. Here's an outline that you can apply to any topic.

- Front cover—The title should describe the contents of the brochure in a way that highlights its usefulness to the reader: *Six Ways to Improve Home Insulation, How to Cut Your Utility Bill by Up to 40 Percent, A Quick and Easy Guide to Window and Door Weatherstripping.*
- Introduction—The introduction presents a short discussion of the problem, explains how the advice in the pamphlet can help solve it, and tells the reader how best to use the tips presented. It can also explain the company's motivation for publishing the information (e.g., as a service to

customers, to ensure proper use of the firm's product, or to educate the public about applications of the product).

- Body—The bulk of the copy presents information, advice, and tips. The best way to present the information is as a series of numbered sections. You should offer the reader anywhere from five to fifteen tips; fewer seems insubstantial, and more is too much for the reader to grasp.
- Tables—If you present a lot of related information, you might help the reader by summing it up in one or two concise tables after the main section of body copy.
- Wrap-up—This section sums up what the reader has learned.
- Product pitch—Although the informational pamphlet should be free of hype, it's okay to mention your products in one or two sentences at the end. Simply say that you have the products available, and invite the reader to call or write for additional information. Don't forget to include your address and phone number.

Order form

If your products can be ordered directly from your catalog or brochure, you should make ordering easy by including an order form and a business reply envelope so that the customer can mail his or her order without the expense of postage. Your local post office can tell you how to obtain a business reply permit and produce your own envelopes. Be sure to follow the instructions; otherwise, the post office may not be able to process and deliver your envelopes.

The order form is a sheet the customer can fill out to order the desired merchandise. The simpler the form, the more orders you'll receive. A confusing or complicated form will turn customers off.

Here is what you should include on your order form.

- Instructions telling the customer to print or type (handwritten orders can be hard to read).
- Space for the customer to fill in name, address, and phone number. Ask for a street address (United Parcel Service does not deliver to box numbers).
- A request for change-of-address information.
- Space to fill in shipping address if it is different from billing address.
- Space for the customer to indicate desired merchandise, including quantity and price.

- Instructions on method of payment.
- List of credit cards accepted; minimum amount for credit card orders.
- Number the customer can call to order by phone.
- Guarantee.
- Return policy.
- Offer specials, discounts, and impulse items for sale directly on the order form.
- Information on packing, shipping, and delivery.
- Information on shipping and handling costs and sales tax.
- Thank the buyer for the order.
- Ask for the names and addresses of friends who would like to receive the catalog or brochure.
- Ask whether the customer objects to your giving his or her name to other companies for mail solicitations.
- Code number (so you know which brochure or catalog generated the order).

Keep the order form simple. Don't confuse customers with an overly elaborate form. Number each step to aid the customer in completing the form. Give clear instructions for completing every step.

Leave enough room for the customer to fill in the desired information. It's frustrating to try to cram a name and address into a quarter-inch space.

Don't hide the order form. Make sure it's easy to find. Make the order form as large as the catalog or brochure page; otherwise, it can get lost among the pages.

Reply card

A reply card is an abbreviated version of the order form. Whereas the order form solicits complete information and an order, the reply card is a response device the reader can use to say, "Yes, I'm interested. Please send me more information or get in touch with me by phone."

Reply cards are postcards with your own address on them. They can require the reader to add a stamp, or they can be business reply cards that require no postage. (Your post office can provide you with complete details on how to get a permit for business reply and produce your own business reply cards.)

The front of the reply card contains either a business reply permit number or a place for the stamp. The back of the card has space for the

☐ We'd like more information. Give us a call.
☐ Not interested right now. Try us again in _____ .
(month/year)

Our industry is:

☐ **Chemical processing**   ☐ **Data processing**   ☐ **Wastewater treatment**
☐ **Pollution control**   ☐ **Electronics**   ☐ **Consulting**
☐ **Plastics processing**   ☐ **Telecommunications**   ☐ **Other:** _____
(specify)

Name _____   Title _____

Company _____   Phone _____

Address _____

City _____   State _____   Zip _____

Figure 10. The prospect fills in the back of the reply card, puts a stamp on the front, and drops it in the mail. In a few days, the advertiser receives the card and can take appropriate action.

reader's name, organization, title, address, and phone number. You can also add boxes to be checked off or space for the answers to a few simple questions. Figure 10 shows the back of a typical reply card.

The reply card has two basic missions. First, it allows the reader to take the next step in the buying process. This can be a request for more information, a product demonstration, a phone call, a sales visit—whatever method you choose. Second, it enables you to solicit some information about potential customers. You can ask readers to tell you how they intend to use your product, when they plan to buy, what products they are currently using, or how much money they can afford to spend. This information allows you to qualify leads and separate nonprospects from serious potential customers.

CHAPTER FIVE

Selling Your Company and Your Product: The Copy

Which comes first, the copy or the layout?

You're familiar with the riddle, "Which came first, the chicken or the egg?" Well, brochure producers are faced with a similar puzzle: Which comes first, copy or layout?

There's no right answer. Different experts have different approaches. I can only tell you the way I do it, and that my method is successful. When I handle a project, the copy comes first. Why? Because brochures, unlike TV commercials and many consumer print advertisements, are primarily a medium of information. And it is words, not pictures, that do the bulk of the work when it comes to communicating detailed, complex facts and ideas.

The sequence of scenes in a TV commercial or the illustration in a print ad must do the hard work of grabbing the attention of a uninterested consumer. But when the consumer reaches for a brochure, he or she is actively seeking information and already has some interest in the product, so there's no need to go to wild extremes to gain attention. The trick is to hold that attention—with interesting, relevant, informative copy.

On most assignments, I discuss with the client in advance the topics the brochure will cover, the rough format (number and size of pages), and whether we'll use photos or drawings. I usually don't submit a formal outline unless the job is unusually complex or the client requests it.

The next step is to write the copy. On brochures that are mostly text and have simple layouts, I submit the copy with a list of suggested visuals (if visuals are to be included). Some of the most effective sales brochures I've written have been all text.

If the layout is complex or the text is heavily dependent upon layouts and visuals, I'll submit my own rough sketch of what the finished piece should look like. A rough layout drawn by the writer is called a *copywriter's rough.* It is not a finished layout; it is a guide that shows the artist the relationship between the text and the visuals and their placement on the pages. The graphic artist, using my crude sketch as a starting point, produces a fairly polished rendering of the layout of the piece.

If you believe, as I do, that the text of a brochure is more important than the design, you should think of the layout as a framework for the copy. The designer's job is to make the printed page attractive, to draw the reader's eye to the text, to make the brochure flow smoothly from page to page, and to make the copy easy and pleasant to read. The layout, or framework, should therefore be designed to accommodate and enhance the copy. The copy-writer dictates the length of each section, the number of words in headlines and subheads, the order of sections of text, and the total length of the brochure. The artist designs the brochure around the copy.

If you take the opposite view—that design comes first—you'll be in trouble. You'll find yourself force-fitting copy to accommodate an existing design. You'll be cutting and condensing and expanding copy to fit a page layout, when in fact it is the copy, not the layout, that the reader is interested in. Doing the layout first is a mistake as far as I'm concerned—no ifs, ands, or buts about it.

Who writes the brochure?

Organizations with limited promotional budgets, and even some with large budgets, know they can save money on a brochure by doing all or part of the work themselves. When the question of which tasks might be done in-house comes up, copywriting is first on the list (photography is second). After all, not many of us know how to specify type or paste up a mechanical, but nearly everyone can write.

Should you write the brochure yourself or hire an outside writer? The answer depends on your budget, your internal resources, and what you hope to achieve with your literature.

As far as money goes, hiring a professional writer isn't cheap. The fee depends on the size and complexity of the project, but you can expect to pay anywhere from $500 to $2,500 for a small or medium-size brochure on a single topic. Some organizations find this a small price to pay for profes-sionalism; for other groups, it's far beyond their means. If you flinch at these fees, maybe you can do the writing yourself, maybe not. It depends on your internal resources. Do you have writers on staff? If not, is there someone else in your organization who has the editorial skills to produce a smooth-reading, persuasive piece of literature? Does this person have the time and desire to handle the project? Is this the best use of this person's time?

An alternative is for you to write a rough draft and turn it over to a professional writer for polishing. Since you've done much of the research and organizing, the writer may handle the rewrite for a lower fee than he or she would charge for doing the job from scratch. Yet the finished copy will still have the flair, style, and crispness of the professional touch.

Finally, consider the nature of your literature and what you hope to achieve with it. An internal pamphlet announcing a company picnic doesn't have to be particularly persuasive (it's not hard to sell a free picnic), so maybe someone in the employee relations department can write the announcement. On the other hand, a new corporate brochure requires a great deal of sophistication, the kind that only a professional writer can bring to the job. Poorly executed, sloppily written copy could result in a corporate brochure that does more to hurt your image than to enhance it.

As for whom to hire and how, Chapter 3 can guide you in the process of choosing an outside writer or agency.

Getting ready to write the copy

Whether you, someone else in your organization, or an outside writer is to write the copy, you need to gather the source material that will provide the necessary background information. Although we've already discussed the need to gather source material, I can't overemphasize the importance of having the facts before you or the writer begins the assignment. Without studying previously published material, an outside writer would have to start from scratch, knowing almost nothing about your organization or your product. And how would the copywriter know what facts must be included and what questions to ask?

The best approach is for the writer to become immersed in previously published material (supplied by you). After doing this, he or she will know much more about your business and will have most of the information required to write your brochure, catalog, or pamphlet. The writer will also have a clear idea of what facts are missing and what questions need to be asked. By doing the homework in advance and writing out a list of specific questions, the writer can get the missing facts in a short conference or phone conversation with you. Marathon meetings, confusion, and incorrect copy will be dramatically reduced.

Here's a checklist of the specific types of materials you should gather for the writer.

Ad reprints
Brochures
Annual reports
Catalogs
Article reprints
Technical papers
Text of speeches and presentations
Film, videotape, and slide show scripts
Press releases
Market research
Marketing plans
Sales reports
Letters from customers
Back issues of the company newsletter
Competitors' ads and brochures

Some organizations say that their product or service is new and that therefore they have no written material to give the writer. But this is nonsense. The birth of any new idea or product is accompanied by mounds of paperwork that can be useful to the writer:

Internal letters
Letters to customers
Product specifications
Manufacturer's literature
Blueprints
Plans
Illustrations
Photos of prototypes
Engineering drawings
White papers and other internal bulletins
Instruction manuals
Marketing plans
Reports
Proposals
Results of laboratory tests and field tests

This is enough to get the writer started. If you want to do even more, you might circle, underline, or highlight passages in the material that relate to the project at hand. This step is optional, but it can save the writer the trouble of plowing through a lengthy report that contains only one or two relevant paragraphs.

Organizing your material

If you're writing the brochure yourself, this section offers tips that will help you organize, research, and write your copy. If you're hiring a writer, you should still read this section to gain an appreciation of what's involved in copywriting and the qualities that make for successful brochure copy.

Faced with a mound of background material, the writer should begin by reading the material thoroughly, studying it, and extracting the facts that will be included in the copy. Some writers underline key material for easy reference later on, but I find it cumbersome to have to search through a stack of literature during the writing stage. For this reason, I recommend that you take notes as you go through the source material and refer to these notes during the actual writing of your copy.

You can take notes either on index cards or on a pad. With the pad method, your material remains in the order you read it. Cards can be shuffled to reorder your notes later on.

If you jot notes on a pad, type them up when you've finished studying the background material. The advantage of this method is that you can condense a mountain of reference material into a couple of single-spaced, typewritten sheets that give you all the facts at a glance. Also, the act of reading the background, writing notes, and then retyping them increases your familiarity with the information.

An alternative is to take notes directly on your typewriter or your word processor. This saves the step of retyping notes from the handwritten version; however, many people find that the act of typing onto a keyboard inhibits their note-taking. It's really a matter of individual preference.

When you take notes on index cards, you should limit your notes to one key fact or thought per card. Then, when you're finished, you can rearrange the cards so that the notes are in the order in which the key points will appear in the final copy.

For a short, simple piece in which organizing the facts is pretty easy, I type my notes on a couple of sheets of typing paper. If I'm uncertain about how to organize the material, or if the brochure contains more information than I can fit on a few typewritten sheets, I use index cards. I also use index cards for modular projects (i.e., those involving a number of separate but related pieces of literature).

Once you've got your pile of note cards, organize them according to the major headings in your outline. One stack may deal with facts on service; another may contain notes on how the product works. If one stack is much thicker than the rest, perhaps it should be divided into two or more separate sections. If a stack contains only a few cards, you might need more information on this subject; or maybe these cards should be included in other sections.

Whether you take notes on cards or on a pad, you should list any questions that come up on a separate sheet of paper. After you've finished studying the source material, look over your outline and notes to see if there are any other facts missing. If there are, add questions about these facts to your list.

At this stage, you're just about ready to write the copy. The only thing remaining is to get answers to your questions, and that's where research comes in.

How to uncover missing facts

Basically, there are four methods of gathering missing facts: interviews, observation, experimentation, and secondary sources.

Don't let the idea of research scare you off. Unlike a scientist, who must unlock the hidden secrets of the universe, or the journalist, who must rake muck and squeeze tidbits out of uncooperative sources, the copywriter and his or her source of information (the client) are working together. Their mutual goal is to produce the best promotional literature possible. So the copywriter doesn't have to fight or scheme to get the facts; he or she has the full cooperation of the client in uncovering them.

The interview is the basic research tool of the copywriter. The easiest, most efficient way to interview is for the writer to call the client and say, "I have a list of questions about the XYZ brochure. Where can I get the answers?" You, as the client, will be able to provide the answers yourself or tell the writer where to find them. Perhaps some of the questions are best answered by sending the writer additional material. For those questions that you can't answer because they deal with a subject outside your own expertise, you can go to other people in your organization or have the writer contact them directly. However, if you do the latter, be sure to give these folks advance notice. Otherwise, they may not feel comfortable giving away company secrets to a stranger over the telephone.

On extremely complex projects or new projects whose direction isn't clear, the writer may need to conduct more in-depth interviews with experts from your organization. In this case, it may be best to schedule a meeting or conference at your facility. Allow plenty of time for the writer and the people being interviewed to get everything done at one sitting and not feel under pressure. If the writer feels rushed, he or she may hurry through the interview and not ask all the necessary questions.

If you are writing the copy, you'll have to do the interviews. There are a few things you should keep in mind. First, unless you're the boss, the person you interview is really doing you a favor. After all, promotion is your job, and the other person is taking time out of a busy day to cooperate with you. So be courteous; schedule an appointment for the interview well in advance and be on time. Come prepared with a list of questions. And do your homework: Don't ask simplistic or basic questions that you could have answered by leafing through a technical bulletin or the company catalog. Ask questions that only this person, the expert, can answer.

Also, find out in advance how much time the person can spend with you, and keep the interview within this schedule as best you can. If the person is looking impatiently at his or her watch, end the interview and continue it another time, either in another meeting or in an informal chat over the phone.

Second, thank the person for cooperating with you. Build good will by explaining the purpose of the interview, and be sure the person gets a copy of your brochure when it is published. If you depend on certain people as regular sources of information, try to do some small favors for them (such as sending them copies of projects they helped with), and be sure to treat them with courtesy. Don't be rude or show impatience if the person you're interviewing has a hard time explaining something. Instead, help by rephrasing the question or asking a more specific one.

If the interview is to gather specific information—numbers, statistics, facts—take notes with pad and pen. If you're interviewing for spicy quotations you can use in a newsletter or bulletin, also use a tape recorder as a backup to ensure accuracy. But first, make sure the person doesn't object to being recorded (some people do).

Studying the source material and asking questions should give you all the information you need. But there are a few additional research techniques that can add to your understanding and appreciation of the product, concept, or organization you are trying to promote.

Direct observation is a useful technique, and it's one that is likely to reveal falsehoods or exaggerations in the information you've gathered so far. For example, the shop foreman may tell you, "Stress quality control in the brochure. I run the best manufacturing line in the business." When you visit the manufacturing plant, however, you observe rusting assembly lines, sloppy workmanship, and a large number of defective pieces rolling off the conveyor belt. From direct observation, you learn that your quality controls are not what they should be. Steps should be taken to correct this, but in the meantime, quality control is not something you want to highlight in your brochure.

Experimentation can give you additional insights into the product. Now, I know you're not a laboratory scientist, and I don't expect you to run the product through a battery of tests. But a few simple, do-it-yourself experiments can tell you a lot about a product and its key selling features.

Here's a story that illustrates this point: A copywriter was trying to come up with an idea for an ad for corn flakes. His corn flakes looked the same as other corn flakes; when he poured two bowls and tried them, he found they tasted the same, too. But minutes later, he discovered that the competitor's flakes had turned soggy in the milk while his client's flakes stayed crisp. He had found his competitive advantage, and the theme of flakes that "stay crisp in milk" became the basis for a successful ad campaign.

I know of male copywriters who, assigned to a panty hose account, have worn panty hose under their business suits to find out what it feels like. And I know one writer who, in the privacy of his bathroom, applied mascara to his lashes so he could better understand the importance of a good applicator. If a mail-order client tells me they guarantee fast delivery of a product, I am likely to order the product and see how long it takes to get to me. A few simple experiments can reveal volumes about a product and how honestly your past promotions have reflected reality.

A fourth technique at the writer's disposal is to go to secondary sources to uncover additional facts about a product, business, or market. For example, if assigned to write a brochure about a piece of chemical equipment, I might first turn to my copy of *Perry's Handbook of Chemical Engineering* and read any articles I find there on this type of equipment. If given the task of writing a flier to promote a vitamin mix containing vitamins A, C, and E, I might consult medical reference books to find out the individual properties and benefits of these ingredients.

Secondary-source research isn't a necessity. Your organization is the best source of information about its products. But you may have omitted or forgotten about a fact that can be the basis of a convincing selling argument. Digging into other sources can help you uncover these hidden features.

"Roughing it"

Remember the copywriter's "rough"? Well, in addition to being helpful to the designer, it can aid the writer in getting his or her thoughts organized. Any piece of printed literature is broken down into a fixed number of pages. When the brochure is closed, we see only one page, either the front or the back cover. When it's open, we see a number of pages at a time (depending on the way it's folded). This grouping of pages is called a *spread.*

As readers turn the pages, the eye and mind take in the words and layout one spread at a time. In a regular 8-page brochure (Figure 11), the reader sees the front cover first. Next is the opening spread, consisting of the inside front cover and the facing page (pages 2 and 3). Then comes the centerfold (pages 4 and 5), and after that, the spread consisting of pages 6 and 7 (the inside back cover). The end of the brochure is the outside back cover.

When planning your copy, think about how the various sections flow from one page or spread to the next. If you have a large table of specifications too wide to fit on a single page, you can put it on a double-page spread (say, the centerfold; you shouldn't break it up by making the reader turn the page to get to the second half of the table.

Use the copywriter's rough to plan the order and layout of the copy. The rough can be a sketch; or, if you prefer, you can construct a *dummy,* a full-size paper model of how the finished piece will look. Figure 12 is a sample sketch of a copywriter's rough for an 8-page brochure. Figure 13 gives you a blank form you can use to produce copywriter's roughs for a variety of promotional pieces.

The key to designing a copywriter's rough is to group similar topics on one page or spread. As the reader turns the pages, it should be easy to see (and read) a logical progression of ideas from point A to point B to point C.

Keep in mind that the copywriter's rough is just an aid to the writer, not a final layout. When you get into the writing, you may discover that a section of copy has to be expanded from one page to two or that the guarantee should go on the back cover instead of on page 6. Go ahead and write it that way; then make the changes on the rough you submit to the artist. But don't let a design dictate the length and direction of your copy; rather, the layout should be changed to accommodate the text.

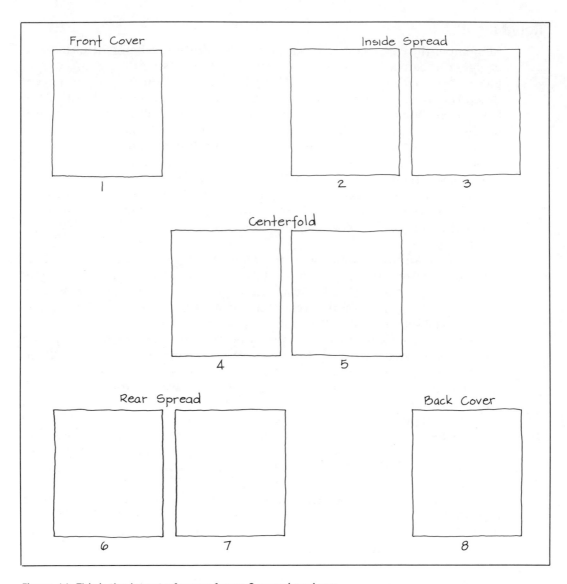

Figure 11. This is the layout of pages for an 8-page brochure.

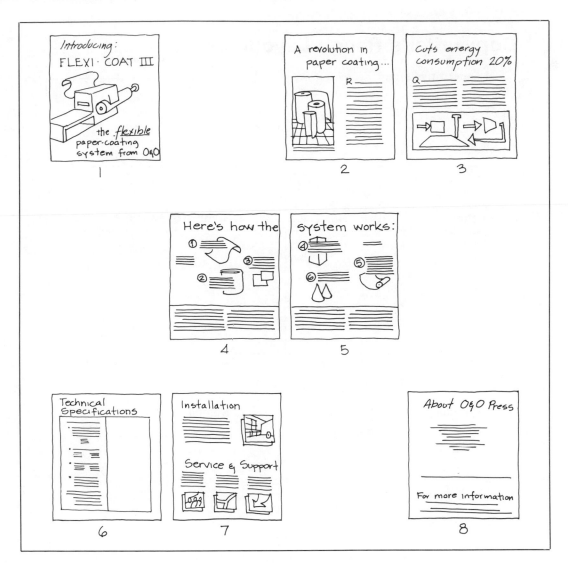

Figure 12. The copywriter's rough is a crude sketch showing the approximate size and location of headlines, subheads, body copy, and illustrations.

Copywriter's Rough Layout for:_____
(project)

[   ] Outer Envelope:

(   ) No. 10   (   ) 6" x 9"   (   ) 9" x 12"

[   ] Letter: (Page Size:_____ Number of Pages: _____)

| Page 1 | Page 2 | Page 3 | Page 4 |

[   ] Circular: (Page Size:_____ Number of Pages: _____

Format: _____)

| Page 1 | Page 2 | Page 3 | Page 4 |

Figure 13. You can use this form to create copywriter's roughs for a variety of projects, including brochures, direct mail, order forms, and print ads.

[   ] **Reply Card: (Size:** _____)

Front	Back

[   ] **Reply Envelope: (Size:** _____)

Front	Back

[   ] **Order Form (Page Size:** _____ **Number of Pages** _____)

[   ] **Space Advertisement (Page Size:** _____)

[   ] **Other Materials:**

Writing the copy

If you've hired a writer, you don't have to worry about the writing process. The writer can struggle with the copy out of sight and out of mind; that's what you're paying for. All you have to do is wait for the typed manuscript to appear on your desk.

If you're writing the copy yourself and you've never written promotional copy before, the process will be new to you, and you may be feeling some anxiety about getting started. Here is some advice that can help.

➤ **Don't be overwhelmed**

The tendency is to say, "I'm not a brochure writer. How am I going to do this?" But you've written many other things: reports, memos, letters to friends and family. That didn't scare you, and neither should writing a brochure. Don't think of it as "advertising." Think of it as a letter to a friend. The friend is your customer, and the letter's goal is to convince your friend to try a great new product or service, which happens to be your product or service. You can even go as far as writing the first draft in letter form, beginning with "Dear Fred" and ending with "Sincerely, Mary." You can always go back and add headings, subheadings, and visuals later.

➤ **Don't worry about getting it right the first time**

Professional writers don't expect a first draft to be a masterpiece. They know that the essence of writing is rewriting and that it takes many revisions to produce a publishable piece of prose. Novices, unaware of this fact, feel they have just one shot, and that they've failed if it doesn't come out right the first time. They agonize over every word they put on the page and become so uptight that they block themselves and are unable to write.

You don't have to get it right the first time. In fact, you shouldn't even try. Your first draft can be as rough and as sloppy as you like. You can put down anything that comes to mind. Some nonwriters even prefer to dictate their thoughts into a tape recorder and have a secretary transcribe the tape. Use any method you please as long as you get something down on paper.

The next step is to revise the copy. Read the text, and change it to make it better. Delete words and sentences that are unnecessary or repetitive; add more material where the copy seems insubstantial. Reorganize paragraphs and sections into a more logical order. Add descriptive headlines and subheads. Break out some material into sidebars (short articles or sections of copy separated from the main text and enclosed in a box or other graphic

device) and tables, and indicate where photos or drawings can help illustrate a point. Add connecting phrases to smooth the transition between
sentences and paragraphs.

The final step is to polish the copy. Once it is in reasonable shape, edit
further to make it sound even better and more persuasive. Carefully read
the words you've written and see if using a different word or phrase can
improve it. Read the copy aloud to make sure it flows smoothly and contains
no awkward passages. If it doesn't read smoothly, fix it. Check grammar,
punctuation, and spelling. Also review for accuracy, consistency, and completeness of information.

➤ Sleep on it

As I've said, a good writer rewrites the copy many times before considering it
finished. One way to make this rewriting process more productive is to put
each version aside for an evening and look at it with fresh eyes the next
morning. When you are refreshed, you are able to review your copy more
objectively and spot mistakes you might have missed when you were
fatigued. If you have the time, put the final draft aside for a few days, and
review it once more before sending it to the designer. You'll probably spot
opportunities for improvements you didn't see before.

➤ Do the easy parts first

We've already talked about how breaking the copy into sections makes the
brochure easier to write (and to read). Most novice writers feel compelled to
write a brochure in order; they begin with the introduction and work their
way through to the back cover. But it doesn't have to be done that way. In
fact, if you have a tough time getting started, I recommend that you start
with the simple sections first—the list of branch offices, the table of technical specifications, the physical description of the product, the corporate
biography. Once you get a few sections down on paper, your writing
momentum will build, and you'll get enough steam up to run right through
the entire job.

Ten tips for better brochure copy

The goal of the brochure writer is to get the message across and have the
desired influence on the reader. Promotional literature doesn't strive for
strict grammatical accuracy or the scholarliness of a Ph.D. thesis. Instead,

the copywriter aims for a friendly tone, clarity of expression, persuasiveness, and content that is complete, informative, and accurate. Here are ten tips to help you achieve these goals.

➤ **Start selling on the cover**

Whether the reader gets your literature in the mail or plucks it off a rack, the first thing he or she sees is the cover. The message on the cover either compels the reader to turn the page or dampens the reader's interest, causing the brochure to be discarded and forgotten.

Yet, the majority of advertisers waste the front cover. They decorate it with the product name, a fancy graphic, and the company logo and hope that their initials and symbol are enough to prod the reader to go on. But these things are not enough.

The cover should convey a strong selling message, usually in the form of a headline. This message can point out a product benefit, highlight the usefulness of the product (or of the brochure itself), identify the audience the brochure is aimed at or the applications the product is designed for, or stress how the product saves time, money, and aggravation. By applying a little thought and imagination to the problem, you can create a cover headline that increases the selling power of the piece. Take, for example, the headline on a pamphlet promoting a bank's Christmas club:

> **Imagine Having an Extra $520 for the Holidays.**
>
> **It's easy.**
> **It's painless.**
> **It's automatic.**
> **It's just $10 a week.**

This headline is more likely to grab my attention than a pamphlet labeled *Christmas Club Account.*

A headline is only one way you can begin your sales pitch on the cover. Another might be to tell a story with one or more dramatic photographs. A booklet used in a fund-raising mailing for the Humane Society, for instance, might feature dramatic photos of mistreated animals.

Most brochure covers feature a headline, logo, and visual only, so another way to make yours stand out is to start your body copy on the cover. Begin the text under the headline. It may not look classy, but it will get people to start reading.

➤ **Make your story flow**

A brochure is in many ways a miniature book, and like a good book, a good brochure tells a story. The story has a beginning, a middle, and an end, and flows smoothly from one point to the next. When you've written the first draft, sit back and read it as you would an article or short story. Does it progress logically? Or are there points where the transitions are awkward, where you are jarred by a phrase or sentence that doesn't seem to belong? If the transitions are clumsy, they'll need to be smoothed. Perhaps the material needs to be rearranged a bit. Maybe an extra subhead or headline or an introductory paragraph will take care of the problem. Or perhaps a transitional phrase can bridge the gap between one sentence and the next.

➤ **Strive for a personal tone**

Imagine going to a restaurant and hearing the head waiter tell you, "Pursuant to our phone conversation of 1/28/85, we have reserved two seats in our dining room as per your request." Sounds ridiculous, doesn't it? But that's just the way many business people sound when they write something to their coworkers or customers.

When you hand a report to your boss, would you say, "Enclosed please find the information requested"? Of course you wouldn't. Yet the insipid phrase "enclosed please find" makes its way into thousands of letters and memos each year, along with such other stuffed-shirt expressions as "herewith," "enclosed herein," "pursuant to your request," and "as per."

Perhaps you were taught by a supervisor or a professor that business writing has to sound this way—puffed up, pompous, and self-important. Well, your supervisor or professor was wrong. When you write pompously, you come across as pompous. And people don't want to do business with a stuffed shirt.

When writing promotional literature—or direct mail, a letter to a customer, or any other business communication—write in a natural, relaxed, friendly style. I don't mean you should be chatty, sound like a yokel, or throw in a lot of *you know*s, *yeah*s, *wow*s, and other slang. Written language has to be more precise, more concise than speech. But you should strive for the easy, conversational tone of spoken language—short words, short sentences, the personal touch. Friendly copy bespeaks a friendly organization, an organization that people will want to do business with.

On the following page is an example of copy written in the overly stiff, formal style so typical of big business.

> Well-designed documentation is a necessary requisite for an optimized hu-man-machine interface. Because the ARC-1 GAT (Graphic Arts Terminal) was designed to be a user-friendly instrument, the structure and accessibility of pertinent documentation become matters of primary importance.

When I read this kind of copy, I don't want to read any further. See how much more effective the same message is when written in language human beings can understand.

> The ARC-1 graphic arts terminal is extremely easy to use. And part of the reason is the set of clear, comprehensive instruction manuals that come with every system. Manuals written in plain English. Manuals that guide you through the system every step of the way.

John Louis DeGaetani of Harvard Business School, in an article in *The Wall Street Journal* (Feb. 8, 1982), describes a simple test he has devised for ensuring that your copy is conversational. "As you revise, ask yourself if you would ever say to your reader what you are writing," he suggests. "Or imagine yourself speaking to the person instead of writing." If what you've written sounds stiff, unnatural, or dull, it's not conversational, and you need to revise it.

> ## Stress benefits, not features

When you are enthusiastic about your job, your work becomes a major part of your life. As a result, your view of what you and your organization do becomes somewhat distorted. You believe the world revolves around your business or cause, when, in fact, it doesn't. You believe people are fasci-nated by every detail of your product, when, in fact, their only concern is what the product can do for them.

Too many promotional brochures stress the features of the product or service—the bare facts about how it works, what it looks like, how it is made, where it is made, who designed it, and so on. Effective copy trans-lates features into benefits. A *benefit* is a reason for the customer to buy the product. A benefit explains what the product can do for the customer. It tells how the customer can come out ahead by doing business with you: how one can save money, improve health, do the job better, protect one's family, save time, earn more money, gain status, feel good about oneself, enjoy life.

Remember, you don't want to settle for telling the reader what the product is. You want to show what the product can do for the reader. Copywriter Luther Brock, writing in *Direct Marketing*, says that effective promotional copy places "100 percent emphasis on how the reader will come out ahead by doing business with you."

➤ **Be specific**

Specificity is the heart of good writing, and that includes brochure writing. Many brochure writers use an elegant style of copy, full of fancy phrases and dramatic statements but short on facts. They fear that facts will bore the reader, so they strive for drama, entertainment, and literary style.

The fact is: People read brochures because they want information. They are quickly turned off by brochures that are long on puffery but empty of content. "Platitudes and generalities roll off the human understanding like water from a duck," wrote Claude Hopkins in his book, *Scientific Advertising*. "They leave no impression whatever." Specifics, on the other hand, stick in the mind. They are remembered, and they sell.

The best writing is superior largely because it presents facts in an interesting, clear fashion. Here, for example, is how *New York Times* reporter Sonny Kleinfield, in his book *The Biggest Company on Earth: A Profile of AT&T* (Holt, Rinehart and Winston), puts together a paragraph describing a subject most people consider rather mundane: the telephone book.

> AT&T's range strays some distance beyond phones. It is a major publisher. Each year, it turns out some 120 million copies of telephone directories (four hundred thousand tons of paper). The Bell System has to keep cranking out directories since about a quarter of all listings change each year. The print in them is a specially designed Bell Centennial, which recently replaced Bell Gothic. Bell Gothic has been used by eye doctors to test vision. The biggest directory in the country is Houston's. It has 2,899 pages and 939,640 listings, 8,350 of which are Smith. The smallest directory is one printed for Farley, Missouri. It has 3 pages and 282 listings, four of them Smith.

A lazy writer would be content to say, "AT&T also publishes a lot of phone books every year." But you can see how the specifics of phone-book publishing add a lot more interest to the subject at hand.

Apply the same techniques to your copy. Don't write "low, low prices" when you can say "50% off all carpets in stock through Sunday." Don't say "We're reliable" if you can tell the customer, "Our repairman arrives within 24 hours, or we fix it free of charge." Don't be content to talk about "a lot of energy saved" if you know your insulation "reduces heating bills by 30 to 50 percent a month." Remember, specifics sell.

➤ **Support your claims**

There is one problem you should keep in mind. Even if you stress benefits instead of features, even if you make specific claims, the customer still may not believe you. In his book *Direct Mail Copy That Sells*, copywriter

Herschell Gordon Lewis describes this phenomenon as the "Age of Skepticism":

> This is the Age in which nobody believes anybody, in which claims of superiority are challenged just because they're claims, in which consumers express surprise when something they buy actually performs the way it was advertised to perform.

How can you overcome skepticism and get people to believe you? There are a number of techniques that work.

Guarantees. Offer a guarantee: money back, free replacement, unlimited service, work redone at no cost. Guarantees allow the customer to try the product at no risk and ensure satisfaction. The message they carry to the consumer is: This product must work; otherwise, the manufacturer wouldn't guarantee it. A guarantee is the most powerful tool for overcoming skepticism. If the guarantee is a strong one, or if it is unusual to offer a guarantee on your type of product, you might stress the guarantee in your copy as a major selling point.

Letter from the president. Many catalogs include a personal letter from the company president to the consumer. In the letter, the president stresses the firm's reputation, the quality of its products, its dedication to service, and its promise to keep its customers satisfied.

People like to deal with the person in charge; this is why you so often hear a dissatisfied customer say to a clerk or waiter, "Let me speak with the manager, please." When the chief executive of an organization speaks, it leaves more of an impression than words from an anonymous copywriter.

Personal tone. The conversational style of writing we discussed earlier in this chapter can help build the reader's trust in you and your product. People would rather do business with people than with faceless corporate entities. Conversational tone conveys a sense of warmth, of caring, of person-to-person communication, even though the customer knows the brochure is a mass promotion. A cold, corporate style of copy sounds aloof and makes readers apprehensive about the treatment they'll receive if they deal with your organization.

Track record. Consumers are distrustful of new, unproven products and small operations that are here today but gone tomorrow. If you buy a new roof with a twenty-year guarantee, you want to buy from the company that's going to be around to honor the guarantee, not the independent contractor who may decide to quit tomorrow and retire to Florida.

Prove your stability and reputation to the consumer by talking about your track record, your past successes. Cite number of years in the business, number of employees, the size of your operation, number of warehouses, number of plants, number of offices, annual sales, profits, reputation. Talk about what you've done, who you've done it for, and how successful you've been. This builds the reader's trust in you.

Explanations. If your copy raises questions in the consumer's mind, you must put this reader at ease by answering them in the same piece of copy.

For example, I know a ghostwriter who writes novels, plays, articles, books, and stories that are published under his clients' by-lines. Many people would hesitate to hire him because his policy is to demand payment in full in advance. So he devotes one section of his pamphlet to explaining the reasons for this policy. When you read the reasons, the policy seems perfectly logical and reasonable, and the pamphlet generates considerable business for him.

Testimonials. A testimonial is a statement of praise or endorsement from a satisfied customer (or, in some cases, a celebrity). The testimonial is written in the customer's own words, appears in quotation marks, and is usually attributed to a specific person. The person's affiliation, title, or city of residence is included (if appropriate). If the person doesn't want his or her name used, you can comply by using the initials and address only ("Here's what E.G. in Florida says about . . ."), but the full name is better for overcoming skepticism. The quotation can range in length from a sentence to a few paragraphs. It's always more impressive to include several testimonials rather than just one, but one is better than none.

Case history. You can publish case histories as separate bulletins or include one or more case histories in condensed form within the text of a brochure. Case histories tell the customer, "When we talk about our service, we're not just being theoretical. Our product really works in the real world. Here's proof!"

Free trial. Some things have to be seen to be believed. So let the customer see your product and use it for a trial period. Traditional mail-order companies, especially magazine and book publishers, use this technique with success. To get you to subscribe to a magazine, they offer to send you the first issue free. If you don't like the magazine, you keep the free issue and cancel your subscription without payment or penalty. Or when you order a book, the publisher sends it to you on a fifteen-day free-trial basis. You read the book, and if you don't like it, you send it back—again, without paying for it.

Many industries are adopting this technique. Take software, for example. No matter how detailed the brochure, the customer can't really appreciate the benefits of the software without sitting down at the computer and using it. So companies that sell programs will offer to send customers a condensed version of the program (known as a *demo*) first. The customer gets the demo free or for a nominal sum. Once the demo proves itself, the customer can feel confident ordering the $395 program by mail.

Demonstration in person. Some products can only be demonstrated in person, either by a salesperson or by a qualified technician. In your brochure copy, you state that you can prove your claims with a live product demonstration, in the customer's home or office or at your facility.

A client of mine sells a $50,000 software system designed for large corporate computers. Her problem isn't explaining how the software works (it's rather simple) but getting people to believe how simple it is and how easy it is to use. The brochure describes the system but doesn't attempt to convince the reader that the description is true. Instead, the copy simply says, "Come in for a short demonstration and you will see for yourself how easy the system is to use." With this statement, the customer's skepticism is partially overcome by the copy alone. After all, reasons the customer, the brochure must be true; otherwise, they wouldn't offer a demonstration.

Demonstration in print. The next-best thing to offering an in-person demonstration is to demonstrate the product in print. For example, I once wrote a flier describing a new four-step dental procedure that was much quicker and easier than the conventional method. The brochure used a series of photos and captions to demonstrate the new procedure step by step. You could use the same technique to demonstrate many products—a blender, a do-it-yourself home repair kit, a tool, a dishwasher, a boiler.

Test results. Has your product proven its superior performance in tests? If so, include the test results in your copy. The best tests for overcoming consumer skepticism are those performed by an impartial third party, such as *Good Housekeeping* or *Consumer Guide.* But be aware that some of these organizations (e.g., *Consumer Guide*) do not allow manufacturers to include their test results in advertising and promotional literature. The second-best tests are field tests: the product performing successfully in an actual customer installation. Third-best are tests you perform in your own research laboratories.

Many advertisers stress the results of their market research. They claim that their product is most popular or that people say it works the best. These claims are based on surveys made by the advertiser or a market research firm it has employed.

There are three reasons you should be careful about placing too much emphasis on market research: First, consumers are skeptical about such surveys. Second, the people you survey often tell you the answer they think you would like to hear, or give an answer that sounds impressive, rather than the truth. Third, sophisticated consumers are aware that the numerical results of most market research surveys can always be interpreted and presented in a way that sheds the most favorable light on the advertiser and hides the negative points.

Show, don't tell. Don't just say your product or service saves money or improves life; show that it does. Say you're selling an energy-efficient air conditioner. Instead of just talking in a general sense about energy savings, provide sample calculations that show exactly how much money buyers can save based on their utility rate, the room size, the air conditioner's BTU rating, and the thermostat setting. Make it easy for the reader to perform the calculation and come up with the amount of money saved based on his or her specific situation.

Compare yourself with the competition. If your product or service clearly beats the competition, you can include comparisons. Be sure all claims of superiority can be substantiated by fact; if in doubt, leave it out. Unless your comparison is completely factual and can be supported by documentation (i.e., specifications taken from competitors' brochures), don't identify the competition by name. Some advertisers play it safe by putting product comparisons in a separate bulletin. If a competitor threatens a lawsuit or changes its product in response to your comparative advertising, you can stop using the comparison sheet while continuing to circulate your main brochure.

Compare yourself with alternative solutions. Many products and services have two types of competitors: direct competitors (similar products and services offered by other firms) and alternative solutions to the same application or problem. For example, a word processor manufacturer's direct competitors may include IBM, Kaypro, Wang, and Apple. But the company also has to sell the word processor as the best solution for achieving more productive writing, as opposed to alternative solutions: electric typewriters, electronic typewriters, hiring a secretary, or using outside typing services. If your prospects are using conventional products, show how your innovative approach is better, faster, and more economical.

➤ **Keep it lively.**

The difference between lively writing and dull writing is easy to spot but difficult to define. If you've ever been unable to put down a good mystery novel or magazine article, you know that lively writing can engage the reader's attention over long periods. If you've ever tried to force yourself to read yet another boring report or memo or textbook, you know that dull writing can turn readers off even when they are interested in the subject at hand.

Here are a few tricks of the copywriting trade to help keep your copy lively.

Vary sentence length. Most copywriting texts say to keep sentences short because short sentences are easier to read. But writing sounds monotonous when all sentences are the same length, so vary sentence length. Every so often, put in a fairly long sentence. Also use an occasional very short sentence or sentence fragment.

Use personal pronouns. Lively writing is personal, not impersonal. Personal pronouns (*we, they, us, you*) make the copy sound less lawyerlike, more like person-to-person conversation. Addressing the reader directly as *you* in the copy adds warmth and creates the illusion in the reader's mind that the copy was written specifically for him or her.

Give the reader news. Thousands of people who would never read a novel or a poem relax in the evening with the daily paper. Why? Because people are interested in what's new. If you can include news in your copy—about a product, a service, a company, an industry, a program, a technology, or a community—do so. It makes for livelier copy.

Tell stories. Human beings have been telling and recording stories since they first drew crude pictures of their hunting experiences on cave walls. Storytelling is an inherently powerful technique for getting your message across, much more so than a dry recitation of mere facts. Think about your own level of interest when you read a book or an article. Don't you enjoy it when a feature article gives a little anecdote or when there is dialogue to break up the narrative? Of course you do. And you can use the storytelling technique to liven up your promotional copy. For example, instead of just stating that your bottle-coating process is superior, tell the story of how one of your customers actually doubled his bottling business because of your better coating.

Use people. People have a great interest in other people. This is why Ann Landers, Dr. Joyce Brothers, and the gossip columns are so popular. You can add interest to your copy by injecting people, real or fictitious. Let's say you were describing a new procedure for employees to follow when making medical claims. Instead of writing "the employee should" or "the employee shall," create an employee and outline the procedure in story form: "Doris, a parts inspector, was feeling overly tired and wanted to get a checkup. First, Doris took her orange form A-12 to Personnel. Next, ..." You get the idea.

Also, when taking photos of a product, manufacturing plant, office, or building, put people in the photos to add interest.

Stress benefits, not facts. Your customers are not interested in what the product is; they are interested in what the product can do for them.

Here is a factual description of a roofing shingle.

225-lb. fiber glass DuraStay shingles. 20-year warranty on materials and installation.

Now here is a discussion of the benefits.

Because they're fiber glass, they stand up to weather. And because they're DuraStay, we guarantee it.

That's right. Your DuraStay roof is guaranteed to be leak-free for *20 years*. If there's ever a drop of water . . . if you even *suspect* a leak . . . we'll rush right over to inspect it and fix it—absolutely FREE.

Which version did you find more interesting?

Use short paragraphs. Long blocks of copy tire readers. Keep paragraphs and sections short. It makes copy easier to read (and easier to write).

Use heads and subheads. Use plenty of headlines and subheads to break up the text. Make the heads and subheads descriptive ("coating system prevents fuming problems"), not just functional ("coating system"). The reader should be able to get the gist of your sales pitch simply by scanning the heads and subheads, without reading the body copy thoroughly.

Separate the bold from the boring. In many pieces of promotional literature, the copy is split between an exciting sales message and a boring recitation of dull but necessary descriptive facts and specifications. Don't let your exciting message get bogged down with dull details. If you have a list of technical specifications, put them in a separate table or sidebar, and keep your body copy lively.

Think visually. Photos, charts, drawings, and diagrams can go a long way toward adding interest to your text. If something is communicated better with a visual than with words, use the visual.

➤ **Keep it relevant**

All copy should be interesting to read. But not everything that's interesting to read belongs in your copy. Copy should be relevant to the message you're trying to communicate. If it is irrelevant, your readers may be entertained, but they won't be hit with the message you want your promotional literature to communicate. And the people you really want to reach—the ones that are likely to buy your product, join your club, take your course, or donate to your cause—are likely to be turned off by copy that fails to get to the point.

For example, a brochure selling heavy-duty and industrial batteries begins with a two-page essay on the history of batteries, ranging from ancient Egypt to the voltaic pile to the invention of the lead storage battery.

Sounds interesting, you say. Yes—to a history buff. But the industrial engineer looking for specific information on battery size and performance is not likely to wade through this unnecessary verbiage to get to essential size, price, and performance information.

➤ **Check the accuracy**

Then check it again. Then have three or four other people in your organization check it, too. A single mistake can mean that you will need to reprint the entire brochure, and that's expensive. So even though proofreading is boring, it's well worth the time and effort.

In addition to accuracy, you should check for consistency. Make sure you've used the correct grammar, punctuation, and spelling and a consistent style for capitalization, numerals, abbreviations, titles, and product names throughout the copy. If you're inconsistent—for example, if you write "GAF" in some places and "G.A.F." in others—you're automatically wrong part of the time.

➤ **Don't forget the details**

One manufacturer spent $2,400 revising and reprinting product sheets only to discover that the company's phone number had been omitted from the new sheets. We devote so much time and energy to the promotional aspect of our literature that we sometimes tend to shrug off the details. But these details can be just as important as sales pitch and graphic image. Review your copy before it goes to the designer. Make sure you have included everything relevant:

    Logo
    Company name
    Address
    Phone number
    Extensions
    Toll-free number
    Store locations
    Directions
    Hours
    Credit cards accepted
    Branch offices

Telex and TWX codes
Guarantee
Disclaimers
Other required legal wording
Brochure date and code number
Permissions and acknowledgments
Trademarks and registration marks

The lack of this so-called fine print can kill the effectiveness of an otherwise fine promotion. For example, one restaurant handed out hundreds of promotional fliers offering a substantial savings on a fine dinner at its grand opening. The flier was widely distributed but brought in little new business. Why? Because the restaurant was in a hard-to-find location, and although the flier contained the address, it didn't give directions. Potential customers couldn't find the place.

More visualizing

Once you finish your copy, you may want to go back to your copywriter's rough (the crude sketch of the layout) to see how your completed copy compares with your original plan. Perhaps some sections have been dropped and others deleted. Or maybe you've written more copy than you planned for one section but less for another. Chances are your finished manuscript isn't exactly what you indicated on the copywriter's rough, so you may want to redraw the rough on the basis of the final copy.

As you redraw the rough, you can produce a more exact version because you now know how long each section of copy is. Take a look at this new layout. Does it leave more room for illustrations than you thought? If it does, go back and reread the copy. Are there additional pictures and drawings you want to include in your brochure to help get your message across even more effectively? If so, indicate them on your layout and your manuscript.

On the other hand, you might have more copy and less room for drawings. If so, consider whether all your proposed visuals are really necessary. Perhaps some of the borderline ones, visuals you like but don't really need, can be deleted. Unnecessary visuals should be cut because each visual costs extra money.

The copy-review process

If you're the boss in your organization, you have the final say on what copy is acceptable and what is not. But if you're not the head honcho, you probably have to get others to read and approve the copy before you can release it to the printer. Here's how to go about it.

If the brochure is mostly text and has a simple layout, you can get approval on copy only. If the layout contains a lot of visuals and the copy depends on both visuals and layout, give the unapproved copy to the designer first, have the designer do a rough layout (see Chapter 6), and then submit both the copy and the layout for review together.

APPROVAL FORM FOR PROMOTIONAL COPY

Dear Reviewer:

Please read the attached draft of our organization's new promotional literature carefully.

You may mark specific comments, corrections, and suggestions directly on the copy or attach a separate sheet if needed.

When you complete your review, write your initials next to your name on the list below. Pass this on to the next reviewer by the date indicated.

The last reviewer should return the manuscript to
_____ by _____.

Thanks for your cooperation.

Name	Initials	Review by

Figure 14. Attach a copy of this form to your manuscript, and circulate it to the appropriate people for approval.

Attach a *copy review sheet* (Figure 14) to the manuscript and circulate it to the reviewers. The sheet lists the reviewers in the order they are to receive and review the manuscript. Review starts with the person of least authority and ends with the person who has final say.

You send the copy to the first reviewer. He or she reads the copy, makes any changes, initials the sheet, and passes it on the the next reviewer. After the last reviewer has read the manuscript, it is returned to you.

Reviewers are people in your organization who are involved with the product or service described in the proposed brochure and therefore have a say in what the finished piece should contain. You may also want to get the opinions of people not directly involved—sales representatives, consultants, distributors, engineers, and others who may be knowledgeable and have something to contribute.

Send these people a copy along with a cover memo that says, "Enclosed is the copy for a forthcoming brochure on _____. I'd like to get your comments and criticisms on this copy. If you have suggestions on how to improve this copy, may I hear from you by ___(date)___?" Unlike the reviewers, these people are being asked for their opinions only, not for approval. You are obliged to make the changes requested by your boss, but you can choose either to heed or to ignore the advice passed on by people who are not official reviewers.

Although it takes a little prodding and reminding people, you'll eventually get your manuscript back with changes and comments. If the changes are minor and specific, retyping may be all that's needed to produce a finished, approved manuscript. But if the revisions are extensive, the writer may have to take the reviewed copy and make the requested changes.

Don't send the writer's revised draft through this approval process again. Instead, send it to all reviewers at once with a cover memo saying, "Here is the revised manuscript for the _____ brochure. It contains all changes and revisions requested. If you have any comments or additional changes, please give me a call or send a marked-up manuscript to me by ___(date)___." This allows reviewers to get a last look and give the copy their final blessing. Otherwise, some irate executive may complain bitterly that you ignored his or her suggestion, when, in fact, you didn't.

CHAPTER SIX

Finding Your Look: The Design

Who designs promotional literature?

As we discussed in Chapter 3, there are many places to turn to for design services: ad agencies, PR firms, creative boutiques, art and copy services, design studios, free-lance graphic artists. All these folks are qualified to handle the job for you. The question is: Do you need their help, or can you do the job yourself? The answer depends on the complexity of the task at hand.

For very simple pieces, such as fliers, sales letters, typewritten newsletters, and folded pamphlets, sophisticated design isn't required. Your copywriter's rough will show where the type, headlines, and photos go. When you take this rough to the typesetter, you can look at books of sample type and paper stock and select the ones you like. From there, the printer can create a *mechanical* (a paste-up of the type and visuals ready for press) and print the piece without a designer's help.

But for more sophisticated promotions, the design of the page, the use of color, the selection of type, the treatment of visuals, and the arrangement of these elements on the page are far more crucial and complex. You probably don't have the skill or the experience to design the piece on your own, so here's where you need the graphic designer.

What's more, a professional will give your piece the professional touch, and that's really what you want. Saving money by doing the layout and paste-up yourself is usually a mistake. Why? Because when it comes to design, you're an amateur, and your fledgling graphics efforts will probably look just that way—amateur.

Sure, hiring artists can be expensive. But it pays in three ways.

First, the quality—and hence the effectiveness—of your print promotions goes way up.

Second, you must weigh the cost of hiring the artist against what your own time is worth per hour and how long it would take you or your employee to do the job. A good designer can charge anywhere from $20 to $50 an hour or more; $35 is the average. Recent estimates place the worth of a manager's time at around $60 an hour. So you save $25 an hour by hiring the $35-an-hour artist instead of doing the job yourself. And the savings is actually greater because the artist can do the job a lot faster (not to mention better) than you can.

Third, there is a psychological advantage to hiring an artist. We feel good when we work hard at tasks we're competent at, but we feel bad and become frustrated doing work we're really not good at. As a business person or an administrator, you're an expert on planning and thinking; that's why I have suggested you plan, outline, and coordinate the production of your brochure yourself. But you're not trained in art, so trying to draw layouts or specify type would probably frustrate you. Better to hire a professional and know the job is being done right.

How to select the right designer for the job

Chapter 3 provided guidelines on how to select and work with a designer. But I'd like to elaborate on them a little more.

The most important factor in choosing an artist is style. Every graphic artist has an individual style. Some produce very slick, modern graphics. Some are almost abstract or surrealistic in their approach. Others produce plain-Jane graphics with clean, crisp, highly readable type and layouts. Still others use lots of warm colors and folksy artwork for a homey, Norman Rockwell look.

Chances are you already know the image you want your literature to convey. And you have a pretty good idea of how your literature's graphic look should fit that image. Be sure, then, to choose an artist whose style is in sync with your own. If you want a homespun image for your mail-order catalog, choose the Norman Rockwell-type artist, not the abstract painter or the high-tech, futuristic designer. But if you're selling satellites, the futuristic look may be just the thing.

Carefully examine the artist's portfolio of sample work. Do you like what you see? Would you feel comfortable having your own literature done in the artist's style, or is it too far-out or fancy or dull for you? Does the portfolio contain samples of published work similar to the job at hand, or does the artist lack experience in your area, be it brochures or catalogs or annual reports? Pick an artist whose style and specialty mesh with your own.

Don't make the mistake of choosing a designer and then trying to force that person to change his or her style of design to fit the look you want. It won't work. Artists can't (and shouldn't be expected to) switch styles any more than you can switch your personality. Choose an artist in whose work you see a reflection of the way you'd like your own literature to look.

The second most important factor in choosing a designer is attitude. To ensure that the design is completed to your liking and on time, choose a designer who brings a businesslike attitude to the job. I give this warning because not all graphic designers are dedicated to handling commercial jobs. Some are serious artists who moonlight in commercial work. And although many of these moonlighters will give your project their best effort, others won't. Some look down on commercial work and tend to be prima donnas in dealing with their clients. Avoid such temperamental types. Hire a person who blends artistic skill with business professionalism. This is the only way to ensure that the job is completed quickly and competently, without headaches or grief.

Here are some other factors to consider when hiring a graphic artist: clients, commercial background, capabilities, price, and the ability to meet a deadline.

➤ Clients

Ask to see a list of clients. Is it an impressive one? Has the artist worked for clients in fields similar to your own? Call some of the clients on the list. Were they pleased with the artist's work? How were their dealings—was the artist a pleasure or a pain to work with? One warning: A graphic artist unable to produce a client list probably does not have much experience in commercial work.

➤ Commercial background

Is the artist knowledgeable in all phases of the design, production, and printing processes? This is important. Skill in design is not enough; the artist must also know how to prepare work that is acceptable for the printing press. An artist/designer must know the limits and constraints, both physical and financial, of typography, artwork, printing presses, and folding and binding machines. Someone who has artistic flair but lacks commercial experience may produce a design that is beautiful but impractical from a production or cost point of view.

➤ **Capabilities**

Make sure the artist has the resources to handle your type of assignment. If you're producing a highly technical brochure, pick an artist who is comfortable working with complicated graphs and other technical illustrations. If you're producing a full-color catalog, make sure the artist knows how to prepare work for a color press.

No artist excels at every phase of graphic arts production. So when hiring someone, choose a designer with the capabilities to handle your specific requirements.

➤ **Price**

Find out how you'll be charged for the job: by the hour, the day, or the project. What is the artist's best estimate for the job? If there are changes, how much will they cost? Will you be billed on completion of the assignment or in stages? Will the artist put a markup on typography and other outside services and products he or she buys for you? That last question is important. You may want to avoid the markup by buying type, paper stock, and other outside products and services directly.

As with hiring copywriters, the more specific you can be about the job, the more precise the artist's estimate of the cost will be. When you meet with a graphic artist to discuss a job and get an estimate, present your copywriter's rough, the current draft of your brochure text, and your completed literature specification sheet (see pages 47-51). This material will make it easier for the artist to give you a firm price quotation.

➤ **Ability to meet a deadline**

Ask whether the artist can meet the deadline you have set. Some designers are in great demand and are booked many months in advance. Others have studios full of assistants and work around the clock to meet the tightest deadlines. Don't pressure an artist into rushing to meet an impossible deadline. Instead, choose a designer who is comfortable working within your time constraints.

Working with your graphic designer

You've hired a designer. Now what? Does the designer go home and send you a finished brochure and a bill two months later? Or do you sit at the designer's side day and night, supervising the positioning of each word of type, each square inch of artwork?

The process of working with a designer falls somewhere between these two extremes. The designer does most of the creative work independently, working at a studio away from your office and watchful eye, but the two of you do get together at various stages of the project to review the work and make sure the direction it takes is to your liking.

This is basically a five-step process: initial consultation, thumbnails, roughs, comprehensive, and dummy.

> **Initial consultation**

The project begins with a briefing. You sit down with the designer to explain your goals and the type of finished piece you're looking for. Discussing design is more difficult than talking about copy because it can be hard to describe the images you have in your mind. Here's how to go about it: Give the designer the current draft of the brochure text. If it's final, approved copy—great. The designer can go directly to setting type. If it's a rough draft, say so. The designer won't set the type but will be able to use the manuscript as a guide to the length of each section of copy and of the brochure as a whole.

The designer should also receive your copywriter's rough. This drawing shows which visuals go with which sections of text and how the copy and art might be divided on a page-by-page basis. Be sure to explain that the rough is just that, a rough guideline only. The designer should feel free to use it, improve it, or discard it altogether if he or she can come up with something better.

The designer will also benefit from seeing your completed literature specification sheet. This gives an idea of your preferences in colors, paper stock, page size, and so forth.

There are two additional tools you can use to communicate your ideas to designers: *sample files* and *circle layouts.*

A sample file is a file of literature you've collected, literature that you sent for by mail or picked up in stores and at trade shows. Before starting any literature project, go through your sample file and pick out any samples with graphic techniques or styles you think might look good in your own work. Then, when you meet with your designer, you can point to a sample to show exactly what you're talking about.

For example, if you like a particular typeface, show your artist a brochure that uses this style of type. If you like an unusual paper stock, show a brochure printed on it. Build a sample file so that you can communicate your likes and dislikes precisely to the artist.

In the circle layout, a technique described by Lewis Kornfeld in his book *To Catch a Mouse, Make a Noise Like a Cheese*, you draw rough shapes—circles, ovals, squares, rectangles—to show the approximate position and amount of space each element of your layout (headline, subhead, body copy, picture, logo, charts, and so on) should take on the printed page. The logic of this technique is that you, the client, dictate the importance of the various components of your message, which is how it should be. The designer can judge from an aesthetic point of view. But the layout should emphasize visuals and text from a promotional point of view, and no one knows the value of your message better than you do.

The advantage of this technique is that it requires no artistic skill. Anyone who can lift a pencil can, in less than a minute, create a circle layout. Figure 15 on the next page presents some samples.

Of course, you are free to use all these techniques or none of them. How much guidance or freedom you want to give your designer is up to you.

The way I work with designers is to communicate my needs as precisely as possible but to make it clear that what I'm really interested in is getting the best design possible, not just a dressed-up copy of my own primitive layout. (If you say this, mean it. Don't tell the artist, "Feel free to create!" and then, when you get the layout say, "Why didn't you draw it the way I told you to?") A good client is clear about his or her expectations but open to new ideas.

➤ **Thumbnails**

After the initial briefing, the artist goes back to the studio to work on your project. You can do your bit by letting the work be done in peace. Don't badger with daily visits or calls to see how it's going. It's going fine; the artist is a professional and can do the job without your supervision.

You and the artist meet again to review the work that has been done so far. At this meeting, the artist will show you some *thumbnails*. A thumbnail is a small, quickly done sketch intended to give a rough idea of the general look and feel of a design. Thumbnails are miniature sketches, about the size of wallet-size photos. They lack detail and are meant to show overall direction only. Don't be put off by their crude appearance; they aren't supposed to have a finished look.

If the designer is relatively certain of the direction the design is to take, you will be shown only one set of thumbnails representing one design

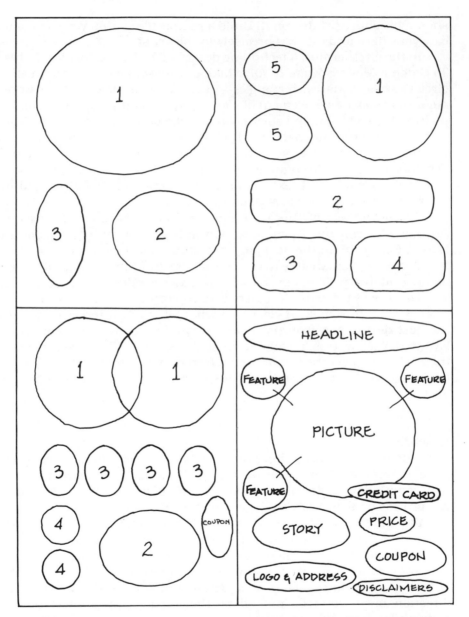

Figure 15. Circle layouts provide a quick and easy way of showing the relative importance of the various elements in a page layout. (Credit: <u>To Catch a Mouse, Make a Noise Like a Cheese,</u> by Lewis Kornfeld. © 1983 by Lewis Kornfeld. Published by Prentice-Hall, Inc., Englewood Cliffs, NJ 07632. Reprinted with permission.)

concept. Or, the designer may show you several sets of thumbnails representing two, three, or four different concepts, with one concept probably recommended as a favorite and the others presented as second choices.

Why bother with thumbnails? Why not just go to the finished layout? Because the nearer to completion the project is, the more it costs to make revisions and changes. (Keep this principle in mind because it applies to all phases of producing literature.) Thumbnails don't take the artist much time to produce, so this step allows changes to be made rather inexpensively. If the literature had already been typeset and pasted up, changes would be extremely costly.

Study the thumbnails. If you like what you see, give the artist your approval to go on to the next step. If you like the basic concept but want some changes, discuss them with the designer. Ask for an opinion on whether the changes would improve the piece or weaken it. Sometimes, the designer will agree with your suggestions. Other times, you may get disagreement. Listen to advice from your designer; don't assume that you always know what's best. After all, when it comes to layouts, your artist is the pro.

When viewing a series of thumbnails, you might pick one version only to find out that your artist prefers another. Again, discuss the reasons for this preference. You may find out that the pro is right.

If you don't like anything you see, don't say "This stinks" or "I don't like any of this" or "You've done a bad job." Instead, explain exactly why you aren't satisfied with the layout and give specific suggestions on how it can be changed to your liking. When you criticize the work of outside suppliers, your criticisms should always be constructive, specific, and stated in a manner that won't insult or offend the person. This, too, is a key principle of brochure production, and it applies to every phase of the job.

If the thumbnails totally displease you, you might ask the artist to go back to the drawing board and submit a new set. But if you approve the thumbnails as is or with modifications, the next step is to look at an artist's roughs.

➤ **Roughs**

A *rough* is a full-size sketch of the layout of each page of the brochure. It shows the position and size of headlines, subheads, body copy, pictures, colors and tints, borders, tables, charts, graphs, drawings, sidebars, footnotes, and any other text or visual elements. Headlines and subheads are written on the roughs so you can quickly determine the subject matter of each page or spread. Body copy is represented by a series of straight or squiggly lines because the actual type won't be set until layout and copy are approved.

When you look at an artist's roughs, you get a good sense of what the finished piece will look like, and this can be a revelation. A graphic technique that sounded questionable when the artist described it suddenly looks great on the page. Or perhaps you discover that the table you crammed onto page 3 would really look better on the centerfold. Or maybe the copy is longer than you thought and needs to be broken up with some additional subheads.

Together, you and the artist review the rough and fine-tune the design. With the rough in front of you, design is no longer an abstract concept; it's real. You can see how each suggested change affects the overall appearance.

> ### Comprehensive

The *comprehensive*, or *comp*, is a tighter rendering of the rough layout. It is as close to the finished piece as a drawing can be. If you made changes on the rough, the comp will give you a chance to see them before the piece is typeset and pasted up. If top management must approve copy and layout, a comp makes it easier for them to visualize the printed piece. Also, the comp serves as a guide to the paste-up artist and printer.

Even at this stage, changes can still be made at a reasonable cost. Remember, a comp is just a sketch; no type has been set, no photos taken, no illustrations rendered. That's why going through these steps is worthwhile; it allows you to change your mind without paying a fortune to do so.

> ### Dummy

Making a *dummy* of the proposed literature is also a worthwhile step. A dummy is a full-scale model of the brochure. It is constructed out of the paper stock on which the brochure will be printed, and it is folded or bound in the same way the finished piece will be.

The dummy gives you an idea of the look, weight, and feel of the brochure, as well as the flow (how smoothly the story unfolds as you turn from one page to the next). As with the rough, holding a dummy in your hands can be a revelation. The lightweight paper you thought was fine when you picked it from the printer's sample book looks cheap and flimsy when stapled into a booklet. Perhaps you need to give the booklet more weight by printing the cover on a heavier stock. Or you may find that your glossy colored stock picks up fingerprint smudges when handled. A different color or coating would solve that problem.

It's especially important to create a dummy if the brochure is to be mailed. There are two reasons for this.

First, you can weigh the dummy and find out the mailing cost based on this weight. You may discover that going to a slightly lighter-weight stock significantly reduces the required postage.

Second, you should see whether the dummy fits into a standard envelope. If it doesn't, you'll need to print a custom envelope, and that's very expensive.

Also, the post office has regulations concerning the size of envelopes, and not all sizes and shapes are acceptable. If your proposed brochure is oversized or oddly shaped, check with the post office to make sure it will be accepted for mailing, and get this clearance in writing. Otherwise, you may spend thousands on your unique booklet only to discover that the post office refuses to mail it.

Design considerations and how to evaluate them

Here are some design factors you'll have to make decisions about, along with some tips on making the right selection.

➤ Number of pages

The number of pages depends on the length of the copy, the number of visuals required, the amount of copy and visuals per page, and, of course, the printing budget.

The copy dictates the size of the printed piece. Obviously, a 3,000-word brochure needs more pages than a 300-word brochure. However, by writing concisely and eliminating unnecessary words, you can cut down the length of the text and, hence, the number of pages. This type of editing saves money because printing costs increase as a function of the number of pages (and typesetting costs increase as a function of the number of words).

Editing also applies to visuals. Use visuals if they enhance and clarify your message, but don't include a picture just because you like it. Each picture adds to the total cost of the job.

Some designers, striving for an elegant, understated look, use a lot of white space (blank space) on each page. The result is often striking but increases the page count and the associated printing costs. Try not to spread your layout too thin. You—and many professional designers—would be surprised to learn how much copy you can put on a page and still make it attractive, eye-catching, and readable.

A client recently hired me to rewrite an 8-page brochure. I received the old draft and a rough of the 8-page layout. By tightening the copy, I was able to recast the layout into 6 pages and save the client a lot of money at printing time.

Of course, budget is the ultimate factor in deciding length. If you have 16 pages of copy but only enough money to print a 4-page brochure, you either have to reduce the number of pages or increase the budget.

➤ Page size

The choice of page size depends, in part, on how you distribute your literature and how your customer makes use of it.

If you can design your brochure to fit into a standard business envelope (known as a number 10 envelope), mailing costs will be lower than for a full-size brochure that must be mailed in a 9-by-12-inch envelope.

Literature that is to be displayed at exhibits or in retail outlets should be designed to fit standard display racks. Travel agents, for example, use racks for pocket-size (4-by-9-inch) folders; full-size literature may not fit.

Pocket-size guides are handy if you want the reader to carry the literature (e.g., a pamphlet on gas-saving tips should fit into an automobile glove compartment). But you should use full-size pages (8½ by 11 inches) for materials that people are likely to keep around the home or office.

An 8½-by-11-inch page size fits neatly into a standard file. A larger brochure may stand out from the crowd but risks being thrown away because it is too big for the file; a pocket-size brochure can get lost in a file. If the reader is a purchasing agent or someone else who might store your literature in a three-ring binder, be sure to leave margins so the three-hole punch doesn't interfere with text or graphics.

Layout also plays a part in choosing a page size. Literature with many sections of very short copy is best suited to a pocket-size folder with 6 or 8 panels; each panel can contain one or two sections of copy. A technical bulletin with large graphs, charts, and tables requires larger pages for adequate display of the material.

➤ Type style

How do you choose a typeface? First, look for readability. Most important, the type must be easy to read and inviting to the eye. After all, the message you want to communicate is contained in the text; if people don't read the copy, your efforts are wasted.

Second, type style has a major effect on the image your literature conveys. Take a look at the sample typefaces in Figure 16. Helvetica Roman has a clean, modern look. Souvenir Medium has a warmer appearance. Eurostile Extended looks futuristic and technical.

There are literally thousands of typefaces available today. However, an individual printer or typesetter typically has access to just a few dozen, which makes your selection somewhat easier. Ask your designer to recommend a typeface and to show you some alternatives in case you don't like the first choice. You may even want to sit down with the designer's type book (a book showing sample typefaces) and see which you prefer.

Also, notice in Figure 16 that there are many variations in the *weight*

Cheltenham Bold	Gill Sans Roman	Serif Gothic Roman
Clarendon Light	*Gill Sans Italic*	**Serif Gothic Bold**
Clarendon Roman	**Gill Sans Bold**	**Serif Gothic Extra Bold**
Clarendon Bold	***Gill Sans Bold Italic***	**Serif Gothic Heavy**
Clarinda Typewriter	**Gill Sans Extra Bold**	**Serif Gothic Black**
Clearface Regular	**Gill Sans Ultra**	Souvenir Light
Clearface Italic	Goudy Old Style Roman	*Souvenir Light Italic*
Clearface Bold	*Goudy Old Style Italic*	**Souvenir Medium**
Cochin Roman	**Goudy Old Style Bold**	***Souvenir Medium Italic***
Cochin Italic	**Goudy Old Style Extra Bold**	**Souvenir Demi Bold**
Cochin Bold	**Grouch**	***Souvenir Demi Bold Italic***
Cochin Bold Italic	Harry Thin Roman	**Souvenir Bold**
Cooper Black	Helvetica Thin	***Souvenir Bold Italic***
Cooper Black Italic	*Helvetica Thin Italic*	Souvenir Bold Outline
Craw Modern	Helvetica Light	**Spartan Medium**
Devinne Roman	*Helvetica Light Italic*	*Spartan Medium Italic*
Devinne Italic	Helvetica Roman	**Spartan Heavy**
Doric Black	*Helvetica Italic*	*Spartan Heavy Italic*
Electra Roman	**Helvetica Bold**	Tiffany Light
Electra Italic	***Helvetica Bold Italic***	Tiffany Medium
Electra Bold	**Helvetica Heavy**	**Tiffany Demi**
Eras Light	**Helvetica Black**	**Tiffany Heavy**
Eras Book	***Helvetica Black Italic***	Times Roman
Eras Medium	Helvetica Light Condensed	*Times Roman Italic*
Eras Demi	*Helvetica Light Condensed Italic*	**Times Roman Bold**
Eras Bold	Helvetica Condensed	***Times Roman Bold Italic***
Eras Ultra	*Helvetica Condensed Italic*	Times Roman Hindu
Eurostile Roman	**Helvetica Bold Condensed**	Trade Gothic Light
Eurostile Bold	***Helvetica Bold Condensed Italic***	*Trade Gothic Light Italic*
Eurostile Extended	**Helvetica Black Condensed**	Trade Gothic Roman
Eurostile Bold Extended	***Helvetica Black Condensed Italic***	*Trade Gothic Italic*
Fairfield	**Helvetica Compressed**	**Trade Gothic Bold**
Fairfield Italic	***Helvetica Extra Compressed***	***Trade Gothic Bold Italic***
Franklin Gothic Roman	Helvetica Outline Compressed	Trade Gothic Condensed Roman
Franklin Gothic Condensed	**Helvetica Bold Extended**	*Trade Gothic Condensed Italic*
Fritz Quadrata Roman	**Hobo**	**Trade Gothic Condensed Bold**
Fritz Quadrata Bold	Italia Medium	***Trade Gothic Condensed Bold Italic***

Figure 16. There are thousands of typefaces you can choose from. Here are a few of the more common ones.

(thickness) of the lettering within a family of type. With Helvetica, for example, you have Helvetica Thin, Light, Roman, Bold, Heavy, and Black, plus italic versions of each of these. You could set body copy in Roman, headlines in Bold, footnotes and other fine print in Light.

In general, it's best to avoid mixing typefaces within a single piece. Stay with one family. I'll get into a detailed discussion on type selection in Chapter 9.

➤ Type size

This one's easier. Type is measured in points. The body copy in promotional literature should be set in 10- or 12-point type; in no case should type be smaller than 9 points. Type size for headlines and subheads depends on their length, but they are usually set at least several sizes larger than the body copy to make them stand out.

➤ Folding or binding

A folded piece of literature, one in which the pages are formed by folding a single sheet of paper, costs less to print than a booklet made by mechanically binding together several sheets of paper. But a piece of paper can be folded only so many times, and therefore the size of folded brochures is limited. If you need more than 8 panels or pages, you'll probably have to use staples, glue, or some other mechanical method of binding. Folding and binding techniques are discussed in detail in Chapter 9.

➤ Number of colors

A *one-color job* is the least expensive and is printed with a single ink. Most one-color jobs are black ink on white paper (e.g., newspapers). But a one-color job could use a different color ink, such as blue or brown.

In printer's jargon, the number of colors (one, two, four) refers to the number of different colored inks used and doesn't take into account the color of the paper. So, by printing a red ink on gray paper, you can create a one-color job that has two colors, red and gray.

A *two-color job* uses two inks (usually black and a color), and is about 15 to 20 percent more expensive to print than a one-color job. Most two-color jobs print black ink on white paper, with the second ink being blue, red, or yellow. But again, you can be more imaginative.

A *full-color* or *four-color job* uses the four basic printing colors—black, blue, red, and yellow—to reproduce artwork and photos in the multiple gradations and hues of full, natural color. Full color can run double or triple the cost (or more) of black and white, depending on the number of color photos included.

When deciding on how many colors to use, keep these cost guidelines in mind. Otherwise, you may not be able to afford the brochure you've paid someone to design.

Image also plays a part. Four-color printing conveys an image of quality, size, and wealth. However, a good designer can create this image with two or three colors and a fine-quality paper stock at much less cost than that of a four-color job.

If photographs play a key role in making the sale, use four-color printing on a glossy white paper stock. This gives the best reproduction of color photographs. Color is important in literature promoting food, fashions, home decorating, travel, collectibles, and other products and services sold primarily on their visual appeal. If, on the other hand, the brochure is all copy, one or two colors are adequate for the job.

➤ **Color scheme**

Don't use color just because you think it looks classy. You're paying extra for color, so make the color work to enhance your message or the visual appeal of your layout.

The Red Devil Company, a tool manufacturer, prints every job in black and red; the red is used to highlight its logo, a graphic of the devil. A recent Bloomingdale's ad featured a photo of a glamorous woman wearing an expensive necklace; the entire ad was black and white except for the necklace, which was shown in full color. The effect was striking and served to draw attention to the item being sold.

➤ **Photographs or drawings**

Photos are useful for showing what a product looks like, for demonstrating its performance, and for adding believability. Drawings, on the other hand, are best for showing how something works, how it is put together, and what it looks like inside (where it would be difficult to take a clear, informative photograph). Drawings are also useful for visualizing products and projects that are planned but not yet completed, such as a new corporate headquarters or the prototype of a new machine. Chapter 7 covers the use of photographs and drawings in great detail.

➤ **Paper stock**

The type of paper you choose—its look, color, weight, and texture—has a major effect on the image your literature conveys. A fine, textured, uncoated stock has an elegant, dignified look and feel, whereas a paper with a reflective metallic coating looks more high-tech.

The best way to select paper is to construct a dummy out of the proposed stock and keep the dummy on your desk for a while. Do you like the way it looks? Does it have enough heft to it, or is it too flimsy? Does the paper stand up to repeated handling, or does it tear, crease, or smudge? For example, black or other dark coated stocks are notorious for picking up fingerprints when handled.

Some pieces of promotional literature, such as flip chart presentations, are subject to unusual amounts of handling and abuse. These pieces should be printed on a heavier stock, such as *cover stock* or thin cardboard, which can stand up to repeated handling. You can even laminate pages with a thin, transparent plastic for added protection.

Paper stock, size, and number of pages are the factors that determine the weight of the piece. So if the brochure is to be mailed, a lighter stock can save you postage costs.

➤ **Amount of text and artwork per page**

Do you want to cram as much text and as many visuals on each page as you can? Or do you want the piece to be light on copy and easy on the eye? This choice depends mainly on your audience. If you are writing for people who read a lot (e.g., teachers), it's okay to have a dense, copy-heavy page, as long as the typeface is easy to read and the page is laid out neatly. But if you are writing for people who are too busy to read much or people who are not readers, cut back on the amount of copy and leave plenty of open space on each page. The space makes the page more inviting to the eye, and the brochure seems less intimidating.

➤ **Use of headlines and subheads**

Used as a design element, headlines and subheads help pull the reader's eye through the body copy. In addition, good heads and subheads allow readers to skim a brochure without reading the entire text and still get the gist of the story. When the artist lays out the page, it may turn out that the writer has not used enough subheads to break up the text adequately. If this is the case, go back and add a few more subheads.

➤ **Cover concept**

The cover can serve several purposes:

- Get the reader to pick up the brochure and open to page 1.
- Deliver a complete message.
- Create a strong identity for the product or the company.
- Identify and select an audience—by market, industry, application, or some other criterion.

The design should be used to achieve the desired goal. For example, a series of brochures describing a family of power tools should have a consistent cover design to build an identity for the product line. This consistency can be achieved in many ways: with a tag line, a style of type, a logo, a graphic device, or even photographs of each tool in a similar setting.

➤ **Attachments**

If your literature is to be distributed with inserts or supplements, you may want to design the central piece with a pocket for holding these extra materials. If the literature is to be mailed with a business card, you can cut slots into a page for insertion of the card. If you want to include cloth swatches or other physical objects with your literature, you might glue these samples to the pages. Any inserts, cards, loose sheets, or three-dimensional objects that you intend to attach to your brochure must be planned for by the designer.

➤ **Pop-ups, die cuts, and other gimmicks**

There are many gimmicks you can use to make your brochure stand out from the crowd. These include *pop-ups* (three-dimensional paper sculptures that pop up when you open the brochure), *embossing* (a technique that raises lettering or other portions of the design), *die cuts* (sections cut out of the page), *varnishes* (to add an extra sheen to photos or bands of color), and *special folds.* And there are new gimmicks invented every day. A recent one is a microchip that you can paste on the page; the chip plays music when you open the brochure.

Because they are expensive, gimmicks should be used sparingly and only when they help to achieve a specific effect. Adding a pop-up or foldout to a small brochure can actually double the cost in many cases.

Gimmicks must be carefully worked into the design to enhance the look and message of the piece. A gimmick used for its own sake is a waste; it draws attention to itself and away from the sales message. Gimmicks should relate directly to the theme and subject of the brochure. For instance, a booklet promoting a typing service could use a pop-up of a typewriter.

Ten tips for designing better promotional literature

➤ **Think of the layout as a framework, not as artwork**
Some artists think of the layout as an end in itself rather than as the means by which the visuals and copy communicate the client's message. That's a mistake. Promotional literature isn't artwork; it's promotion. An aesthetically pleasing layout is a waste if it doesn't present the copy and pictures in an appealing, easy-to-read format.

Unfortunately, some graphic artists are more interested in winning design awards than in winning readers. You can spot them by their layouts, which are full of graphic techniques that look slick but hinder the readability of the copy. Here is a partial list of such techniques.

Copy set in far-out typefaces
Type printed over a tint or a visual
Reverse type (white type on black background)
Type set completely in italics
Type set entirely in uppercase letters
Overuse of white space
Type set too small to read
Pages consisting mainly of color bands, borders, or other design elements
Several pages left blank or used for graphic effect only
Use of abstract artwork
Photos not directly related to the subject of the brochure

The point to remember is that the layout is a communications tool. Its sole purpose is to make the brochure more inviting and easier to look at and to read. A good layout does not call attention to itself; rather, a good layout calls attention to the subject matter of the piece. Stick with layouts that are functional, not fanciful.

➤ **Start selling on the cover**

If any part of the layout is most subject to randomly applied creativity on the part of designers, it's the cover. The cover should be used to select an audience, grab attention, state a strong message, and get the reader to turn the page. It should not be designed as if it were a painting to be hung and admired in an art gallery. Yet many designers design covers just that way.

The first brochure I ever wrote described a sophisticated radar system designed for airport use. If I were to give you the assignment of designing a cover, you'd probably come up with a pretty workable suggestion—a benefit-oriented headline, a picture of the radar operator sitting at the scope, a picture of the radar antenna in operation at an airport, a picture of planes in the sky.

Yet the staff artist assigned to design the cover produced a monochromatic piece of abstract art. The painting was done in orange. The artist explained that it represented a plane, guided by radar, avoiding a storm and flying to clear skies. Unfortunately, no one looking at the painting had the slightest idea of the meaning the artist had intended. To make things worse, the artist refused to allow the product name or a headline to be used on the cover because it would destroy his art. I argued, and he consented to put the company logo and the product serial number in small type in one corner of the cover. Of course, no one looking at the cover could figure out what the painting meant or what type of product the brochure described. And since air traffic managers are more concerned with airplanes than with abstract art, few bothered to read or keep the brochure.

➤ **Emphasize the important points**

It's not enough to cover all the important points in the copy. Unless you highlight the key points, your readers may miss them. If you don't believe me, consider this story, as reported in the *TWA Ambassador* (November 1980):

The Northwestern National Bank in Minneapolis wanted to see whether customers read the fine print in the informational booklets it mailed to them. So in one booklet, they included an extra paragraph offering a free $10 bill to any depositor who asked for it. However, they buried the paragraph in 4,500 words of technical information. The booklets were mailed to one hundred customers, but not a single person asked for the free $10.

The bank never tested a mailing in which the free offer was highlighted in the booklet. But I'm sure that if they sent a mailing with the words "GET A FREE $10 BILL—DETAILS INSIDE!" splashed across the outer envelope and a brochure that talked about the offer on the cover and in the lead paragraph, the response rate of people requesting the money would be 100 percent or something very close to that.

A good layout highlights and emphasizes key copy points. Here are some graphic techniques you can use to achieve this emphasis.

Underlining key words and phrases
Setting key words and phrases in italic type or boldface type
Using short handwritten notes in the margins
Printing selected paragraphs in a colored type
Surrounding a section of text with a border
Printing a section of text against a tinted background (keeping the tint light to ensure readability)
Printing copy in capital letters (for short phrases only)
Calling attention to specific sections of copy with arrows, circles, or asterisks
Setting key points apart as call-outs or *bursts* (a burst is a star-shaped graphic containing a special message)
Putting information in the form of tables
Using lists, with items separated by numbers or bullets
Printing copy on foldout flaps or pages
Printing copy in the margins, separate from the main text
Using more than one style of type, with the second type used sparingly to highlight selected sections of copy
Separating sections of copy from each other by lines, color stripes, or other borders
Leaving space between paragraphs

As I've already pointed out, not everyone will read your copy straight through. Some readers will merely flip through the pages and scan the text. Graphic devices such as boldface type, underlining, call-outs, and the other techniques I've just listed can make key points jump out so that even a casual reader can get the gist of the story at a glance.

➤ **Keep it simple**
Graphic artists are under constant pressure, from both their own egos and their clients' demands, to continuously come up with layouts that are new

and different. Certainly, a clever layout can sometimes make a brochure stand out from the crowd; but most of the time, the simplest layout is the most effective.

Why? Because our reading habits are formed by books, newspapers, and magazines; and these publications use simple, clean layouts, unadorned by fancy graphic tricks and techniques. In fact, a complex layout can reduce a brochure's readership, because many readers are uncomfortable with the unconventional.

One mistake I see all the time is the use of a series of complicated folds to form a brochure with a nonstandard page layout. Such a piece looks interesting at first glance. But unconventional folds usually inhibit reading because people are unable to figure out the sequence in which the pages should be unfolded and read. You're better off with a standard layout in which page 2 comes after page 1—less creative, but more effective.

> **Readability comes first**

A layout can be many things—slick, neat, colorful, eye-catching, inviting, exciting, dignified, even beautiful. But the designer's first priority should always be making the copy easy to read.

Choose a type style that is highly legible and pleasing to the eye. Experiment with type size until you find the one that's easiest to read. Be sure to choose a type that will reproduce clearly on the printing press. Some types with thin letters won't reproduce heavily enough; other types with thick letters may look like blotches when certain inks and papers are used.

Set dark type on a clean, light background. Black lettering on white paper is best. Don't obscure type with colors or tints or by printing it over photos or drawings. Use standard layouts: two or three columns per 8½-by-11-inch page. A single column is usually too wide for easy reading.

Don't be afraid to speak up if your designer proposes a layout that achieves an interesting look by sacrificing readability. Such a sacrifice isn't worth it. Remember, people pick up brochures largely for the words they contain. Those words should be easy and enjoyable to read. Never make the reader strain or work to extract your message from a messy layout.

Also, keep in mind that many sales brochures are photocopied and circulated to numerous people within an organization. Brochures printed on dark paper or with oversized pages or complicated folds won't reproduce cleanly on an office copier.

➤ **Choose visuals that make a point**

Edit visuals the way you edit your copy. Ask yourself, "Does this picture transmit information, tell a story, or prove a point? Or is it just for decoration?" Omit visuals that adorn but don't communicate. Make every picture count.

You improve your literature by including visuals that tell a story. Here are some examples.

> Pictures of the product
> Pictures of product installations
> Pictures of the product in use
> Pictures of people enjoying the benefits of using the product
> Pictures of your organization's manufacturing facilities, research labs, or other operations
> Tables of applications and uses
> Pictures showing how to use or assemble the product
> Tables of product specifications
> Graphs showing performance, efficiency, and growth
> Pictures of product components or raw materials
> Pictures of the product package
> Diagrams showing how the product works or how it is put together

Here is a list of some frequently used visuals that are of questionable value when included in promotional literature. I'm not saying they should never be used. In fact, sometimes they are just the thing. But if you find these visuals in your layout, ask yourself if they are really contributing anything to the effectiveness of the piece.

> Pictures of company personnel
> Pictures of company headquarters or other exterior building shots
> Picture of the board of directors
> *Borrowed-interest shots*—pictures of subjects not directly related to your message (e.g., a steel company brochure showing a picture of a football game to represent corporate team spirit)
> Organizational diagrams (except in corporate brochures and annual reports)
> Historic photos of early products, facilities, and company founders
> Photos of unimportant facilities (company cafeteria, dumpster in back of building, shipping clerk's office)
> Abstract artwork
> Decorative photos (e.g., ocean scenes, blue skies with white clouds, and other stock photos) used to adorn brochure covers and interiors

➤ **Use one important visual per page**

It's better to have one central photo per page than many small photos. A large color photo of good quality is a real attention-getter and gives the page a focal point, a graphically interesting area that draws the eye to the page.

With many small photos, there's no central point for the reader's eye to focus on. Also, from a printing point of view, one large color photo is much cheaper than three or four small ones.

An occasional photo montage can be striking. But, as a rule, your layout should have one central visual dominating each page or spread.

➤ **Be consistent**

The design should be consistent throughout the brochure. If page 2 uses headlines in boldface Helvetica type, so should pages 3, 4, 5, and 6. Continuity from page to page pulls the many elements of the layout together into a cohesive design. Different publications within a series of booklets or brochures should also have a similar, family look.

➤ **Avoid clichés**

There are visual clichés that appear constantly in just about every type of promotion. Some of the more popular ones include the wide-eyed administrative assistant staring at the screen of her new computer, the gray-haired team of business executives debating around the conference table, and the hard-hat engineer staring blankly into the camera lens as he gives testimonial to the latest ball bearing or piston pump.

These visuals were fresh once, but now they're tired and overused. Try to think of a new way to get your message across graphically. You'll wake up bored readers and create a lot more interest in what you're trying to say.

➤ **Don't design over budget**

The designer has to work within the limitations of your project budget. Choice of colors, use of visuals, selection of paper stock, and arrangement of pages all have a major effect on the cost of producing and printing the piece. Therefore, be honest with your designer. Present a budget to work within, and let the designer know whether (and by how much) it is flexible. A designer knowledgeable in printing and production techniques will create a layout that can be produced within your budget guidelines.

I recommend that you have the artist create a layout that can be produced and printed for somewhat less than the amount you've budgeted for. With the extra cash, you can afford to spend a little more on production to ensure a first-class job.

However, if your artist produces a layout that's a little more costly than what you had in mind, you may have to stretch to pay for the job. And if money is tight, you might have to go with the least expensive vendor, who may not produce the highest-quality work, which is generally a mistake. A layout that looks great as a comprehensive can be ruined by a second-class printing job.

In general, it is better to do a first-class production job on a less ambitious design than a shoddy printing job on an elaborately conceived layout.

CHAPTER SEVEN

Getting the Picture: Illustrating Your Promotional Literature

To illustrate . . .

One of the main advantages of brochures, catalogs, and booklets over letters and memos is that promotional literature can be illustrated. You can use photos and drawings to tell a story, transmit information, clarify the text, provide a visual change of pace, build an image, prove a claim, or create a mood.

Properly used, photos and drawings are powerful sales tools. Terry C. Smith, a communications manager at Westinghouse, outlined some of the advantages of using visuals in his book *How to Write Better and Faster* (Thomas Y. Crowell):

> People *believe* in illustrations. A diagram of a proposed organization is more "believable" than a word description. When presented in graphic form, rough estimates seem more precise than they really are. An artist's concept of a revolutionary new piece of equipment makes its development seem just over the horizon. And, of course, nothing beats an actual photograph for adding authenticity.

You know from your own experience that many products simply cannot be sold in print without a picture or drawing. Can you imagine, for example, an ad for a new fashion line that didn't show the clothing? Or how about a brochure on a new car that didn't include pictures of the auto's roomy interior and stylish exterior? Most product literature is more effective when illustrated.

Of course, there are problems with using photos and artwork, as well as advantages. Anne Eisenberg, a teacher and writer, talks about one of these problems in her book *Effective Technical Communication* (McGraw-Hill):

> Illustrations are tricky. They can be so effective that they transcend the text, or so poorly conceived that they cloud the message.

Whether they succeed or fail, however, they do have one thing in common: all are expensive to produce. And therefore most illustrations are subject to the question, Is this illustration window dressing, or will it help the reader?

If all pictures were worth a thousand words, there would be no problem; but this is rarely the case. Instead, illustrations range from the useless to the superb; you . . . will need to cast a cold eye upon them.

As I mentioned in Chapter 3, hiring a photographer for a day's shooting costs an average of $500. Commissioning an illustrator to draw a piece of equipment or paint a portrait in full color can run you $1,000 to $2,000 or more, depending on the complexity of the assignment. For this reason, the key to illustrating your literature at reasonable cost is selectivity. As Anne Eisenberg points out, you must evaluate each proposed photo or drawing. Does it pull its own weight? Does it enhance the brochure enough to justify the cost? If it doesn't, take it out, even if you love it. Otherwise, your budget will quickly get out of control.

Do you need visuals?

Properly used, visuals can greatly enhance the effectiveness of promotional literature. But an unnecessary visual, one that doesn't do anything to get your message across, creates clutter and weakens the piece.

Some brochure producers are under the impression that every brochure or flier must be illustrated. That just isn't true. There are many subjects that can't or shouldn't be illustrated, subjects that are more effectively promoted with an all-copy brochure.

How do you know when to omit visuals? Here are some tips to help guide you.

You are selling a service. For many services, showing a picture of the service would be boring, meaningless, or both. Take accounting, for example. How would you illustrate a brochure promoting the services of a free-lance accountant? With a photo of the accountant punching buttons on a calculator or writing figures in a ledger? That's boring. Would you show a close-up of a completed income tax return? Also boring. You could possibly show some of the refund checks the accountant's clients have received from the Internal Revenue Service, but that would be misleading and is probably illegal.

If I were given the task of creating a brochure for an accountant, my initial plan would be to create an all-copy brochure. Later, as I worked on the project, I might discover a fresh, exciting way of visualizing the service and its benefits. But if I didn't, I would stick with an all-text treatment rather than force in a photo that didn't fit or, worse, was boring or a visual cliché.

You want to transmit information that does not need to be visualized. Many nonfiction books, for example, contain no illustrations and do an excellent job of communicating information to the reader. If your topic naturally lends itself to illustration, then of course you should illustrate your pamphlet. But if the copy can get its message across without the aid of pictures, leave it alone. Don't clutter your pamphlet with extraneous drawings that serve as decoration only and don't help you communicate with the reader.

You're selling an intangible. Why, for example, does a person choose one doctor over another? Trust—in the doctor's ability and integrity. But trust is an intangible; you can't draw it or photograph it. When selling intangibles, your words have to make the reader grasp the intangible and believe in it.

You're selling benefits, not features. Perhaps what you are selling is, as the saying goes, "the sizzle, not the steak." In many cases, the reader is more interested in the benefits of the product (what it can do for him or her) than in what it is, how it works, or how it is put together. Accounting software is a good example. Accounting software can turn your business from a sea of paperwork into a smoothly running, efficient, profitable operation. It can turn a jumble of numbers and ledgers and spread sheets into a lightning-fast information system that can put any figure or fact at your fingertips in seconds. This is the benefit of accounting software, and this is its appeal to entrepreneurs and executives.

Your literature for such software could show sample screens of information or sample reports produced by the system, but such illustrations deal with the nitty-gritty and really don't reflect the benefits. Not only do they fail to support the main sales message; they may actually detract from it by picturing those dreary rows of numbers the executive hopes to escape from. A smart marketer may decide to use an unillustrated brochure rather than include the typical illustrations of screens and reports.

The suggested visuals are clichés. A cliché is a visual that had meaning once but has been seen so often that it has lost all impact and effectiveness. Here are some examples I'm sure you'll recognize: the smiling family enjoying the newest frozen food at the dinner table, the two housewives having an in-depth discussion about floor wax, and the happy secretary who is ecstatic about getting a new computer or typewriter that will let her do even more work during the day.

Avoid these clichés. If the only visual you can come up with is the one everybody else has already used, consider dropping it and going to an all-copy brochure.

You don't have the budget. Unless you have enough money to produce quality visuals, you are better off choosing an all-copy treatment. You should use either first-rate photos and artwork or no photos and artwork. It is better to omit visuals altogether than to ruin your literature by using messy, sloppy, amateurish, second-rate efforts.

The material you have on hand is of poor quality. Perhaps you have photos and artwork available, but they're dreadful. Don't use them. If you can afford to get new ones, do so. Otherwise, omit illustrations from your brochure.

Simplicity

If selectivity is the number-one factor in successfully illustrating your promotional literature, simplicity has to be a close second. Simple illustrations are the best illustrations. Photos, drawings, and diagrams should not contain too many subjects or be cluttered with unnecessary detail. Photographs should be crisp and clear; drawings, clean and uncluttered. Messy, sloppy, busy visuals are unappealing to the eye, and people tend to skip over them. A simple visual, one with a striking, clearly defined subject, is what draws the reader's eye to the page.

The ten basic types of visuals

Visuals used in promotional literature fall into one of ten basic categories. Here are the categories, along with tips on how each type of visual is used.

➤ **Drawing**

A drawing is a freehand pen, ink, or pencil rendering used to show what something looks like. Use drawings instead of photos to illustrate subjects that are not easily photographed or that can't be photographed at all. In a booklet on fossil fuels, you may want to get across the idea that fossil fuels are the decomposed remains of dinosaurs. To dramatize this point, you might show a color drawing of a brontosaurus grazing on ferns or perhaps a Tyrannosaurus rex battling it out with triceratops. You can't photograph these creatures, of course, because they are extinct.

➢ **Photograph**

Like the drawing, the photograph is used to show what something looks like. The difference is that photos make the subject seem more believable, more real. If you are raising funds for a new hospital wing under construction, a prospective donor might ask, "Where's the proof that my money is going to such a project?" An architect's drawing of the proposed wing can help convince the reader that the project is real, but a photo of the girders going up offers irrefutable proof.

➢ **Map**

A map shows where something is located. The most common use of maps in promotional literature is to impress the reader by showing the number of manufacturing plants, branch offices, sales reps, warehouses, and other facilities you have. Let's say you have forty-three offices worldwide. Just saying "we have forty-three offices" may not make much of an impression, but showing the offices as forty-three red dots on a map of the world immediately communicates the scope of your operation. In many cases, visuals can have much more of an impact than words, and this is an example.

Another use of maps is to show connections between things and places. A map marked with a series of crisscross lines could be used to show the routes covered by an airline, the pipelines of an oil company, or perhaps the phone lines linking a telecommunications network.

➢ **Schematic diagram**

A schematic diagram is a detailed drawing of the interior or exterior of a product, system, or process. It is used to show how the product, system, or process works.

Let's say you want to explain the operation of a trash disposal unit installed in a kitchen sink. You could draw a picture of the unit with parts cut away to show the interior. *Call-outs* (captions with lines pointing to various sections of the diagram) explain how it works step by step. If the explanatory text is too long for call-outs, you simply number the diagram at various points; these numbers correspond to a series of numbered paragraphs in the main portion of your text. A sample of a schematic diagram is shown in Figure 17 on the following page.

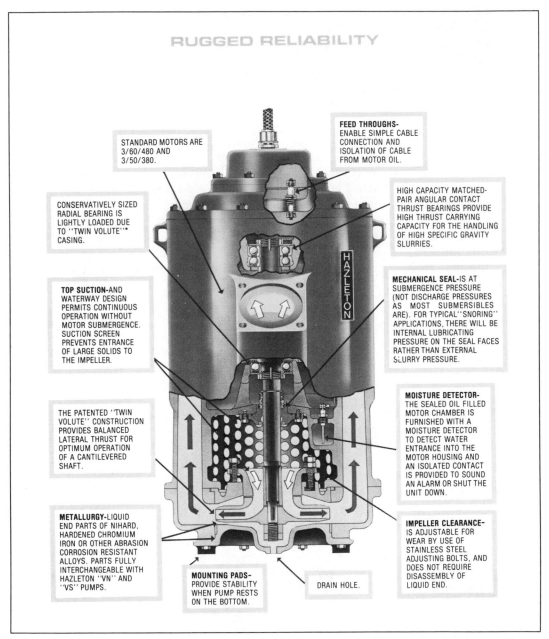

RUGGED RELIABILITY

STANDARD MOTORS ARE 3/60/480 AND 3/50/380.

FEED THROUGHS- ENABLE SIMPLE CABLE CONNECTION AND ISOLATION OF CABLE FROM MOTOR OIL.

CONSERVATIVELY SIZED RADIAL BEARING IS LIGHTLY LOADED DUE TO "TWIN VOLUTE"* CASING.

HIGH CAPACITY MATCHED-PAIR ANGULAR CONTACT THRUST BEARINGS PROVIDE HIGH THRUST CARRYING CAPACITY FOR THE HANDLING OF HIGH SPECIFIC GRAVITY SLURRIES.

TOP SUCTION-AND WATERWAY DESIGN PERMITS CONTINUOUS OPERATION WITHOUT MOTOR SUBMERGENCE. SUCTION SCREEN PREVENTS ENTRANCE OF LARGE SOLIDS TO THE IMPELLER.

MECHANICAL SEAL-IS AT SUBMERGENCE PRESSURE (NOT DISCHARGE PRESSURES AS MOST SUBMERSIBLES ARE). FOR TYPICAL "SNORING" APPLICATIONS, THERE WILL BE INTERNAL LUBRICATING PRESSURE ON THE SEAL FACES RATHER THAN EXTERNAL SLURRY PRESSURE.

THE PATENTED "TWIN VOLUTE" CONSTRUCTION PROVIDES BALANCED LATERAL THRUST FOR OPTIMUM OPERATION OF A CANTILEVERED SHAFT.

MOISTURE DETECTOR- THE SEALED OIL FILLED MOTOR CHAMBER IS FURNISHED WITH A MOISTURE DETECTOR TO DETECT WATER ENTRANCE INTO THE MOTOR HOUSING AND AN ISOLATED CONTACT IS PROVIDED TO SOUND AN ALARM OR SHUT THE UNIT DOWN.

METALLURGY-LIQUID END PARTS OF NIHARD, HARDENED CHROMIUM IRON OR OTHER ABRASION CORROSION RESISTANT ALLOYS. PARTS FULLY INTERCHANGEABLE WITH HAZLETON 'VN' AND 'VS' PUMPS.

MOUNTING PADS- PROVIDE STABILITY WHEN PUMP RESTS ON THE BOTTOM.

DRAIN HOLE.

IMPELLER CLEARANCE- IS ADJUSTABLE FOR WEAR BY USE OF STAINLESS STEEL ADJUSTING BOLTS, AND DOES NOT REQUIRE DISASSEMBLY OF LIQUID END.

HAZLETON

Figure 17. This schematic with call-outs highlights the rugged construction of the Hazleton submersible pump. (Courtesy of Barrett, Haentjens & Co.)

➤ **Exploded view**

An exploded view is a drawing of a machine or other product with its component parts *exploded* or pulled away from the center to show how the machine is put together. If you've ever looked at the instruction sheet for a plastic model car or plane kit, you've seen an exploded view. Exploded views are most often used in the operating or assembly instructions for stereo cabinets, bicycles, food processors, desks, and other products that you put together or assemble yourself.

➤ **Block diagram**

A block diagram consists of a series of boxes linked by connecting lines. The lines indicate the relationships between the boxes, and the boxes are labeled to represent people, places, products, or other items in a family of related items. The block diagram is used to show how a family, organization, plan, or system is organized. The familiar family tree that traces a family's origin is an example.

In promotional literature, block diagrams are most frequently used to depict the organization of a corporation or the ranking of its chief officers. For example, the top box could represent the chairman of the board. The box underneath represents the chief executive officer, and underneath him or her is the president. A line coming out of the bottom of the president's box branches off into several boxes, each representing a vice president of a different division or functional area (manufacturing, operations, finance, research, marketing). Lines coming out of these boxes go to officers lower in the hierarchy, such as division managers, branch managers, and supervisors.

➤ **Graph**

A graph consists of a curve or series of curves framed by horizontal and vertical axes. (The horizontal is known as the *x axis* and the vertical as the *y axis*.) Graphs are used to show how one value varies as the function of another value. A table of numbers can also show this, but the graph dramatically highlights trends. For example, a graph showing how your electric bill increases for each degree you lower the setting on your air conditioner paints a more dramatic picture of costs than merely listing or describing the numbers in the text.

One major application of graphs is to highlight data on the performance of a product—for example, fuel efficiency, product life, storage capacity, power consumption. Graphs are also handy for helping the reader size and select a product. If you're selling an expensive industrial boiler and want to give the reader a quick, rough estimate of what it will cost, you could show a graph of cost as a function of boiler size. Calculations in the text show the customer how to pick the proper boiler size; the graph provides a quick fix on what that particular boiler will cost.

➤ **Pie Chart**

A pie chart is a circle that, like a pie, is cut into slices. It is used to show proportions and percentages. The slices are cut and sized according to the percentage of the total pie that each represents. To add more visual separation, artists often make each slice a different color or shade. Let's say you sell VCRs and want to compare your share of the market with your competitors' shares. If you have 25 percent of the market, your slice is one-quarter of the pie. Your major competitor, unfortunately, has 50 percent of the market—half the pie. Six smaller manufacturers make up the rest of the market, and each gets a small sliver.

In an exploded pie chart, one slice is pulled away for emphasis. If you wanted to use the pie chart to highlight your share of the VCR market, you could pull your 25 percent slice away from the rest of the pie.

Figure 18 shows (a) a regular pie chart and (b) the same pie chart with an exploded slice.

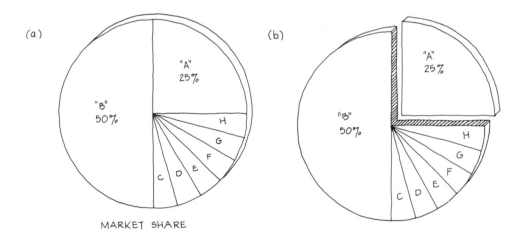

Figure 18. (a) This pie chart shows percentage of market share. (b) In the exploded pie chart, a slice is pulled away to highlight market share of company A.

➤ **Bar chart**

A bar chart consists of a series of horizontal or vertical bars placed side by side. The relative length or height of each bar varies with the quantity the bar represents. Bar charts are used to show comparisons among quantities. In an annual report, you might want to talk about how sales have increased over the past five years. To illustrate this point, you have a bar chart with five bars, one for each year's sales. If 1985 was your best year, that bar is longest. If sales in 1984 were only half those of 1985, the bar for 1984 would be half as long. This type of graph quickly allows the reader to see the changes that have been taking place from year to year.

➤ **Table**

A table is a body of data. It is used to handle a large amount of data too cumbersome to be covered in the copy. Very short tables, those with one or two columns and only two or three items, can be run in the columns of text. Anything longer must be treated as a separate visual.

Tables don't have to be boring. You can, for example, print various sections of the table against different tints of color to add interest. Another technique is to separate each row of numbers or text with a slightly different band of color. Just be sure the colors and tints are light so that the table remains readable.

Drawings or photos: How to decide

The decision on whether to use artwork or photos is sometimes clear-cut and sometimes a tough call. I can't make a real recommendation without seeing your specific project, but I can provide some rough guidelines to help you decide.

Here is a list of situations in which you should use a photograph.

The product is sold primarily on visual appeal. Designer clothing, sports cars, cosmetics, and jewelry fall into this category.

The product is so new or unheard of that prospects require proof of its existence. Examples are a new restaurant, a new personal computer, a new model car.

Your prospects are skeptical. Sometimes you will have to prove the claims you make. For example, if you claim that your chemical treatment makes swimming pool water crystal clear, your readers may be skeptical. You must *prove* your claim by showing before-and-after photographs of a pool treated with your compound.

Photographs will show your product's benefits. Some benefits are a direct result of the product's design and appearance. For example, a photograph of the Apple IIC computer shows its portability. A photo of a jeep shows the rugged construction. A photo of an open refrigerator shows the roomy interior. Use photographs in these cases because showing a benefit is always better than just telling.

The product is attractive. Many products are designed and packaged much more attractively than the competition. If this is the case with your product, why not show off its superior visual appeal in an eye-catching photo? If using a certain photo is optional, the decision may come down to whether the subject is attractive. Let's say you're producing a booklet on a charity foundation and are being pressured to include a photo of the foundation's acting president. If he's a friendly, kind-looking man, great! His picture will help bring in donations. If his appearance is passable, use the photo anyway. It will give him a much-deserved ego boost. But if he's an evil-looking codger who looks more like the head of a cult than a charity, you might consider leaving out the photo, or at least taking a new one that makes him look a bit more acceptable.

A series of photos can help demonstrate the product. Demonstration is a powerful sales technique for many products, especially those that the consumer is required to operate in some way (e.g., food processors, micro-wave ovens, squeeze mops, venetian blinds, dishwashers). A series of photos showing how to use the product step by step can greatly increase the selling power of a brochure or flier.

Good photos already exist. After you make a list of the photos you want to include in your new brochure, you may discover that you already have some of these photos in your files. That's a compelling reason for deciding in favor of photos. After all, the greatest reason to decide against photos is the cost. But if you already have the photo in hand, you eliminate the photographer's fee.

Photos cost less. If you're undecided about whether to use a photo or a drawing and either would be equally appropriate, cost may be the deciding factor. For a simple subject, an illustration may be less expensive, especially if you have to pay a photographer to travel to a distant shooting location. But a complex color painting will probably cost more than a color photograph of the same subject.

There are many situations where an illustration will be more effective than a photograph. Here are some examples.

Art costs less than photography. As I said, in some cases (those in which art and photography are equally appropriate), hiring an artist may cost less than hiring a photographer. If you can save money without sacrificing effectiveness, use an illustration.

Artwork already exists. Perhaps drawings created for previous promotions can be used as is or with minor modifications for your current project. If so, go ahead and use them. You'll save a lot of money by recycling artwork this way.

You need a certain kind of concept. Maps, diagrams, graphs, and charts are best for illustrating location, function, construction, organization, quantity, proportions, trends, and similar concepts.

You want to symbolize an idea or object. Symbols can be a convenient shorthand for communicating ideas and messages. For example, electrical engineers use simple symbols made of lines, squiggles, and circles to represent the various components used in circuits. A catalog of electronic components might use symbols at the top of each page to quickly identify the type of component listed on that page.

The product is unattractive. A good illustrator can create a realistic drawing that accurately depicts the product while masking its ugliness (at least partially).

You need to prove the seriousness of your plan, proposal, or project. Many printed promotions try to sell people on projects and products that haven't been completed yet. A drawing can help convince the reader that the project is under way and fast becoming a reality. For example, in New York City, the housing market is so tight that developers are now selling—and people are buying—apartments that are still on the drawing board. To make the sale, developers must create promotional literature that helps the prospective buyer visualize what the finished apartment will look like. The basic visual technique for illustrating apartment advertising is to show a layout of the floor plan with dimensions. This gives the prospective buyer a good idea of size and layout. But the New York developers are doing more in their ads and literature. Some hire artists to produce realistic renderings of the buildings and apartments that rival photography for realism. A few go so far as to build scale or even full-size model apartments, photograph these, and show them in their promotional folders.

Your visuals are designed to convey information. A schematic diagram or exploded view can tell you a lot more about the inner workings of an automobile engine or an attic fan than any photo can. Illustrations can have a much higher information content than photography. Use them to support text that explains complex systems, concepts, and technology.

You want to show the reader how to do something. Suppose you want to explain how to tile a floor, cut carpet, clean a fireplace, or install a screen window. It's hard to highlight the finer points of product construction or installation techniques with photographs. Illustrations are usually more effective for showing the reader how to install or use a product.

You want to create an atmosphere. Photographs are more limited in range of subject matter and style than drawings because photos, after all, must reflect reality. An artist, on the other hand, can put on paper the wildest scenes his or her imagination can generate. When you want a piece of printed literature to evoke a powerful mood or atmosphere—somber and solemn, fun and frantic, solid and powerful—illustrations are the most effective tool you can use.

The product cannot be photographed. It is impossible, for obvious reasons, to photograph an underground sprinkler once it has been installed. But an artist can easily create a rendering of the sprinkler as it is positioned under a lawn. The drawing can show how deep the sprinkler is laid, how it connects to the house plumbing, and how it delivers water to the lawn surface.

How to hire and work with illustrators

In Chapter 3, I talked about how to hire and work with outside vendors. Now, I'd like to give you some advice that applies specifically to illustrators. An *illustrator* is a person who draws or paints. This is different from a *graphic artist,* whose job is to design and prepare printed literature for publication. Some graphic artists are also illustrators, but many are not. A graphic artist essentially determines the style of the elements in a publication (type, art, photography, paper, color) and the positioning of these elements on the page. The graphic artist orders typography from an outside vendor (the typographer) and illustrations of a particular subject and style from an illustrator.

Unless you have a hidden talent for drawing or have been studying oil painting at a local art school, you'll have to hire an illustrator to produce artwork for your literature. Here are some suggestions on how to get the best results for the most reasonable fee.

➤ **Know what you want**

How many drawings do you want to commission? Are they simple or complex? Do you need color paintings or black-and-white line art, rough sketches or realistic portraits? Outline your requirements as specifically and completely as possible. Without a clear definition of your needs, you can't judge whether an artist is right for the job, and the artist can't give you an accurate cost estimate.

➤ Know where to look

Most illustrators are free-lancers. Even advertising agencies and art studios hire free-lancers to handle much of their illustrating work.

Here are sources of potential artists for your job.

Publications. While leafing through a magazine, newspaper, or book, you might come across a drawing that impresses you. Perhaps you can hire this artist to handle your project. If the drawing is signed, you may be able to find the artist through the local phone book, national directories, or the publication. If the drawing is unsigned, call the editor of the magazine or the publisher of the book and ask for the artist's name and phone number.

Referrals. Check with ad agencies, book publishers, art studios, newsletters, PR firms, and other organizations that use free-lance illustrators. They might know just the artist to handle your job. Don't be bashful about picking up the phone and calling these folks; most will be glad to help.

Directories. There are many published directories that list free-lance illustrators. One of the best is your local Yellow Pages. Others include *The Creative Black Book* and *The Adweek Art Director's Index*. (See Chapter 3 for more information on these books and how to obtain them.)

Ads. Many free-lancers advertise their services in *Adweek*, *Advertising Age*, *DM News*, and other advertising journals. You can also run a help-wanted ad in these journals or in your local newspaper. Free-lancers are always on the lookout for good clients, so such an ad ("Free-lance illustrator wanted") will probably draw a large response.

➤ Know how to choose the right artist for the job

First, ask for a résumé and client list. Has the artist studied at a good art school? Does he or she have a broad range of experience in handling commercial assignments? Who are the artist's clients? What kinds of work did the artist do for them?

Next, meet with the artist and take a look at the portfolio of sample work. There are four things to consider when evaluating a portfolio: first impressions, style, type of work, and personality.

First impressions. Do you like what you see? You should be comfortable with the quality and appearance of the work the artist has produced to date. Don't think that with the right coaching, a poor artist will perform miracles for you. Chances are, it won't happen.

Style. Does the artist's style mesh with your own? Is the style of illustration you see in the portfolio the style you want in your published brochure? Hire an artist who draws the way you want your artwork to look. Don't hire someone who draws a different way and then try to force that artist to change styles. It won't work.

Type of work. If you need architectural drawings, look for a portfolio containing good architectural drawings. If you need a diagram of a complex machine, hire an artist who has done extensive industrial and technical illustration. If you are putting out a brochure in comic book form, hire an artist who has free-lanced for Marvel or DC Comics. Choose an artist who has handled projects similar to yours.

Personality. You should never hire anybody you think you can't work with in relative peace and harmony.

➤ **Provide complete background material**

When you commission an artist to produce a drawing, provide as much background material and guidance as you can. If you want a rendering of a proposed corporate headquarters, provide all existing architect's drawings, blueprints, plans, and schematics. If you want a stylish version of a graph, have an engineer provide an accurate original the artist can work from.

Sit down with the artist and go over your preferences (if you have any) as far as style, color, size, and tone are concerned. Go to your clipping file and select samples of the look you are trying to achieve. You stand a better chance of getting what you want if you communicate your needs precisely—with both words and pictures.

➤ **Discuss fees in advance**

Get a written cost estimate in advance, and send the artist a purchase order before the work begins. Also, make sure you agree on how the job is to be charged. Do you pay for changes and revisions? Does the artist bill you after the job is completed or in stages? Do you pay on completion or on acceptance of the job? What constitutes an acceptable job, your subjective opinion or that of the artist or an outside expert? These provisions should be settled now, in writing. Otherwise, they may be settled later—in court.

➤ **Build in review steps**

Have the artist submit the work in progress for your approval in several stages. Stage one could be a rough sketch; stage two, the half-completed painting or drawing; stage three, the finished work. By reviewing the work in stages, you are assured that the job is proceeding according to your wishes. If you want to make changes, they can be done at a reasonable cost—much more reasonable than the cost of having the artist start over from scratch after the whole job is completed.

➤ **Explain your production requirements**
In order to produce a usable picture, the artist must be aware of how the drawing will be used and how it will be reproduced. Your best bet is to have the artist talk directly with the graphic designer. This ensures that the artist will produce an illustration that fits the layout and can be reproduced by the printing press.

➤ **Know how to judge artwork**
Has the artist done a satisfactory job? Usually, they do. Once in a while, though, you may be unsure of the results. How do you judge? First, compare the drawing with your expectations. If it looks like what you asked for and is on the same level as the other work in the artist's portfolio, you got what you paid for.

Another criterion is: Will it do the job? Maybe the drawing isn't as beautiful or as exciting as you thought it would be. Don't worry. Most artwork prepared for publication looks better in the finished brochure than it does as an original pasted to a piece of art board. Your main concern, though, is whether the artwork does what you want it to do—whether that task is to transmit information, show off a product's design, explain how something works, or explain how to use the product.

➤ **Try for consistency**
Have the same artist do all the artwork for a single piece of literature. An exception to this is literature with two or more types of illustrations that are drastically different. For example, if your brochure will use both color portraits and technical graphs, a portrait artist might be unable to handle the graphs, and a second artist will be needed.

Consistency is also a desirable virtue in a series of booklets or brochures. Try to use the same artist to illustrate the entire series; this gives it a family look.

Alternatives to hiring an artist

There are basically three alternatives to commissioning an original drawing from a professional artist: doing it yourself, using clip art, and buying reproduction rights.

➤ **Doing it yourself**

As I said earlier, unless you're a highly skilled amateur, forget it. A crude, unprofessional drawing can ruin an otherwise fine piece of literature. And even if you are good with watercolors or oil paints, you probably lack the graphic arts know-how required to produce a picture suitable for a commercial job. However, if you are good enough to do your own artwork, consult with your graphic designer first. Have him or her outline any special requirements for the preparation of the artwork—size, proportions, color, and so on.

➤ **Using clip art**

Your local art supply store or dealer can sell you books of *clip art:* ready-to-use artwork that you can clip out and paste onto your own layout. Most clip art is black and white, but a few of the newer clip-art services are including color drawings in their books. The problem with clip art, of course, is that it is ready-made; hence, it covers subjects of a general nature and cannot be used to illustrate specific products, services, people, or organizations. A free-lance writer looking to add a visual to a letterhead might find a usable line drawing of a typewriter in a clip-art book. But if you need a more specific visual, such as a diagram of your product, you'll have to produce it yourself.

➤ **Buying reproduction rights**

Occasionally, a trip to an art gallery or a glance at an art book may uncover a painting or drawing that would be perfect for your next brochure. If you can locate the artist or the artist's representative, you may be able to buy the right to reproduce the artwork in your literature. In such cases, you pay the fee, and the artist supplies you with a color slide or print from which you can reproduce the work. The fee is based on the type of literature the art is to be used in and how many copies are to be printed. Your agreement with the artist may include a limit to the number of years you can use the work.

Twelve ways to get better photographs at lower cost

Most brochure producers use photographs as much as or more than they use artwork. Here are twelve tips for getting the best photographs at reasonable cost.

➤ **Hire the right photographer for the job**

Fees charged by free-lance photographers vary to an amazing degree. A top fashion or advertising photographer may command $2,000 or more for a single color shot. But a moonlighter from your town paper might be happy to put in a day's work and bill you only $200 for it. And why not? That day's fee may equal the photographer's regular weekly paycheck.

Of course, it's vitally important to hire the right photographer for the job. The newspaper photographer is the right choice for taking publicity photos; nobody is in a better position to know what appeals to editors. A family photographer may be best for shooting portraits of company officers because part of the job is knowing how to pose people to make their good features come through. A wedding photographer would be the one to capture the company banquet on film; wedding shots provide experience in handling groups at parties.

➤ **Plan a shoot list in advance**

A *shoot list* is a list of photographs that must be taken. It helps you coordinate travel, sets, and props so that the photographer can cover more ground in less time. And if you can reduce the time it takes to shoot your photos from two days to one, you cut your photography fees in half.

Organize the list so that you complete all the shots in one area or location before you move on to the next. Schedule location shooting so that you move to the nearest location each time, rather than hop back and forth. For each shot, indicate what props, costumes, products, and models are required so that everything will be on hand when you arrive.

Even if you're working on only one or two brochures now, try to anticipate future photographic needs and get those photos taken now, too. The more you get done in a single session, the more money you save. So if there's even a possibility that you'll need a certain photo, take it. You can put it in your file for later use, and chances are that someone will request it sooner than you think.

➤ **Get all the necessary permissions**
If you want to use a photograph of a person in your promotional literature, you must get that person's permission in writing. Otherwise, you can be sued by the subject for unauthorized use of his or her likeness. This applies to professional models as well as company employees, the photographer's friends and family, and people on the street.

Let's say you find an old photo that is perfect for your new brochure. If the photo has people in it and you can't track them down to get their signatures or find signed release forms in your file, don't use it. Otherwise, you will be leaving yourself open to a lawsuit.

Here is a form for obtaining permission to use a person's photograph in your literature. Make copies of it, or have your attorney create a form for you. Then get signatures from everyone appearing in your photographs. I suggest you get signed release forms before the photo session starts, not after. If a person appears in the day's batch of photos and then refuses to sign the form, you will have to scrap the photos and shoot them over again.

MODEL RELEASE FORM

CONSENT OF SUBJECT OVER AGE _____

For a fee of $_____, which I have received, I consent that the photographs taken on ___*(date)*___ or any reproduction of these photos, may be used by ___*(name of organization)*___ or by anyone to whom they give permission, for the purposes of illustration, advertising, promotion, publicity, or publication in any manner. I also consent to the use of my name in connection with these photographs.

Name_____ Date _____
    (signature)

Address _____

City _____ State _____ Zip _____

Witness _____

➤ **Prepare the set**

Preparing the set or location is the responsibility of the photographer, but you should be aware of what's involved so that you can spot mistakes or suggest improvements when you supervise the photography session. Preparing a set or location for shooting requires great attention to detail. The details are important because even the smallest irregularity can ruin an otherwise fine photograph.

Here is a list of some things to consider when supervising the preparation of a photo shoot.

Use classic styles. Everything in the scene should have a classic, timeless look. Objects that are fixed to the year or period quickly date the photograph. For example, I once had the task of assembling a new brochure on a high-tech mixing device. While flipping through the photo file, I discovered a wonderful shot. To show that the mixer could be manufactured in large sizes, the manufacturer had photographed a giant-size model next to a car. That huge piece of curved metal, which dwarfed the car next to it, indeed, made a dramatic impression. Unfortunately, the car was a 1956 model, but the brochure was to be published in 1979. There was no way we could use this photo because it would have destroyed the high-tech image we were trying to convey. Had the manufacturer used an elephant instead of a car, there would have been no problem.

Wipe sweat. Sweat on a lip or forehead can reflect the light from the photographer's flashbulb and cause a glare or *hot spot* in a photo. If your models sweat, wipe the sweat and apply a little "pancake powder" to keep them dry.

Starch collars. I paid a professional to take a picture of me for the jacket of my first book. When I received the proofs, I was horrified—the left side of my collar was sticking out like a diving board. The photo appeared on the book and in many trade magazines, and to this day people ignore my good looks but continue to laugh at that stuck-out collar. So make sure collars are starched, ironed, and fixed in the proper position. Costumes and clothing with button-down collars are best because these collars can't pop up.

Start early. Shoot the people photos early in the day when your subjects are fresh, their clothes are unwrinkled, and the men's faces are unmarked by 5 o'clock shadows. People look tired and worn by midafternoon, but products and other inanimate objects aren't bothered by time. Save the product shots for last.

Look for contrast. Contrasting colors result in sharper-looking photos, whether you're shooting color or black and white. But if colors blend, the photos, especially the black-and-white shots, will come out dull and muddy.

If you're shooting a male model in a white computer center, dress him in gray or black.

Make sure there is continuity. If your brochure contains a series of related photographs, there should be continuity. Continuity simply means that the background and the appearance of the models and props are the same from shot to shot. For example, if you're using a series of photos to show how to operate a binding machine, the model shouldn't be wearing a pink blouse in one frame and a gray sweater in the next.

Keep it clean. Clean up the set before you shoot. This means emptying the ashtrays, picking up the trash, moving boxes out of the way, taking down bulletins and posters, repairing peeling paint, hiding broken furniture. A single dirty item or piece of trash may seem insignificant now but will stick out like a sore thumb when the photo is developed.

Avoid lettering. Amateur photographers often try to label items in their photos with placards and signs. Don't. This lettering won't be legible when the photo is reproduced in the brochure. If you have to label the photo, have an artist add the labels to a print by hand.

➤ **Make it appealing**

A key reason for using photographs is to add visual appeal to the pages of a piece of printed literature. Therefore, it pays to make your photos as interesting to look at as possible. One way to add interest is to use photos that tell a story. For example, most cologne ads show a bottle of cologne. But one recent ad showed a young man lying in his bed and talking on the phone. The bed was in an artist's loft, and unfinished canvases dotted the room. The bed covers were half off, hinting that the man was naked. Who was this man? Who was he talking to? What went on in that room the night before? The photo began to tell a story that the copy went on to complete.

Even if you don't tell a story, you can heighten a photograph's appeal simply by adding people to it. If you're going to photograph a shirt, show someone wearing it. If you're taking a picture of a gourmet treat, show people eating and enjoying it. Do not, however, photograph people or parts of their anatomy in extreme close-up. People are repelled by a face full of pores or a dirty thumbnail.

People like to know the size of a product, but you can't get a good grasp of size if you photograph the product alone against a plain background. Add a familiar object to the photo to give it a sense of scale. For example, if you want to show the reader how compact a microchip is, photograph it next to a penny or a postage stamp.

One of the most popular subjects for photographs is attractive women. Bikini-clad beauties have been used to sell everything from saunas to stereos to vacations to industrial products. Is this an effective ploy? It can be, but only when the photographs are relevant to the product. A firm, healthy body can be used to highlight the benefits of many different products and services—for example, membership in a health club or spa, an exercise machine, a diet plan, a diet soda, a Caribbean cruise, tight-fitting clothing, skin-care products, and vitamins. But using buxom women to promote, say, industrial equipment is a poor approach. It is sexist and amateur. Male engineers may enjoy the photos, but this type of promotion doesn't really persuade them to buy the pump, compressor, valve, or whatever it is you're selling.

➤ **Frame the shot**

Use your layout to guide the photographer in framing the shot. He or she will frame it differently depending on whether you need a horizontal or a vertical shot. Also, keep in mind what portion of the photo might be *cropped* (cut out) in production. Shoot so that you can crop the photo without cutting into the main subject matter; cropping should cut out extraneous background or borders only.

Volume 3, Issue 9 of the newsletter *Communications Briefings* reports that when cropping a photo, you should try for a height-to-width or width-to-height ratio of 3 to 2. This ratio is most pleasing to the human eye. Other pleasing ratios are 3 to 1, 5 to 3, and 8 to 5.

➤ **Decide on color or black and white**

To ensure having the right kind of film on hand, let your photographer know in advance whether you need color or black and white. If you need both, the photographer may bring two cameras and shoot with both color and black-and-white film.

Find out whether the printer can produce better color printing from slides or from photographs. If slides, have your photographer use special slide film; if photos, photo film. (Most printers prefer to work from slides for color printing and prints for black and white.) You always want your printer to work from original slides or prints; duplicates do not retain the clarity and sharpness of the originals.

➤ **Decide how much to shoot**

In deciding how many shots of a single setting or product to take, my philosophy is "the more, the better." If you've taken multiple poses in a day's shooting, you have a greater variety to choose from when creating your mechanical. Have the photographer take many different shots, trying different angles, using both posed and candid people shots, changing the filters and lighting, using different lenses—anything to add variety and avoid the ho-hum of ordinary, bland, straight-on product photography.

➤ **Decide on a sales point**

Each photo should add to the selling effectiveness of the brochure or catalog. If it doesn't, throw it out and use a different photo. Say you're producing a college catalog. The purpose is to get high school students to apply to the school. What photographs can be used to entice them? A shot of students getting a tan on the quad on a sunny day has its appeal. So does a photo of the science labs. A photograph of the power plant, on the other hand, may be a source of pride to the school's operating staff, but it won't bring in the applications. Make sure every photo you use has sales appeal.

➤ **Avoid clichés**

As in the case of illustrations, avoid clichés when planning and taking photographs. "There's always that person with a piece of paper who has to be photographed," laments photojournalist Arthur Rothstein, "a student with a diploma, a president of a corporation giving a check to someone. You've got to avoid cliché shots of these repetitive, routine situations by looking at them in a fresh, imaginative way." One way of doing this, says Rothstein, is with a candid shot.

➤ **Get the right prints**

The prints you make should be large, preferably 8 by 10 inches. You will lose the sharpness of your image if you have to enlarge a print more than 150 percent when you reproduce it in the finished brochure. Ask for prints with a matte (dull) finish instead of a silk (glossy) finish; matte prints reproduce better. Do not mount the print on a cardboard backing; many printing processes require that the print be flexible.

➤ **Use special effects**

The appearance of photographs can be altered with a variety of special effects. Two of the most popular are *airbrushing* and *screening.*

An airbrush is a paint atomizer powered by an electric motor. It produces a fine spray of paint that the airbrush artist, also known as a *retoucher,* applies to a color print. Airbrushing can be used to alter the photograph so that it shows things that weren't there or hides things that are. For example, let's say you photograph a glass full of whiskey and then decide that the glass should have been half empty. You send the print to the retoucher, and when it comes back, the glass is half empty. You cannot tell that the print has been retouched.

If you examine newspaper photographs with a magnifying glass, you can see that they consist of a series of closely spaced dots. The dots allow the photo to have shades of gray as well as black and white. Any picture in which the shading is achieved through the use of dots is called a *halftone.* Halftones are made by converting regular photo prints with a *dot screen.* But by using a *line screen* instead of a dot screen, you can turn an ordinary photo into a special effect.

To begin with, the line screen eliminates shades of gray, leaving only a stark image of black and white. By using different screens, you can create different patterns in the photo: straight lines, wavy lines, spirals. You can even order a customized screen to etch a special pattern into photos—your corporate logo, for example.

Line screens are an especially effective technique for breathing life into dull or poor-quality prints. A picture that seems flat and boring as a regular halftone may make an intriguing graphic when it is processed with a line screen.

Photo resources

Here are some of the places you can turn to when you need photographs.

➤ **Free-lance photographers**

The most common and practical method of getting good-quality photos for your literature is to hire a free-lance photographer to take them. Chapter 3 explains how to hire free-lancers and where to find them. The key consideration, as I've said, is in selecting the right photographer for the job. Be especially careful not to overhire. Paying a $2,000-a-day fashion photographer to shoot a black-and-white photo of your new sales manager for the employee newsletter is a waste of money. You could probably get someone to do the job—and do it well—for $200 or less.

➤ **Staff**

If you have occasional need for photography, you might recruit an employee who is good with a camera to be your organization's unofficial part-time photographer. Photography is one of the most popular hobbies in the United States, so chances are good that you'll find someone who is able—and willing—to do the job. Of course, this person should be capable of producing professional-quality work.

If your needs increase, it may pay you to hire a full-time staff photographer. The staff photographer can give you quality work at a small fraction of the cost of hiring free-lancers. And staff photographers are available whenever you need them. But don't hire a full-time photographer if you don't have enough work to keep him or her busy forty hours a week. Having a staff photographer just sitting around is a waste of your money.

➤ **Do it yourself**

If you are so inclined, perhaps you can become your organization's unofficial part-time staff photographer. With the automatic 35-millimeter cameras on the market today, even an amateur can take good color photos and slides. If you want to improve your skill, take photography courses at the local community college, or read introductory books on photography. One I highly recommend is Tom Grimm's *The Basic Book of Photography* (New American Library). But don't take on the job until you're good enough to turn out top-quality photographs.

➤ **Stock house**

A stock house is a firm that maintains a large library of photos covering almost every subject imaginable. When you need a picture of a particular subject—a clown, a group of children, a blue sky with clouds, the beach at dawn—get in touch with a local stock house. They'll send you a number of representative shots to choose from. If you see something you like, you tell the stock house how you plan to use it (type of publication, number of copies), and they'll quote you a fee. This can range from $100 to over $1,000, depending on the application.

➤ **Other sources**

Stock houses are not the only source of stock photography. Government agencies, public libraries, newspapers, wire services, nonprofit organizations, museums, and corporations all have photo files that may be available to you. For example, NASA sells striking color photography of space shots and moon missions at a very reasonable cost. Manufacturers often provide free photographs to their dealers and distributors for use in local advertising and promotion. A magazine or newspaper that does a story on your firm may be willing to let you use the photos from its article in your own sales literature and promotional publications.

CHAPTER EIGHT

Special Marketing Problems (And How to Solve Them)

"I want to include prices in my brochure. But although my products stay the same, my prices change frequently. If I put in the prices, my costly brochure will be out of date three months from now. What do I do?"

"We sell our product to six different markets. Does that mean I need six separate brochures, one for each market? Or can I use the same brochure for all six groups of customers?

"Our services are related but can be sold individually. How can we produce literature that presents a unified theme while allowing our sales people to isolate one specific service and sell it to a client?"

When I help clients plan brochures, I get questions like these all the time. Although for many organizations the production of promotional literature is a simple, straightforward affair, for some it is not. Some organizations have special marketing problems that affect the design, writing, and production of their literature.

Consider Andy H., a professional painter who wants to print a simple flier about his services. He has two markets: the residential market, consisting of homeowners and landlords, and the commercial market—local businesses, schools, and state agencies. Andy provides the same service to both markets: He paints buildings. But experience has taught him that each market hires painters for different reasons. Homeowners are most concerned with cost and usually hire the painter with the lowest bid. Local businesses, on the other hand, want to deal with a painter who is able to provide routine maintenance painting (touch-ups) on a regular basis. Service and reliability are their key concerns.

Andy sits down to write a headline for his flier. He is faced with a dilemma. Which feature should he highlight, maintenance and service or low cost? Can he give them equal billing and still have an effective headline?

Perhaps he needs to produce two separate fliers, one for each audience. But that would double his printing and production costs. What is he to do?

The painter's marketing problem is not complex, yet you can see that some extra thought will be required to resolve it. You may find yourself facing a much more complex problem, one that does not have an obvious solution.

Fortunately, the types of marketing problems that affect the planning and production of promotional literature fall into identifiable categories. The same situations come up again and again, and through experience, people have learned how to cope with these situations.

Naturally, your promotion is unique, and no two marketing problems are exactly alike. I can't give you a definitive solution to your problem without knowing the specifics of your particular situation, but I can list the categories of common marketing problems, along with suggestions on how to plan, write, and design literature that overcomes the problem. Here, then, are common marketing problems and some proven ways of solving them.

The product is changing rapidly

This is a major headache for high-tech companies. Their products are in a state of constant change or evolution, and therefore any published material quickly goes out of date. For example, consider IBM's personal computers. Every few months, IBM announces yet another model or added feature. At first, there was just one model, the IBM PC. Next came the IBM XT, and all PC literature had to be revised to mention the availability of this enhanced version. Then, in rapid succession, IBM announced the PC*jr*, PC Portable, PC AT, IBM "Local Area Network," Xenix operating system, Topview software, and several major releases of IBM applications software. Each announcement required updating of product literature, ad copy, and catalogs.

What is the high-tech marketer to do? One solution is to wait until the product becomes relatively stable in design and function before publishing any literature on it. Because they are reluctant to spend money on a brochure that will be obsolete a month after it is published, some conservative high-tech companies have a policy of not printing any literature until the product matures in the marketplace. But that's a mistake. Without literature, your advertising and promotion campaign is crippled. The fact is, many consumers and almost all business buyers won't make a purchase without first receiving some type of printed material. Without a product brochure, you lose these sales.

The second solution is to publish a *temporary* brochure. The temporary brochure is an interim publication, a small, inexpensively produced piece that the company can use until it feels secure in spending the money for a "real" brochure. This strategy is better than no literature at all, I suppose, but not much better. The interim brochures I've seen are usually shoddily designed, hastily written, cheaply printed affairs more likely to hurt a product or company's image than to enhance it. The interim brochure gives salespeople and dealers the literature they so desperately need to conduct an aggressive sales campaign, but if it is poorly produced, it can cause prospects to doubt the reputation and stability of the firm.

The third solution—and this is the solution I recommend—is to produce a first-class brochure as soon as you put the product on the market but to design it in a way that will allow you to make revisions quickly and inexpensively in order to accommodate expected product changes.

Let's say you are introducing a new computer to the market. To distribute literature that's anything less than your best effort is to build an image of shoddiness and cheapness for your product. Quality literature conveys an image of a quality product and a quality firm.

If you expect the product to change significantly, you may have to redo the brochure fairly often. But with some advance planning, the process won't be as costly as you think.

When you publish the brochure, print fewer copies than you normally would. For example, if you envision a major product update in six to eight months, don't print more than a six-month supply. Normally, I recommend that you print many more copies than you think you'll need, but if your brochure will be outdated soon, order fewer copies so that there will be less waste.

When you plan the brochure, create a layout that leaves room for changes and revisions. Leave extra white space on the page so that you can add to the copy without redoing the page layout. Leave room to expand tables, charts, and lists that will get bigger as your product line expands. If the basic design of the computer is set and only certain technical specifications will change, put these specifications in a separate table so that you can update them without resetting the type for the entire text. In other words, plan for change so that the copy and layout can be updated without having to redesign the brochure from scratch.

The product doesn't exist yet

Yes, I've been asked many times to write copy for a product that hasn't been built or produced yet. Take mail-order publishing. Most mail-order publishers run advertisements offering books that haven't been written yet. If the ad is successful in generating orders, the publisher commissions a writer to produce the book. If the ad flops, the publisher has saved money by not producing a book that wouldn't have sold.

Because of the long lead time required to produce and implement an advertising campaign, many manufacturers start producing literature, ads, and other materials before the product is actually built. When a major manufacturer hired me to write a brochure describing a new electronic filing system, the only such system in existence was the crude experimental model set up in the manufacturer's test lab. The exterior design of the equipment hadn't even been decided on.

Of course, the copywriter isn't hampered by the lack of a real product that can be held in two hands. As long as the facts about the planned product exist—the technical specifications of the electronic system, the outline and table of contents of the mail-order book—the copywriter can do the job.

The artist, on the other hand, has difficulty creating illustrations for a nonexistent project. The problem is how to show the customer what the product looks like without letting on that it hasn't actually been built yet. There are several ways of doing this.

One way is use photographs of a *prototype.* A prototype is a full-size, functioning, experimental version of the product. If the actual manufactured product will be a carbon copy of the prototype, you can use photos of the prototype to illustrate your brochure. Readers have no way of knowing that the machine they are looking at was the only one of its kind at the time. If the actual product will not look like the prototype, photos of the prototype should not be used. The product the reader sees in the literature should look exactly like the one available to the buyer.

The next best thing to a prototype is a *mock-up.* This is a model of the product; it looks exactly like the product will look, but it is a fake, with no parts, wires, or gears inside. Use mock-up photos only if the mock-up looks 100 percent authentic; a phony-looking mock-up photo is easy to spot.

But whether you show a prototype or a mock-up, try to include some sort of product photograph in any literature for a new product. Photos convince customers that the product is real, whereas new-product literature with drawings only gives the impression that the product doesn't exist.

In some cases, you may not be able to photograph a prototype, model, or product sample, and you will have to use artwork to depict the new product. Your illustrations should be as realistic as possible so that they create the illusion that the product is real. Use blueprints, engineering drawings, exploded diagrams, or a high-quality color illustration. Avoid rough sketches, line drawings, and abstract or stylized artwork that can give literature a phony look.

The product is sold to multiple markets

There are some products that appeal to different groups of customers for different reasons. Recently, I was hired to write a brochure describing a system used to spray a protective coating on glass bottles. The project was relatively simple because the system could be used by only one specific type of customer: bottle manufacturers. I was able to write strong copy directed at the needs of my reader because I knew precisely who my reader was. But the next week, I got an assignment to write literature on a moisture analyzer (a machine that detects even the slightest bit of moisture in air, gas, liquids, or solids). This time, I was faced with a problem: The device was used in many different industries and applications—utilities, rubber plants, chemical plants, food processing, textiles, natural gas pipelines, tobacco curing—and each of these customers buys moisture analyzers for different reasons.

If your product appeals to a variety of different prospects, and each group is motivated by different product benefits, you must ask the question: "Can a single brochure be effective in selling to all markets, or do I need a separate piece of literature for each group of buyers?"

It depends. If, as in the case of the moisture analyzer, the product offers unique benefits to each market, you may want to create a series of folders, each highlighting how the product meets the needs of a particular group of buyers. In some cases, the basic reason for buying the product is the same for all buyers, but you may want to highlight specific applications in each area. Here, there's no need for separate brochures. Instead, you can devote a page of your brochure to listing these applications by market. Finally, there are products—light bulbs, for example—that are bought for the same reasons regardless of the market (schools, industry, offices, consumers), so there's no need to create market-specific literature.

The product is sold to multiple markets that want to believe it is designed especially for them

Ego is involved here. Each market buys the product for basically the same reason but wants to believe they are getting something special. The brokerage firm buys a business phone system for the same reason a manufacturer does: to communicate. But brokers are like most of us; they think they are special. They want to buy a phone system designed specifically for brokerage houses.

Don't rush out and create a special brochure for this market just yet. There's a better way: You can create the impression that a brochure is aimed at specific markets by printing one basic brochure with different covers. For example, a different cover photo could be used with each version. The brochure meant for brokerage houses shows a stock broker surrounded by ticker tape and talking on the phone system. A different version aimed at plant engineers shows a supervisor wearing a hard hat and talking with workers on the shop floor.

You can add to this differentiation with other techniques. The color of the cover, for example, could be different for each version—green for brokerage houses, blue for manufacturers, yellow for utilities. Also, you could print a line of copy on each cover to identify the specific market (e.g., "The communications tool for brokerage firms" or "The system that lets manufacturers communicate").

The product is sold to multiple buying influences within an organization

Packaged goods such as soap, shampoo, cereal, and soda are bought by one person: the consumer who uses them or buys them for the family. With other consumer products, you have to appeal to more than one customer. For example, toy advertisements must make the children want the toy and convince the parents that the toy is safe, educational, wholesome, and worthwhile.

When you sell products and services to business, the situation becomes even more complex. Business purchases are usually made by committee, not by individuals. For example, if you are selling a $500,000 pollution control system to a chemical plant, many people are involved in the purchase: the plant manager, the purchasing agent, the company president, the pollution control expert, and possibly others. The problem is that each of these people has a different level of interest in and understanding of your product. The purchasing agent is primarily concerned with cost. The plant manager is worried about installation and maintenance. The pollution control expert will analyze whether your product can handle the requirements in terms of removing chemicals and particles from the air. And top management is concerned with the reputation and reliability of your firm.

If you want to influence a wide range of buyers, you have to take this into consideration when you plan your literature. Some advertisers find it advantageous to create two or more levels of literature. The first brochure is more sales-oriented and is aimed at managers, purchasing agents, and others who want compelling reasons to buy your product but don't have the time or patience for the nitty-gritty. The second brochure is more detailed; it is aimed at operators, technicians, engineers, and other experts who hunger for complete knowledge. It gives them the numbers, figures, graphs, and curves that would not be of interest to less technically oriented buyers.

A more economical approach is to create a single piece of literature that is interesting and appealing to a broad audience. This takes some extra planning in the design and copywriting stages. For example, the copy style must be readable enough to catch the interest of a busy manager, but it must not be so general or full of fluff that it turns off the technical reader. Highly technical material should be collected and displayed in a separate section of the brochure (such as the centerspread) so that technical readers can easily find it while executives can skip over it.

Creating a lot of different pieces of literature is expensive, so I recommend that you try to produce a single brochure which tells the whole story and appeals to all audiences. If your audience is so diverse that this approach is too cumbersome, additional pieces of literature may be necessary. But before you commit yourself to a second or a third or a fourth piece of literature, ask yourself, "Is this really necessary? Or is there some way to say it all in my central brochure?" If you cut down on the number of pieces of literature you publish, you'll save time and money.

The sales cycle has multiple steps

The number of steps in the sales cycle is determined by counting how many times there is contact, in person or via promotion, between seller and buyer. In fund-raising direct mail, for example, the fund raiser sends a letter to you requesting a donation. If you believe in the cause and are moved by the letter, you send your donation by mailing a check or a pledge card. The sale is made in one step. But let's say you are in the market for a new car. There may be many steps between your initial interest and your final purchase. The first step is seeing a car commercial on TV. The second step is visiting the dealer's showroom. The third is studying the manufacturer's brochure on the car and thinking about it at home. The fourth step is going back to the showroom, negotiating a deal, and writing a check for the down payment.

Generally, the number of steps involved increases with the cost of the product. And often, the advertiser is unsure whether to try for a quick sale or to reduce the pressure on the buyer by adding some steps to the cycle.

For example, I know of a firm that sells home-study foreign language courses (cassettes and workbooks) by mail. Although it has been successful with its mail-order ads, the company wondered whether there wasn't a large number of buyers who required more information before making a decision. So the firm created a new ad that seeks to generate a sales lead rather than a direct sale. This new ad offers a free catalog to people who respond; the catalog contains complete descriptions of the various courses the company offers. When the company receives an inquiry, it mails the catalog and follows up by phone. This two-step approach is still being tested, so it is too early to say whether it is more effective than the one-step mail-order ad. But you can see where the length of the sales cycle plays a vital role in a marketing campaign.

You must, therefore, consider your sales cycle when you plan your promotional literature. If the cycle has multiple steps, can one piece of literature be used to satisfy all requirements? Or will you need a separate piece of literature for every step—one brochure to respond to inquiries, a second to offer more detailed information, a third to be used by salespeople during sales calls, and a fourth to close the sale? The answer, naturally, will depend on your particular product, customers, and selling methods. Only you, after a careful analysis of your situation, will know how many brochures you need and what type.

One tip: When possible, make one piece do double or triple duty in your sales cycle. For example, many companies use a very brief, general brochure to respond to inquiries and a more comprehensive brochure for sales calls. But there's really no reason to make the inquiry piece so general; after all, the person requesting it has demonstrated an interest in your product. By adding more meat to the inquiry piece, you can create a brochure that can work in both environments.

The product remains basically the same over the years, but new features are added periodically

The periodic addition of new features can render a product brochure obsolete. For example, this is the case with automobiles. The 1985 Chevette is, after all, just a variation of the 1984 model. Yet, the differences are significant enough for General Motors to produce new brochures each year to describe the latest models. Of course, you are not General Motors, and producing a brand-new four-color brochure every twelve months would probably be a strain on your budget. What can you do?

The first thing to ask yourself is whether you really need a new brochure in the first place. Perhaps the change is so insignificant that it doesn't need to be described in your literature. Or, maybe it can be handled with some type of separate insert sheet or envelope stuffer. If not, you can still save money by recycling your old brochure rather than scrapping it and starting all over again. For example, some product changes are purely cosmetic: a new package, a new label, a new case or housing; what's inside remains the same. So you can keep your copy and layout. Just photograph the new product and substitute these new photos for the outdated ones in the brochure. Yes, you'll have to change the printing plates, and printing a new batch of bulletins is costly. But it's not nearly as costly as setting new type, doing new page layouts, and writing entirely new copy.

Other changes, although substantial, do not change the essence of the product or your sales pitch. Making these changes can be as simple as changing the numbers in a table of product specifications or adding a couple of paragraphs of copy to the brochure. Again, you pay for redoing the printing plates and printing new bulletins, but it costs less than a complete rewrite and redesign.

Unfortunately, some changes completely alter the nature of the product and therefore of your sales pitch. In such cases, there's no choice but to redo the brochure. But you can still save money by recycling as much of the old brochure as possible—cover design, photos, tables, charts, illustrations, even sections of type.

The company's various products are not related in any logical way

At first glance, this doesn't seem to be a problem at all. Why not just create a separate brochure for each product, and distribute the brochures to the appropriate buyers? But selling a random selection of products and services creates confusion among your customers.

Consumers tend to form an image of a company in their minds: Apple is a computer company, Ford a car company, and Gerber's a baby food company. But what if Ford suddenly started marketing a personal computer? Mass confusion! People would say, "Hey, wait a minute. What does this have to do with cars and trucks?" And they would stick with the traditional makers of computers, like IBM, Apple, and Wang.

So it is with your organization. People know you by your products, services, or goals. If you add new products or services that don't fit in with your current line, people will become confused. To overcome this confusion, try to find a common element that can link seemingly disparate products, a unifying theme that provides a consistent identity.

For instance, a mail-order firm I deal with sells *planning boards* (oversized wall calendars used to organize and schedule the work flow in a department or organization). Recently, this company began offering books by mail. When it added books to its catalog, it created confusion: Why is a manufacturer of planning boards in the publishing business?

Then the company saw that the common element of the books and the boards was that both products help companies improve productivity through better organization, planning, and thinking (the books dealt solely with business topics such as management, marketing, and communications). A new theme was created for the catalog based on the slogan "Planning tools to help you increase productivity." The theme made sense out of the combination of books and boards and eliminated confusion among the customers.

When you add a product or service, study it to see if you can discover a relationship between it and your established line. If you can't, if there is absolutely no tie-in, perhaps the product is wrong for your company.

The product consists of modules or components that can be sold in a package or individually

Two of my recent projects fell into this category. The first was a corporate brochure for a major bank. My task was to describe the overall capabilities and business philosophy of the bank as well as to outline the various services it offers to its customers. Some of the bank's customers buy a package consisting of every service, but many others are interested in only one or two.

To make matters even more complex, the bank has a special accounting system through which every service is handled. This is a major advantage of using the bank because the system generates extra interest for the customers using the service. In addition to this benefit, which is common to all services, each service has its own unique advantages over the competition.

How did I handle this? I created a central brochure that described the bank, its philosophy, and its unique accounting method and how that method makes using the services more profitable. The information in this central brochure stressed the bank's superiority as an organization and talked about the individual services only in general terms. The last page of the brochure contained a pocket. Into this pocket were inserted seven fliers, each describing a specific service of the bank in detail. The fliers also briefly mentioned the advantage of the special accounting system. But they didn't explain it in depth because the central brochure took care of that.

The bank's sales representatives could use the individual fliers to sell specific services to select customers. The customer interested in service G could get all the necessary information in a brief flier, without having to plow through a huge brochure on services A, B, C, D, E, and F first.

In addition, the bank adds and changes services from time to time. Now, when a service is added or updated, the bank simply reprints one of the inexpensive fliers rather than the expensive corporate brochure.

The second project involved a computer system consisting of a minicomputer and sixteen individual software modules (programs). The modules can exchange information and work together, if needed. They can be purchased as a package or individually; the customer can buy just a few modules now and add more later.

I used an approach similar to the one that worked for the bank. The central brochure gave an overview of the system and described how the software was designed to work together or separately. Sixteen fliers, inserted into a pocket built into the back page, described the individual programs in detail. This modular approach allows the computer firm to promote modules as individual products, and it also prevents the brochure from becoming obsolete when a new module is added or an existing program updated.

The product is too complex to describe in writing

A few years ago, I received a call in response to an ad I ran offering my services as a free-lance copywriter. The conversation ran something like this:

"Mr. Bly, my name is Mike Guterl. I read your ad and would like you to prepare a sales letter promoting my business."

"Fine," I replied. "Just send some of your previous letters and literature, and I'll get started."

"We don't have any literature," Guterl said.

"You mean you're in business and you don't have a single piece of printed material describing your operation?" I asked, shocked. I had never encountered an organization without some sort of printed literature on itself.

"That's right."

"Okay," I said. "Why don't you tell me about your business."

"I can't," Guterl replied.

"Why not?"

"Because there's no way to describe what we do," he said.

"Then how do you sell your product or service to your customers?" I asked. "What do you tell them?"

"Well," he said after a long pause, "we can't really explain our business to them. They sort of have to *experience* it."

I sighed. Then I explained to Mr. Guterl that if he truly believed that his business was incomprehensible, I certainly couldn't write about it, and I politely declined the assignment.

It was a ridiculous conversation. Why? Simply because there is no human endeavor—no business, no product, no service, no concept or cause or idea—that cannot be explained in plain English by a competent, clear-thinking individual.

Do you protest? Do you believe that your business, ideas, or activities are beyond comprehension or communication? Then you're fooling yourself. You're building an aura of mystery around your activities to make them seem more impressive. But the customer—or the copywriter—won't be impressed when you tell him or her that you can't explain your business, just angered, insulted, and totally turned off.

So if you're worried that your product or idea is unexplainable, stop worrying. Go out and hire a good copywriter. The professional will explain it to your customers for you.

The brochure cannot adequately sell the product

Print does have its limits. Try, for example, to write a paragraph describing the scent of a rose, and you'll immediately see these limitations at work. But don't be frustrated by this. Rather, try to understand what printed promotional literature can do—and what it cannot do.

Let's say a TV manufacturer asks you to produce a brochure describing its new color TV. Your brochure can show pictures of the set and the screen. But what it can't do is demonstrate the product; a printed photo is a poor substitute for seeing the set in operation. This may frustrate you until you stop to consider that no one is going to order an expensive color TV sight unseen, anyway. People will go to the store and watch the TV; the brochure is just something they can take home and study at their leisure before making a purchasing decision.

By the way, advertisers are becoming more and more ingenious in overcoming the limitations of printed literature. Some cosmetics companies include "scratch and sniff" cards with their literature; when you scratch the card, you smell the fragrance. Many mail-order record companies, realizing that you don't want to buy a record until you've heard part of it, bind in small plastic demonstration records in their mailings. If the prospect likes the demonstration record, the next step is to send for the full-length record or set.

The product or service can't be illustrated

How do you illustrate financial planning, free-lance writing, life insurance, career counseling, legal counsel, a seminar, or the preparation of income tax forms? There are many products and services that don't easily lend themselves to illustration. And there are two ways to overcome the problem.

The first is to hire a designer clever enough to come up with visual concepts for these hard-to-illustrate products. Even if you are unable to make any suggestions, don't worry. Just present all the background information, and let the designer go to work. When you see the thumbnail sketches of the initial ideas, you can judge whether the artist has hit the target or missed the mark.

The second solution is simply to omit visuals and have an all-text brochure. I have seen (and written) many successful brochures that consisted solely of words. Look at magazine ads and in your mailbox. You will find many mail-order promotions that contain hundreds, even thousands of words with only the simplest of illustrations or no illustrations at all. Such mail and advertising has sold billions of dollars in goods.

Students in my advertising classes at New York University often ask, "But isn't it true that people won't read a page unless there are pictures?"

No, it isn't. A powerful headline splashed across the page can do as much to gain attention as the boldest graphic or the most striking photo. And once the prospect's attention is gained, he or she will read your copy and continue to read as long as the words are interesting, compelling, and relevant to his or her situation.

The product is ugly

You may be faced with the tough task of selling a product that is not designed and packaged as attractively as it could be—a book with an ugly cover, a cosmetics set in an unattractive wrapper, a computer with a plain, boxlike terminal. What can you do? Here are three options.

Don't show the product. A book is bought more for its contents than for its cover. If you're writing a promotion to sell a poorly designed book by mail, don't show a picture of the cover in your flier. Although an unattractive cover may prevent people from buying a book, once they do make a purchase based on the book's contents and merits, they are highly unlikely to return it just because the cover isn't fancy. So if your product is ugly, don't show it.

Use a sketch. Although I prefer photos to drawings, one exception is for products that are ugly. A carefully executed sketch can accurately portray the product while making it appear more attractive than it really is.

Redesign the product or the package. If the merchandise is really that hard to look at, maybe you should redesign the product or the package before you put it on the market.

Lawyers tie your hands and rewrite your literature

A funny thing happens when people go to law school. They are transformed from ordinary human beings into people who write things like this:

> Subject to the terms and conditions contained herein, the Author hereby transfers to the Publisher during the full term of the copyright and all extensions thereof the full and exclusive rights comprised in the copyright in the Work and all revisions thereof (hereinafter called the "Work") including but not limited to the right, by itself or with others, throughout the world, to publish, republish, and distribute the Work and to prepare, publish, and distribute derivative works based thereon, in English and in other languages, in all media of expression now known or later developed, and to license or permit others to do so.

I suppose this kind of language is okay for legal contracts (which is where I got the sample). But the problems start when "lawyerese" finds its way into promotional copy—something that I've seen happen too many times. After months of planning, writing, and approvals, an organization has a manuscript and layout they are happy with. Before it is published, someone suggests they "run it by legal."

The brochure copy is sent to the lawyers. A week, then two, then three go by. The advertising manager begins to worry. Then, one morning, he gets the manuscript back on his desk. Attached is a memo informing him that legal approves the copy "as per the revisions indicated on the manuscript."

And some revisions! What started out as a lively, powerful, persuasive piece is now a dull, turgid, dead document, copy written by lawyers instead of writers. The lawyers have taken out all the specifics and all direct claims, watering the prose down with generalities and hedge words. The result is something so stiff and lifeless that no prospect or customer would dream of struggling through the copy. It is a document that pleases legal but no one else.

Don't let this happen. If you feel that it's necessary to have your legal department or outside counsel review your copy, fine. Have them do it. But don't let the lawyers rewrite copy. Instead, have them outline the specific factual changes they recommend. Go over each revision to make sure the change is necessary from a legal standpoint and is not just the personal whim of the attorney. Then, have the copy revised by a writer or an editor. Writing should be repaired by writers. Don't let your lawyers moonlight as copywriters.

You can't give away too many trade secrets

"No, we can't say this, we can't talk about that, and we don't want to publish these statistics," you tell your copywriter as you slash sentences from his manuscript.

"Why not?" he protests.

"Because of our competitors," you explain. "We don't want them to find out this information. It's secret."

Many organizations are afraid of being too specific in their literature because they don't want the competition to learn their trade secrets. But if promotional literature lacks facts and specifics, it becomes weak and ineffectual. What can you do? My advice is to write the best, most fact-filled literature you can and not worry about the competition.

Why? Because if your competitors want to learn more about your product, they will. For example, they can, using a false identity, buy your product, go to your dealership, or even pump your salespeople for information over the phone. So there's no point in crippling your promotional literature by holding back the facts that can help the literature sell.

My rule is this: Don't, of course, publish trade secrets that are secret even to your customers. But you should publish a piece of information if it helps you make the sale. Remember, if it's something you'd say to a customer in confidence, it's something your competitors could learn if they really want to. So quit worrying about spilling the beans, and concentrate on creating great promotional literature.

The product is new and therefore unproven

The consensus among most advertising professionals is that consumers want new products, new services, and new ideas. If a product or service is new, the ad agency makes the most of it by stressing its newness in promotional copy with words like *New, Announcing, Introducing, Just Published, Amazing Breakthrough, Revolutionary, At Last,* and so on.

But I'm not sure that newness is all it's cracked up to be. Take automobiles, for example. When General Motors came out with its new front-wheel-drive X-cars, a lot of people became excited and immediately went out to buy them. But I know of many others who said, "If it's new, they haven't gotten all the kinks out of it yet. I'll let you buy one first. Then, if it works okay for you, maybe I'll consider it. If it doesn't, I'll have saved myself a lot of money and headaches."

This is the real problem with new products. True, new means exciting; but it also indicates a product that is untested and unproven, one that has not demonstrated its ability to perform as advertised.

In the same way, many people are afraid to buy from new companies. They reason, "This new company is a small, fledgling enterprise competing among established giants. Its future is uncertain. If I buy its product and it goes out of business in a year, I will be stuck with a product that no one will service or support."

You see the problem that the brochure writer faces. Should the writer stress newness, thereby generating excitement and interest but raising questions about the product's reliability and performance? Or should he or she skirt the issue of newness, thereby eliminating the questions but also the opportunity to generate excitement?

My answer is this: Go all out in stressing the newness in your brochure.

Splash the cover with words like *Introducing, Announcing,* and *Now Available.* Make a big to-do about the product being new and different. It will make your brochure—and your product—stand out from the crowd. Then, in your copy, take pains to offset the questions of reliability and proven performance that the aura of newness raises. Here are some ways to do it.

- Mention that although the product is new in the United States, it has proven its performance for five years in Europe and other countries overseas.
- If the product is an industrial product adapted for consumer use, say so. Let's say you're selling a scaled-down version of an industrial paint sprayer designed for home use. Explain that although the new version is being offered to the consumer market for the first time, it is based on a machine that has gained great favor among professional painters over a period of many years.
- Many products are first test-marketed on a small, local scale before being offered nationwide. If this is the case with your product, say so. Explain that hundreds of buyers in Kansas or Ohio or Florida have been delighted with it and that therefore you are making it available to people in all fifty states.
- Some products have been around for years but have never really been promoted. If yours is such a product, you can announce it as new. Then explain that although it is new in the sense of being marketed nationwide for the first time, it has delighted a limited but loyal group of customers for many years.
- Maybe your product really is brand-new. Maybe it hasn't been sold to a single consumer. But I'm sure it has been thoroughly tested in your laboratory and in the field. Highlight these test results in your copy to show that the product has indeed proven its performance under rigorous conditions.

Your product is going to change soon

You know what the changes are. Should your literature describe the product as it is today or as it will be? This is a tough one. Here are the guidelines I follow in such a situation.

- *Avoid using future-tense references.* People become uncomfortable if they keep reading about features that "will be available" or are "soon to come." They expect a brochure to tell them about a product as it really is now, not as the manufacturer dreams it will be. Your brochure should reflect reality.

- *Make an occasional promise.* It's okay to talk about one or two forthcoming improvements or features as long as you don't overdo it. The reader can accept a few promises if they are isolated and if the copy makes clear that they are planned improvements, not existing features. Just make sure that 95 percent or more of your copy is grounded in the present.

- *Don't dream out loud.* Talk about only those planned improvements that are on the drawing board and fast on their way to becoming reality. Give the reader a preview of next year's model if you wish, but don't make your brochure a "wish list" of all the conceivable features you'd like to add but may never get around to designing. People have long memories when it comes to broken promises.

- *Be careful about discussing planned changes in the present tense.* Some clients tell me, "Write about this planned feature as if it already exists. After all, by the time the brochure is published, we'll have it." If you pursue this tactic, be absolutely certain that the product change will be made according to schedule. If something goes wrong and the change discussed in the literature isn't made, you may be stuck with a pile of brochures that contain a lie.

CHAPTER NINE

Production Time:
Paste-Up and Printing

Your role in production

Congratulations! The job is nearly done. After just a few final steps—typesetting, paste-up, and printing—you'll have the finished literature in your hands. Your role in this final leg of our journey is that of supervisor and checker. You must carefully supervise the work of your outside vendors to make sure the job is being done properly and according to your specifications. And, you must check the work every step of the way to ensure that the brochure will be accurate and error-free. There will be a lot of proofreading to do at this stage.

Here, briefly, is what's going to happen next.

Your graphic artist will have the text of your brochure set in type. He or she will buy the type from a place known as a *type house, typesetter, typographer,* or *compositor.* You can, if you wish, deal with the type house directly, but buying type is not as simple as it seems, and your artist has more experience at it than you do.

The type—body copy and headlines—will be pasted up on pieces of stiff cardboard known as *art board.* The size and location of all visuals will also be indicated on this board. Such a paste-up of copy and art is known as a *mechanical.*

The printer takes the mechanical and reproduces your literature on the paper you selected. If your literature includes full-color photography, the printer will have to send the job out to a *color separator* in order to reproduce these pictures.

You pay the printer and get your literature. Everybody lives happily ever after.

Let's take a look at how you can control quality and cut costs at each step of the way.

Typography

Typography (called *type* for short) is lettering printed as black characters on a glossy photographic film. The film can be cut apart, pasted on art board, and reproduced on the printer's press.

To get your brochure set in type (a process known as *typesetting*), take the manuscript to the typesetter or have your artist do it for you. The typesetter will retype your manuscript onto a computer keyboard. The keyboard activates a special phototypesetting machine that produces a copy of your text set in type. The type comes out in one long sheet. The typesetter sends over a *galley* (proof copy) of this sheet for your approval.

Because the typesetter may have made mistakes when retyping your manuscript, you must carefully proofread the galley to catch any errors. (When correcting galleys, use the proofreader's symbols shown in Figure 19 on page 194.) The galley is returned to the typesetter, the corrections are made, and your artist receives clean, error-free type to work with.

The artist cuts the type apart and pastes it up on the art board according to the layout. For a little extra money, the artist can order a duplicate set of type along with the original. This is a wise thing to do, because an accidental slip of the artist's knife can cut through the lettering, and the project will be delayed until a new sheet of type is delivered.

How to specify type

The phrase *to specify type* means to order type in the size, style, and format you want. This should be done by the artist because there are so many variables involved. However, you should be aware of the basic information to be provided to the typesetter.

Size. Size refers to the height of the lettering. It is measured in *points*, and there are 72 points to an inch. Most newspapers are set in 8- or 9-point type; most promotional literature in 9 to 12 points. Another commonly used measure is the *pica;* 1 pica is equal to 12 points. Some artists also measure in *agates;* there are 14 agates to the inch.

Style. There are hundreds of *families* (basic styles) to choose from. Figure 16 on page 135 shows some of the most popular styles, including Helvetica, Souvenir, and Times Roman. The two basic categories of type styles are *serif* and *sans serif.* Serif type has little lines and curls on the ends of the letters; sans serif doesn't. The text of this book is set in a serif type, and the headlines and subheads are set in a sans serif typeface. Serif is generally believed to be more readable than sans serif.

Typeface. You also need to specify the particular typeface within the family with respect to thickness of the lettering (light, medium, or bold), width of the characters (some families offer a variety of condensed or extended faces), and slant or *posture* (the angle of the type).

Case. This term refers to whether the letters are uppercase or lowercase.

Kerning. The spacing between the letters in a word is called kerning. If there is too much space, the type looks thin and airy; if there is too little, it appears scrunched.

Spacing between words. You can choose regular spacing or narrower (*French*) spacing.

Leading. This refers to the space between each line of type. Unlike typewriters, which offer only single, double, and triple spacing, typesetting machines can adjust spacing from 1 point to as many as you choose. Most graphic artists space lines of type 1 or 2 points apart.

Justification. The type is justified when the completed line is filled and both right and left margins are *flush* (even). If it is not justified, one or both margins (commonly only the right) are *ragged* (uneven). Both the left and right margins of this book are flush, so the book is set with justified type.

Column width. This is measured in inches, picas, or characters (number of letters and spaces). In a brochure with full-size (8½-by-11-inch) pages, the columns are about 2¼ inches wide if the type is set in three columns and 3½ inches wide (about the widest a column should be) if type is set in two columns. If a column is any wider, the text becomes difficult to read.

Indentions. An indention is the number of spaces (called *em* spaces) by which lines (such as the first line of a new paragraph) should be indented.

Paragraph spacing. Some designers prefer to leave an extra space between paragraphs to make the copy a bit easier to read.

Five ways to save money at the typesetter

You can hold typesetting costs down by paying careful attention to a few commonsense rules.

> **Provide clean copy**

Before handing your copy over to the typesetter, type a clean draft and make sure you've proofread it to eliminate all errors. The typesetter *keys* (enters your copy into the typesetting machine) text exactly as you have written it— errors and all. So if your manuscript has typos, they'll show up in the galleys, and you'll have to pay to have them corrected. Also, if you submit a sloppily typed manuscript full of cross-outs and handwritten corrections, your typesetter will have a hard time deciphering your instructions and producing a clean, accurate galley. There is often a penalty charge for this.

After the manuscript is retyped, proofread it as a final check for errors. If there are mistakes, you can correct them by neatly marking the manuscript with the proofreader's symbols shown in Figure 19 (see page 194).

➤ Do it in one shot

If you're completing a long project in stages, do not submit it for typesetting a section at a time; instead, wait until the entire manuscript is completed, and submit the whole thing at once. Katie Muldoon, writing in *Zip* magazine (Sept., 1984), explains how this can save you money.

> Type is set by a computer which, in a way, must be programmed. If all information is supplied at one time, it's one program. Each time additional info must be fed to the "type computer," there is an additional set-up charge.

➤ Use standard typefaces

Although there are thousands of typefaces, a dozen or so lead the list in popularity and are used nearly as much as all the rest combined. These include Helvetica, Times Roman, and Souvenir. Standard typefaces are more readily available and hence cost a bit less than exotic, hard-to-get styles.

➤ Get competitive quotations

The typesetting fee for a given job can vary as much as 50 percent (or even more) from one typographer to the next. Get job estimates from a number of local typesetters, and then choose the one who will do the best job for the lowest-possible cost.

➤ Use your personal computer

Much of the cost of typesetting goes to paying the typesetter to key your copy into the typesetting machine. Now, thanks to the personal computer, you can eliminate this costly step and enjoy big savings at the typographer's. Copy typed on your office computer or word processor can often be entered into the phototypesetting machine directly in electronic form; there is no need to retype it. The copy can be transmitted over the phone line via modem or handed to the typesetter as a floppy disk.

OPERATIONAL SIGNS		TYPOGRAPHICAL SIGNS	
ℐ	Delete	*lc*	Lowercase capital letter
⌒	Close up; delete space	*cap*	Capitalize lowercase letter
ℐ	Delete and close up	*sc*	Set in small capitals
#	Insert space	*ital*	Set in italic type
eq #	Make space between words equal; make leading between lines equal	*rom*	Set in roman type
hr #	Insert hair space	*bf*	Set in boldface type
ls	Letterspace	*wf*	Wrong font; set in correct type
¶	Begin new paragraph	X	Reset broken letter
no ¶	Run paragraphs together	⊙	Reverse (type upside down)
☐	Move type one em from left or right		
⊐	Move right	**PUNCTUATION MARKS**	
⊏	Move left	⌄	Insert comma
⊐⊏	Center	⌄	Insert apostrophe (or single quotation mark)
⊓	Move up	⌄⌄	Insert quotation marks
⊔	Move down	⊙	Insert period
=	Straighten type; align horizontally	*(qst)* ?	Insert question mark
‖	Align vertically	;|	Insert semicolon
tr	Transpose	:|	Insert colon
(sp)	Spell out	|=|	Insert hyphen
stet	Let it stand	$\frac{1}{M}$	Insert em dash
⊥	Push down type	$\frac{1}{N}$	Insert en dash

Figure 19. These proofreader's symbols are used to indicate corrections both on manuscripts before they are sent to the typesetter and on proofs after they have been typeset. (Reprinted from the <u>The Chicago Manual of Style, 13th Edition,</u> copyright © 1969, 1982 by The University of Chicago, publisher.)

This drastically reduces the errors that normally crop up during the keying process. And because it saves labor, you save money. Most typesetters will take 15 to 25 percent off your type bill if you submit your copy electronically rather than as *hard copy* (typed on paper).

If you already have a personal computer, find a typesetter whose equipment is compatible with yours and who is willing to offer a discount for electronic copy. Compatibility shouldn't be a problem because manufacturers now design typesetting equipment to be compatible with most brands of personal computers.

If you don't have a computer, find out which machines are compatible with your typesetter's operation, and buy one. Expect to pay between $1,000 and $2,000 for the computer, $700 for the special typesetting software you will need, and $400 to $1,000 extra for a printer. The printer is useful in printing hard copies of your manuscript for internal review and distribution.

If you decide to create an in-house graphics or advertising department, you may want to obtain your own phototypesetting system. Using a personal computer and one of the less expensive typesetting machines, you can set up a complete system for between $10,000 and $15,000. If your type bill is $1,000 per brochure, the machine will pay for itself after fifteen projects.

Alternatives to type

On small projects, your budget may not allow for phototypesetting. There are four alternatives for lettering your copy: hand lettering, typewriter type, press type, and headline machine type.

➤ Hand lettering

A person who prints or writes neatly may be able to do passable lettering for invitations, menus, posters, and fliers. Calligraphy can even add a classy look to formal documents. But for any document with a significant amount of body copy (brochures, catalogs, reports, proposals), hand lettering quickly becomes tiresome and hard to read and is therefore unacceptable.

➤ Typewriter type

Typewritten copy can be cleanly reproduced on an offset press and therefore can be used as a substitute for typography in printed promotions. For certain promotions, typewriter type is sometimes more appropriate than phototype. Sales letters are set in typewriter type to make them more closely resemble personal letters. Newsletters set in typewriter type have an immediate, urgent, newsy look, whereas newsletters set in phototype sometimes look too promotional.

A manual typewriter cannot produce acceptable type because the characters are of uneven darkness. You need a good electric typewriter such as the IBM Selectric. An electronic typewriter is even better because it produces a perfect, error-free page.

Of course, phototype still has a number of advantages over typewriter type. First, phototype is generally considered more readable; according to a study conducted at Boston University, phototype can be read 27 percent faster than typewriter type with no loss of comprehension.

Second, typeset documents look more impressive, more professional. Typewriter type can cheapen the appearance of a brochure or booklet. People might actually wonder whether your company is too poor to afford typeset literature.

Third, phototype is much more versatile and flexible. There are thousands of styles, and the type can be set or cut into any shape or layout imaginable. Typewriters are limited to just a few type styles, and the spacing and format of the type they produce is severely limited.

➤ **Press type**

Press type, also known as *rub-on type* or *transfer type*, is transferred from a plastic sheet to the page by pressure; rubbing causes the ink to adhere to paper or art board. Such type can be purchased in a variety of styles from your local art supply store.

Press type is used primarily for headlines and subheads, not for body copy. Using press type is a slow, tedious process, and the letters often develop cracks that cause them to reproduce poorly. Still, it is an inexpensive alternative to phototype for signs, posters, fliers, proposals, reports, and other documents.

➤ **Headline machine type**

For $1,000 or so, you can purchase a headline machine. Although it is not a true phototypesetter, it can produce camera-ready headlines in a variety of styles and sizes.

Unlike phototypesetting equipment, which is computer-controlled and extremely fast, headline machines are painfully slow. You dial an *alphabet wheel* to the appropriate position, pull a lever, and a letter is applied to the film. To print the next letter in the headline, you redial the wheel and pull the lever again. It can take you three minutes to produce a one-sentence headline this way. However, the machines are easier to use than press type, and they produce a better-quality type.

Proofreading type

Proofread type carefully, and do it twice—at least.

The first proofreading is done when the galleys come back from the typographer. Go through the copy and neatly mark all changes and corrections. You should also proofread the galleys against the original manuscript to make sure that nothing has been changed or left out.

If the printer has made a typo, there is no charge for the correction. But if you decide to change the copy at this point, this change is known as an *author's alteration,* or *AA,* and you must pay for it. That's why the copy should be finalized and approved before it goes to the typesetter. No rewrites should be allowed after that point.

You return the corrected galley proof to the printer. Your changes are keyed, and a corrected galley is printed and sent to you or your artist. You also get a copy of the corrected galleys. Proofread them to make sure all mistakes have been corrected according to your instructions.

The artist pastes up the type to create the mechanical. At this point, you should proofread the entire text again, being as careful as you were when you read the galleys. Why? Because the artist, in cutting apart and pasting up the galleys, may have inadvertently left out a paragraph, switched a sentence, or transposed a word. It's your job to catch and correct these slip-ups.

The artist will place a *tissue* (an overlay of thin, transparent paper) over the mechanical to protect the type. Some people like to proofread the actual mechanical and mark changes on the tissue. I prefer to make a photocopy of the mechanical and proof this copy. With a photocopy, you don't have to worry about accidentally damaging the boards.

Proofreading tip: Try reading the copy backwards. This slows you down and forces you to read one word at a time. Using this technique, you can often catch spelling errors you might otherwise have missed.

Preparing photographs for the printer

The graphic artist is responsible for this step, but you should be aware of the basics.

- *Never write on the back or front of a photograph.* The impression made by your pen or pencil will show up as an unsightly streak or line in the printed brochure.
- *Make sure the printer gets original color slides and black-and-white prints.* Reproductions made from reproductions lose sharpness and clarity.
- *Specify the degree to which the photo is to be enlarged or reduced.* This is indicated by percentage: 50 percent means you want the printed image to be half the size of the original; 80 percent means a reduction four-fifths the original size; 100 percent means the same size as the original; 150 percent indicates an enlargement one and a half times; and 200 percent means an enlargement twice the size of the original.
- *Tell the printer how you want to crop the picture. Cropping* involves cutting out sections you don't want to appear in the printed piece. All cropping is done from the edges inward; you can't cut out part of the middle. The easiest way to tell the printer how you want a picture cropped is to make a photocopy and draw lines on the photocopy indicating which portions are to be eliminated.
- *Do not paste original photos directly on the mechanicals.* Although typography is pasted up directly, original photos are handled differently. The artist indicates the position of each photo by drawing and labeling boxes on the mechanical. Photo A goes in box A, and so on down the line. The easiest way to label photographs is to write out a label on a piece of paper and tape it to the back of the picture. If you are using slides, simply write the label notation on the frame.

Mechanical checklist

Before you release the finished mechanical to the printer, ask yourself the following questions:

- Does it follow your approved layout? If not, why not?
- Are all logos, trademarks, registration marks, and other symbols properly sized, positioned, and typeset?
- Have all logos, trademarks, and proprietary product names been capital-

ized and given registration marks ® or trademarks (TM) where appropriate?

- Have all disclaimers, standard paragraphs, and other fine print been placed in the appropriate positions?
- Have all proper names and titles been accurately spelled and capitalized?
- Have all form numbers, copyright lines, country of printing, and other standard information been typeset and placed according to requirements?
- Have all elements been securely mounted on the paste-up?
- Are all elements positioned and cut squarely? Are they neatly aligned?
- Have all separate pieces of art associated with the paste-up been properly keyed to the job? (Are their positions, sizes, and proportions properly indicated?)
- Does the numbering of the visuals match the captions and text references? Do all visuals appear on the pages where they are first discussed in the text?
- Have all pencil marks, smudges, and excess bits of rubber cement been removed?
- Is there a fresh tissue overlay with proper instructions for printing?
- Are samples of the paper stock to be used attached to the mechanicals?
- Are swatches showing the colors to be used attached to the board or tissue?
- Has each board been labeled on the back with the name of the job, company, and address?

Choosing paper

Although you may have selected your paper earlier, you can still change your mind. Most printers have a wide selection of paper you can choose from. If they don't have a particular paper in stock, they can order it; however, ordering paper not in stock may delay the job. That's why you should order paper several weeks before you're ready to go to press—but only if you're absolutely certain about your choice.

Let your printer and graphic artist guide you in the selection of paper. Printers know, for example, which papers are best for showing off photos and which are best for taking up certain types of inks or coatings. Many times, they can save you money by suggesting a paper they can get at a discount from their special sources and suppliers.

Paper is graded by weight. Heavy papers are stiff and thick; lighter papers are thinner. Paper weight is measured in *pounds* (with the pound measurement referring to the weight of 500 sheets, not a single sheet). Newspapers are printed on 30-pound stock; résumés, on 50- or 60-pound stock; some magazine covers, on 80- or 90-pound stock.

Another factor that affects stiffness is the thickness of the paper. Paper thickness is measured in *mils;* one mil is equal to one-thousandth of an inch.

Paper may be smooth and uniform in composition, or it may have an interesting weave or texture running through it. The surface may be dull, high-gloss, or somewhere in between. Paper is available in many variations of white and in an almost infinite variety of other colors.

Another consideration is *opacity.* Can you see through the paper when you hold it up to the light? Will ink printed on one side bleed through to the other? Opacity is determined by thickness, weight, and the manufacturing process and chemicals used to make the paper.

The most common grades of paper are bond paper, coated stock, text paper, cover stock, book stock, and offset paper.

- *Bond papers* are used for stationery and business forms. Bond paper is easy to write on.
- *Coated stock* has a glossy finish. It receives ink well and is the stock to use when you are reproducing color photographs in your literature. Coated stock is ideal for high-quality jobs such as annual reports and corporate brochures.
- *Text papers* have a rich texture and feel to them. They are used in booklets, brochures, and other print promotions.
- *Cover stock* is a heavier paper used mainly for brochure and booklet covers. It can be cut and embossed and stands up to heavy abuse. You can make your literature feel more substantial by printing the cover on cover stock and the inside pages on a lighter paper.
- *Book stock* is a less expensive grade used, as its name implies, in books, including this one.
- *Offset paper* is similar to book stock and is used for résumés, cover letters, and other quickie printing jobs done on small offset presses.

Although it helps to know about paper, don't spend your time becoming an expert in the subject. Instead, lean on the expertise of your printer and artist, and let them guide you.

Pick a grade of paper that does justice to the project because, to a large extent, the look and feel of the paper determine the first impression the reader receives from your literature. And first impressions, as you know, are important when it comes to doing business or making a sale.

Fortunately, the difference in cost between poor and good paper is not as great as you might imagine. Calvin York of Danbury Printing estimates that to print 20,000 eight-page color catalogs of standard size (8½ by 11 inches), the cost would be $1,200 on inexpensive paper and only an additional $230 for good-quality paper.

One way of saving money is to buy paper in large quantities. Let's say you print a newsletter on a special gray-blue stock. Each issue has a press run of 5,000 copies, and you print six issues a year. Buy 30,000 sheets (one year's supply) at once instead of just 5,000. The savings will be substantial.

Another money-saving technique is to use paper the printer already has on hand. Because the printer loses money on paper he can't sell, you may get a better deal on existing inventory than on paper that has to be ordered especially for you. Also, many local printers often offer for sale the remainders of odd lots of paper. These sales allow you to buy perfectly good paper at incredibly low prices.

How to select a printer

Commercial printing today is a $27-billion industry. And you will shortly be contributing to its profits. Printing can account for between 25 and 75 percent of your production budget, and the cost of the job can vary by as much as 30 percent or more from one printer to the next. Therefore, it pays to choose your printer with care. Here is some advice for doing it right.

➤ **Get a referral**

The best way of finding potential printers for your job is through referral. Just about every organization uses the services of local printers at some point. Ask your associates at other firms to give you the names of two or three good printers they can recommend. If referrals don't yield enough names, you can find numerous printers listed in the Yellow Pages. Also, printing is a competitive industry, so chances are various local printers will mail you samples of their work or other direct mail in the hope of soliciting your business. File such mailings away for future reference. Then, when the need for printing services arises, you will have a file full of suppliers right at your fingertips.

➤ **Use local printers**

The printer should be located within a one-hour drive from your office. During the printing process, you will have to visit the facilities many times to check on the job and oversee the work. If the printer is far away, these visits can quickly eat up your time. Also, printers, like other professionals, must be compensated in some fashion for their time, and if they have to travel half a day to see you, they'll factor this travel time into your bill.

➤ **Go as far as the suburbs if you have to**

As a rule, suburban and rural printers charge much less than printers located in major cities. However, the rural printer may be so far away that the cost savings isn't worth the extra time, so your best bet is a printer in a nearby suburb. The fee will be substantially less than that of a city printer, and if the printing plant is near a bus route or major highway, the extra travel time will be minimal.

➤ **Check out the printer's operation in person**

Don't just be content to meet with the printer's sales representative in your office or have the printer mail you some samples. Check the operation out carefully. Visit the facilities, have the printer explain the equipment and the operation's capabilities to you, meet with the people who will be handling your job. Hire a printing firm whose people you feel you can trust with the important task of printing your publications correctly and on time.

➤ **Choose a specialist**

Some printers specialize in particular types of projects: annual reports, catalogs, direct mail. Others specialize according to printing process: offset, letterpress, gravure. A third group specializes according to the size of the *run* (the number of copies you need). Choose a printer set up to handle your specific task. The advantage of using specialists is that they can often do a better job at significantly lower cost.

➤ **Get three bids**

Once you've narrowed the field, select your three favorite printers, and have them bid on the job. The information they'll need for an accurate price quotation includes the quantity to be printed, page size, number of pages, type of binding or folding, paper stock, colors, number of halftones, and deadline. The literature specification sheet (Figure 8) that you completed in Chapter 2 will give printers all this information and more. You should also give the printers a copy of your layout.

Getting three bids ensures that you will pay a fair price for the job. If you solicited only a single bid, you would have no way of knowing whether it was reasonable or sky-high. When you get three bids, you can immediately see whether one is out of line with what the others are charging.

➤ **Get it in writing**

Insist on written proposals from your printers. The proposal should reiterate all the specifications you've outlined along with the deadline, number of copies needed, and price for the job. A written agreement eliminates misunderstandings and protects you if the final bill is higher than the estimate or the job is not as you ordered it.

The printing process

Once you hand over the mechanical to the printer, your work is nearly done. Here's what happens from that step on.

The printer's job is to reproduce your mechanical on a printing press. A printing plate is made. Then, before the copies are run from the plate, the printer gives you a *blueline* to check.

A blueline is a final proof of the work. It derives its name from the fact that it is printed as dark blue lettering on light blue photosensitive paper. The blueline gives you one final opportunity to proofread for typos and check for mistakes. Take full advantage of this opportunity. Occasionally, pieces of type fall off the mechanical or photos are placed upside down, and the printer does not notice. Proofing the blueline lets you catch and correct these mistakes before the job goes to press (unfortunately, making changes at this stage is very expensive). You should also check the blues for correct placement of color (in two-color jobs), broken type, splotches, smears, and spacing.

On full-color jobs, an additional step is involved: color separations. In a color separation, the original color picture is photographically or electronically separated into four basic colors: red, yellow, blue, black. Each is made into a halftone printing plate. When the four plates print on top of one another, the result is full, natural color reproduction.

In color work, you commonly proof what is known as a *color key*. The key is four translucent sheets, each chemically treated with a pigment in one of the four basic colors. By placing the four sheets together, you see an image closely resembling what the final print will look like.

A more accurate (albeit slightly more costly) method of proofing color work is to make a *cromalin*, which uses a single sheet of paper instead of four acetate sheets. Cromalins have a much closer resemblance to the finished print than color keys.

If you are unhappy with the appearance of any color photos in the keys or chromalins, you can tell this to the printer. Changes can be made by adjusting the application of the four basic colors of ink.

On major color jobs, you might also consider checking *press proofs* at the printing plant. A press proof is an actual printed version of the plates run as a final quality check prior to gearing up the presses for the full run. Some printing experts swear by press proofs; others feel they are not worth the expense and, in addition, are not a reliable method because the press proof is often run on a different press than the final version will be.

After you approve the proofs, the printer duplicates the plates on the press. The pages are cut, folded, or bound according to your instructions, and boxes of finished literature are shipped to you. And that's it.

Eleven ways to get good printing at low cost

Here are my rules for keeping printing costs under control.

➤ **Submit a perfect mechanical**

A perfect mechanical is one the printer can work with directly without having to clean it up, create additional artwork, or redo any part. If the printer has to touch up the mechanical because it's dirty or sloppy or improperly prepared, you'll be charged extra for it.

➤ **Use the printer as a consultant**

Get the printer's advice on what works and what doesn't. Involve the printer in the early stages of planning and design, not after the fact. The printer may be able to suggest alternative ways of designing and producing the piece, and these suggestions could save you a bundle at press time.

➤ **Get great photographs**

Photos should be sharp, clear, and full of contrast. If your photos are of poor quality, the printer can correct for that in the printing process to a degree. But no printer can make up the difference 100 percent. That's why good printing starts with good photography.

➤ **Submit transparencies**

In color printing, better reproduction quality can usually be obtained by working from slides rather than color prints. So use color slide film when you shoot, and submit original color slides to the printer.

And regardless of whether you're using slides or prints, color or black and white, submit originals, not copies. A *second-generation print* (a print reproduced from the original print rather than from the negative) will not reproduce as well as the original print. A *third-generation print* (a print made from a second-generation print) is even worse. Reproduction quality declines in direct proportion to the generation of the print or slide.

➤ **Use full frames, not silhouettes**

A silhouette is a visual in which a picture of an object is cut out of a photograph and reproduced as an outline figure using the white space of the page as background. But silhouettes add extra cost to the job. Using a regular product photo, one showing the product against the background in which it was photographed, is more economical.

➤ **Use basic colors**

The printer stocks standard inks or can buy them off the shelf. When you print in unusual colors, such as maroon or lavender, custom inks have to be mixed specially for your job, and that can increase printing costs by 15 to 25 percent or more.

➤ **Catch mistakes early**

The earlier in the production process you catch mistakes, the easier and less costly they are to correct. So when you proof the mechanical, proof it carefully, and try your best to eliminate all errors. Although you can make corrections if you spot typos in the blueline, it's expensive. Concentrate on your early proofing so that your blueline will be letter-perfect.

➤ **Think big**

Try to use one large photo per page rather than many smaller ones. The reason? The fewer photos you use, the less the piece costs to produce. On average, each additional color photo you use adds $200 to $300 to the printing bill.

➢ **Print in large volumes**
Printing becomes more economical in larger volumes. Also, a large press run dramatically lowers the cost per piece. If you're not sure whether you'll need 5,000 or 10,000 pieces, order the 10,000. Having a few left over is much less costly than not printing enough and having to go back to press for an additional 5,000.

➢ **Fold smaller pieces**
Folding is less costly than binding, so if you can form your brochure by folding one piece of paper into panels instead of binding several pieces of paper together, do so. Popular folds and binding methods are illustrated in Figures 20 and 21.

➢ **Take delivery at multiple sites**
If your supply of literature is to be split among several locations, have the printer deliver the proper amount directly to each location. This is cheaper than having all the brochures sent to your office and then reshipping them in cartons to your various branch offices or dealers.

Where to go for more information

A complete discussion of graphic arts techniques, procedures, and equipment is beyond the scope of this book. For more information on design, layout, paste-up, and printing, you can turn to the following reference books:

- *Graphic Arts Encyclopedia*, George A. Stevenson (New York: McGraw-Hill), 483 pages, $41.50. This is a comprehensive reference work on creating and reproducing graphic images. It discusses the latest machinery, processes, and techniques.
- *Graphic Designer's Production Handbook*, Norman Sanders and William Bevington (New York: Hastings House), 208 pages, $9.95. Over 110 subjects are covered, from preprinting preparation and halftone reproduction to lithography and finishing operations.
- *Graphics Master 3*, Dean Lem (Santa Barbara, CA: Dean Lem Associates), $57.50. Lem covers a broad range of graphic arts topics, including typography, computerized phototypesetting, proofreading, photography,

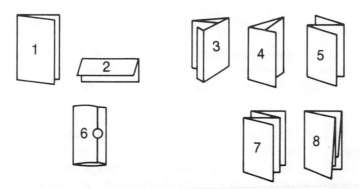

Figure 20. Some popular folding styles are shown here: (1,2) 4 pages, (3) 6 pages with flap, (4,5,6) 6 pages, (7,8) 8 pages. (Credit: From <u>How to Promote Your Own Business,</u> by Gary Blake and Robert W. Bly. Copyright © 1983 by Gary Blake and Robert W. Bly. Reprinted by arrangement with New American Library, New York, NY.)

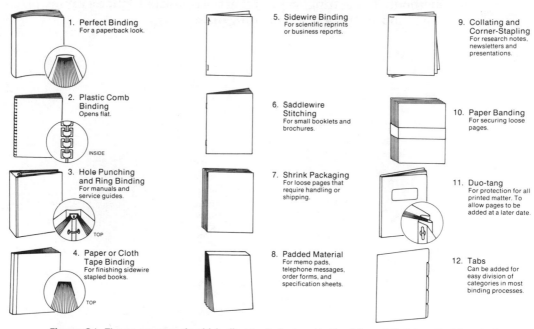

1. **Perfect Binding**
   For a paperback look.

2. **Plastic Comb Binding**
   Opens flat.

3. **Hole Punching and Ring Binding**
   For manuals and service guides.

4. **Paper or Cloth Tape Binding**
   For finishing sidewire stapled books.

5. **Sidewire Binding**
   For scientific reprints or business reports.

6. **Saddlewire Stitching**
   For small booklets and brochures.

7. **Shrink Packaging**
   For loose pages that require handling or shipping.

8. **Padded Material**
   For memo pads, telephone messages, order forms, and specification sheets.

9. **Collating and Corner-Stapling**
   For research notes, newsletters and presentations.

10. **Paper Banding**
    For securing loose pages.

11. **Duo-tang**
    For protection for all printed matter. To allow pages to be added at a later date.

12. **Tabs**
    Can be added for easy division of categories in most binding processes.

Figure 21. These are standard binding techniques. Method 6, saddlewire stitching, is the most popular method for binding brochures and booklets. In saddlewire stitching, staples are forced through the backbone or <u>spine</u> of the booklet to hold the pages together. (Credit: From <u>How to Promote Your Own Business,</u> by Gary Blake and Robert W. Bly. Copyright © 1983 by Gary Blake and Robert W. Bly. Reprinted by arrangement with New American Library, New York, NY.)

halftone screens, color, papers, printing, binding, and finishing. Includes a glossary.

- *In Print*, Frank N. Levin (Englewood Cliffs, NJ: Prentice-Hall), $6.95. This guide to graphics and printing explains the procedures for obtaining print cost estimates, preproduction, typesetting, artwork, and mechanicals.
- *Mastering Graphics*, Jan V. White (New York: R. R. Bowker Co., 1983), 180 pages, $24.95. This is a guide to design and production for people who publish newsletters, magazines, newspapers, tabloids, and house organs. Topics include logo design, masthead design, cropping and scaling of halftones, and preparation of mechanicals for printing.
- *Pocket Pal: A Graphic Arts Production Handbook* (New York: International Paper Company), 204 pages, $3.75. This popular handbook was first published in 1934 and is now in its twelfth edition. Chapters provide in-depth discussions of a wide range of graphics topics, including printing methods, typesetting, copy and art preparation, photography, platemaking, binding, paper, and printing inks.

CHAPTER TEN

Keeping It Going: How to Manage a Successful Promotional Literature Program

When you're having more than one . . .

Opening a carton and pulling out a freshly printed, glossy booklet or brochure can be a very satisfying feeling, especially if you had a hand in its creation. But in most organizations, you can't rest on your laurels. At some point, the brochure will become dated, and you'll need a new one. Or else you'll have to produce additional literature to cover other areas or to supplement the original.

This chapter gives you tips and advice on a miscellany of topics related to managing a successful program of promotional literature. You will get advice on how to generate customer interest in your literature; how to get salespeople and top management enthusiastic about your literature program; how to distribute, store, and reprint literature; how to create a successful series of brochures; and how to get the most out of existing copy, type artwork, and photographs.

How to sell your program to top management

Unless you're the boss, you need to convince top management to fund your literature program. Chances are, you will be required to submit some sort of promotional budget for approval. The budget outlines the projects you want to do and the money required for each.

If you've never done this before and you expect to get instant approval for your ambitious plans, you're in for a shock. Management may, for example, think $8,000 is excessive for a brochure and cut that item to $2,500 ("Do we really need four-color illustrations?"). Projects you think of as essential may be eliminated altogether ("Let's use last year's brochure until sales go high enough to justify printing a new one").

Ranting and raving that management doesn't understand the importance of good literature won't change their minds. Although they may indeed not understand the need for quality brochures, that lack of understanding is your problem, not theirs. It's your job to make them understand, to prove your case and defend your budget.

How do you get management to approve your budget and see your point of view? Here are eight suggestions.

➤ **Educate your managers**

Part of your job is to provide your management with an ongoing education in the value of advertising, publicity, and promotion. After all, they have many other things to worry about, and they may not spend as much time thinking about promotional literature as you do.

How do you educate management? One way is to read advertising and business magazines and clip any articles that pertain to promotional literature. Distribute copies of the articles, along with brief memos, to key managers. Also, many printers, advertising agencies, and other vendors occasionally sponsor educational seminars or meetings for their customers. If you get invited, try to take some of your managers along. They'll gain an appreciation of what it takes to create a successful brochure or booklet.

➤ **Be cost-conscious**

Frankly, some advertising and publicity directors, in their zeal to do a first-class job, are not as cost conscious as they should be. Top management, on the other hand, is most impressed by a manager who can achieve goals as economically as possible. Become cost-conscious, and let your management know the steps you're taking to conserve promotional dollars. For example, if you prepare detailed cost estimates for each project, circulate these estimates to your managers. This will give your management a clearer picture of the expenses involved and will also show them that all budget requests are well thought out.

One technique to make the cost of producing literature seem more bearable is to state the cost in terms of the price per piece rather than the price per project. Let's say it cost you $10,000 to produce a brochure, and you printed 10,000 copies. Don't say the cost is $10,000; say it is $1 per copy.

As I mentioned in Chapter 9, the cost of printing does not increase in direct proportion to the number of copies printed. Although a press run of 10,000 copies costs $10,000, a run of 20,000 copies might cost only $12,000. By printing the extra copies, you lower your cost per copy from $1 to 60 cents.

➤ **Track the competition**

Collect samples of the competition's literature. Circulate these samples to your management. When management is aware of what the competition is doing, they'll be better able to appreciate why your own literature has to look at least as good. (Also, they will appreciate the effort you're making to gather valuable information on the competition's products and marketing efforts.)

➤ **Show the piece before and after**

When you update or redo an old piece of literature, circulate the old brochure with the updated version. This side-by-side comparison dramatically demonstrates that the extra effort and cost involved in producing first-class literature pays off. Your management will immediately see and appreciate the difference in quality, image, and communications effectiveness. This will help pave the way for future efforts.

➤ **Get supporting opinions**

If your customers and salespeople think highly of your literature, ask them to say so in writing. Then show these letters of praise to top management to prove the popularity of your new promotional efforts.

➤ **Demonstrate customer interest**

Keep track of the number of brochures you distribute each year. Then, if management questions the effectiveness or need for literature, you can back up your claim that your brochure is in demand with a hard statistic (e.g., "2,400 requests for our catalog this year").

➤ **Measure effectiveness**

Try to make some measurement of the brochure's readability, persuasiveness, and communications effectiveness. This is difficult but possible. (More about this later.)

➤ **Divide the cost**

If a project is too expensive for one department or division, perhaps the cost can be shared by several groups within the organization. For example, the annual report is used not only by the public relations department but by marketing, sales, advertising, and human resources as well. Splitting the cost among various groups makes the price tag affordable to the managers of these divisions, who would hesitate to foot the whole bill themselves.

In the same way, you can make an art or photography budget seem more palatable if you can show how the cost can be spread over several projects. Five hundred dollars for pictures to be used in a slide presentation might seem excessive to some managers. But if you explain that the same photos will also be used in publicity, literature, and print advertising, the manager can see his or her way clear to approving your request.

How to get your salespeople enthusiastic about your literature

If your organization sells its products or services through an inside sales force, sales reps, agents, distributors, or dealerships, a major application of your literature will be as a sales aid to support their efforts. It follows that the first step in creating successful promotional literature is to create literature that the salespeople will want to use. Gaining sales force acceptance of your literature begins in the planning stage, not after the fact.

Before you outline your brochure, talk to some of your dealers and salespeople. Find out what they think should be included in the literature—and what should be omitted. If you've already written an outline or draft or have designed a rough layout, show it to your salespeople. Do they think the proposed brochure would be useful in their sales activities? Or do they complain that you're creating an expensive *puff piece* (a fancy but overly general brochure that fails to include any real information or sales talk)?

Take these criticisms and complaints for what they're worth. You don't have to agree with every comment. But remember: The salespeople are the ones who have to go out and sell the product every day. They can give you a lot of guidance about what sells—and what doesn't. Incorporate the best of their thinking into the finished piece.

If you follow this procedure, you'll gain speedy acceptance of your literature by salespeople for two reasons. First, the literature will reflect their need for an effective sales support tool. Second, they'll appreciate the fact that you took the time to consult with them on the project.

Be sure to distribute an adequate supply of literature to all branch offices, dealerships, manufacturer's representatives, and inside salespeople. Let them know that additional copies are available, and make it easy for them to request these extra copies.

Keep in touch with the sales force so that you can get feedback on your literature's success. Experience in using the literature may provide additional ideas on how to improve it for the next press run. For example, maybe you didn't include a fact because you thought it was unimportant, but your salespeople report that every customer is asking about this fact. In the next edition, you can highlight this fact up front.

Using publicity to generate interest in your brochure

Is the publication of your new catalog or brochure news? Not to the *New York Times* or the *Wall Street Journal*, perhaps. But there are many specialty publications whose readers want to know about the availability of your new literature.

The best way to publicize the publication of new promotional literature is with a *new literature release.* This is simply a short press release announcing the publication and availability of your new brochure, catalog, booklet, or handbook.

The new literature release begins with a headline announcing the publication. The text of the release describes the contents of the literature in a way that makes it most interesting to editors and their readers. The closing paragraph explains how the reader can obtain a free copy of the publication being discussed. The press release is typed double-spaced and is usually one page long, two pages at most. A typical new literature release is shown below.

Do editors print these releases? The answer is yes, many do. There are thousands of specialty magazines covering every conceivable field, from agriculture and aerospace to television broadcasting and industrial training. *Bacon's Publicity Checker* is a book listing these thousands of magazines. It is published by Bacon's Publishing Company, 14 East Jackson Boulevard, Chicago, IL 60604, (312) 922-8419. The reference room of your local library probably has a copy on its shelves.

The press release is typed, reproduced (by offset printing or as photoco-

FROM: Kirsch Communications, 226 Seventh Street, Garden City, NY 11530. For more information please call: Len Kirsch, (516) 248-4055

FOR: Globe Electronic Hardware, Inc., 32-02 57th Street, Woodside, NY 11377. Contact: Patrick J. Dennehy, President, (212) 278-2400

FOR RELEASE: October 20, 1985

GLOBE OFFERS NEW CATALOG
FOR ELECTRONIC HARDWARE

A new 188-page catalog containing complete engineering dimensions, specifications, materials, and finishes for its entire line of electronic hardware components has been published by Globe Electronic Hardware, Inc., Woodside, NY.

According to Patrick J. Dennehy, president, the new catalog provides new and revised data for all of the company's standard products, rearranged for easier selection and specification by design engineers. Products featured include...

(description of products)

Copies of the catalog are available without charge from John Choberka, Globe Electronic Hardware, Inc., 32-02 57th Street, Woodside, NY 11377, telephone 1(800) 221-1505 or (212) 278-2400.

#

Note to editor: Cover photo, copy of catalog enclosed

pies), and mailed to any magazine or newspaper that might possibly have an interest in it. Your local paper probably won't be interested in your new ball bearing catalog, but the readers of *Machine Design, Design News, New Equipment Digest,* and other journals aimed at design engineers would be very interested indeed in obtaining it. The editors, knowing this, may very well publish a short feature item describing your catalog. Some editors like to illustrate these items with a picture of the literature, which is why you should include the actual catalog or a photo of its cover with your release.

When the release is published, people will read it, and many will send for a free copy of your brochure. In this way, publicity generates sales leads at practically no cost, because you do not pay the magazine to run your release.

Using direct mail to generate interest in your brochure

Direct mail is another vehicle that is effective in generating requests for your literature. How do you go about it?

First, obtain a list of the names and addresses of qualified prospects, people who would be interested in your product and should receive a copy of your brochure. The best list is probably your customer list. Second-best is your list of prospects, people who have shown interest in your products or organization but have not yet made a purchase. Third-best is a list compiled by another organization and rented to you for mailing purposes. You can rent such lists from trade journals (subscription lists), professional societies (membership lists), trade shows (attendee lists), and special companies known as *list brokers.* Many list brokers advertise their services on the pages of *Direct Marketing* magazine (224 Seventh Street, Garden City, NY 11530, (516) 746-6700).

Second, create the direct-mail piece. The simplest format is a one- or two-page typewritten letter and reply card mailed in an ordinary business envelope.

If you have a word processor and the list is available on floppy disk, you might want to personalize your mailing. But if you don't have a computer and a computerized list, you will probably have to make do with a form letter. That's okay because form letters can still be extremely effective.

Outside print shops and *letter shops* (printers specializing in direct mail) can also produce personalized direct mail for you. But this is not economical for mailings of under 10,000 letters.

The letter highlights the benefits of the product and urges the reader to send for the free brochure by completing and mailing the reply card. Each reply card you receive represents a hot sales lead, someone with immediate interest in your product.

Direct mail is more expensive than publicity. But it is also more of a sure thing. With a press release, there is no guarantee that an editor will run it, hence no guarantee that your message will reach your prospects. But with direct mail, you have precise control over who receives your mailing. Also, by mailing only to qualified prospects, you generate higher-quality sales leads than you would with publicity, which reaches a more diverse audience.

The key to getting the best response to your mailing is to concentrate on the offer of the free literature rather than the product or service itself. Here's a sample letter designed to get the reader to send for a free pamphlet called *Life Insurance for Children.*

There's no gift
more meaningful . . .

. . . for the children you love, than the one discussed in a new free pamphlet. It is yours with my compliments if you'll just mail the card enclosed.

You'll be surprised at the gift, I am sure. Most people are—at first. For that gift is "Juvenile Life Insurance."

Before you object that children rarely die young and so life insurance is depressingly inappropriate, let me surprise you again by saying that people invest in life insurance for children precisely because they expect these children to *live!*

But you'll appreciate the good sense of this, with this informative pamphlet in your hands. Just complete and mail the card and it's yours. . . .

[list of product benefits as described in the pamphlet]

The free pamphlet contains the little-known facts. You may decide against this gift, of course. But I am sure you'll want to know why so many millions of devoted men and women do give this gift—every single year. Please complete and mail the card—and see.

Sincerely,

© Stanley J. Robens Corp.

Integrating your literature with your advertising program

A powerful technique for increasing the response to your advertisements is to offer free literature to people who respond to the ad. To take advantage of this technique, your advertising people must be kept informed about the promotional literature you have available now as well as the pieces you're planning to publish in the near future.

Here are some tips for making your advertising and literature programs work together more effectively.

- *Make sure you have literature appropriate for fulfilling inquiries from your ads.* If you create a new ad campaign based on a service theme and your existing product literature doesn't talk about service, you may need to revise the literature or create a separate piece to highlight the service capabilities.
- *Include helpful information as well as product information in your literature.* People are more likely to request a booklet that contains useful advice and tips than a brochure that is purely a sales pitch. By including some useful information of a general nature, you make your brochure more valuable, thus increasing the number of inquiries generated by your advertising.
- *Give the literature an attractive title.* Your literature's title should imply value and make people want to have a copy. For example, if your pump catalog gives tips on product selection, call it *Pump Selection Guide* instead of *Pump Catalog.* The word *guide* implies helpful advice and information, while *catalog* sounds more like a blatant sales pitch.
- *Use a coupon in your ad layout.* A coupon increases response by 25 to 100 percent. The coupon belongs in the bottom right-hand corner of the ad. It should be large enough for the reader to be able to fill in the required information (name, address, phone number).
- *Use a toll-free number.* Clipping a coupon takes effort. Many people do not have stamps and envelopes handy. A toll-free number provides a quick and easy way for people to request your literature.
- *Use the closing paragraphs of ad copy to describe the booklet and entice the reader to send for it.* For example, say something like this: "To get the full story on our complete line of hobbyist telescopes and accessories, phone or write for a free copy of our new, full-color booklet and product directory, *A Layman's Guide to the Stars.*"
- *Show a picture of the booklet.* Don't make it the central visual, of course. But showing a photo of the booklet at the bottom right-hand corner near the closing copy will increase response. Put a caption under the photo to

highlight the value of the literature. For example: "20-page color catalog of telescopes and accessories—yours *FREE*."

- *Don't try any funny business.* People are wary of trickery. Be sure to stress that the booklet is sent free, with absolutely no obligation on the part of the consumer.
- *Do not mention any follow-up.* If you plan to follow up your mailing with a phone call or visit by a salesperson, do not mention this in your ad copy. Saying that a salesperson will call drastically reduces response.

Creating an inquiry fulfillment package

Naturally, you're not in business to publish free brochures and mail them. The purpose of generating inquiries and fulfilling them is to bring you one step closer to making a sale. But too many times, the mailing of the brochure does not lead to a sale. Instead, the brochure is thrown away, and a hot sales lead quickly turns cold.

Why? Part of the reason is that the brochure alone is not enough to move the prospect to action. You need more than just a brochure. You need a complete *inquiry fulfillment package.*

An inquiry fulfillment package is used to respond to leads generated by advertising, direct mail, publicity, and other promotions. It consists of a group of coordinated materials designed to hook the prospect's interest, provide the requested information, and get the prospect to take the next step in the buying process. There are five items in the package: the outer envelope, the brochure, the reply element, the dealer list, and the cover letter.

➤ **Outer envelope**

Even the design of the envelope that the brochure is mailed in has an effect on whether the prospect reads the enclosed material or throws it away. An envelope used for mailing inquiry fulfillment materials should be imprinted with the words "Here is the information you requested" or a similar message. This alerts the recipient that the envelope contains material that was requested, rather than the type of unsolicited advertising matter that people often refer to as *junk mail.*

➤ **Brochure**

"The proper literature—what the respondent is asking for—is the most important part of the package," says Larry Whisenhant, advertising manager of Koch Engineering, a manufacturer of chemical equipment. The fulfillment package should include all the material the prospect requested along with any additional literature that can answer questions or help make the sale.

➤ **Reply element**

The reply element is a device the reader can use to initiate the next step in the buying process, whatever that step may be. The reply element can be a reply card, an order form, a questionnaire, or a specification sheet.

The most common reply element is the business reply postcard. On the back of the card is space for the prospect to fill in name, address, and phone number. There are also boxes to check to indicate the recipient's level of interest. The front of the card contains your name and address and a postage-paid business reply permit number. The prospect simply completes the card and tosses it in the mail—no need for a stamp. The card comes back to you, and you take the appropriate action.

➤ **Dealer list**

Most people prefer to buy from a local store, agent, or dealer rather than direct from the manufacturer. If you use local dealers, agents, or outlets, the fulfillment package should supply the prospect with the name, address, and specific location of the nearest dealer.

There are several ways to handle this. One is to include a cover letter signed by the local dealer and written on the dealer's letterhead. Another way is to have a cover letter from the manufacturer but to attach the dealer's business card or give the dealer's name and address in the text of the letter. A third way is to print a listing of all dealers and include it in the inquiry fulfillment package. Such a listing is best organized by state. You can circle the name of the appropriate dealer in red pen to make things even easier for the prospect.

➤ **Cover letter**

The cover letter ties the package together. The literature concentrates on selling the product, but the cover letter concentrates on telling the reader about the next step in the buying process and on urging him or her to take it.

A good cover letter starts off by thanking the prospect for his or her interest in the product. Next, it highlights specific product benefits or gives a brief overview of the enclosed literature. Then it describes the next step in the sales cycle. Finally, it urges the reader to take action.

Here's an excellent example of an effective cover letter for an inquiry fulfillment package.

Dear Mr. Moore,

Thanks for your interest in our Pelletizers. Literature is enclosed that will give you a pretty good idea of the simplicity of our equipment and its rugged, trouble-free construction.

The key question, of course, is the cost for equipment to handle the volume at your plant. Since the capacity of our Pelletizers will vary slightly with the particulates involved, we'll be glad to take a look at a random 5-gallon sample of your material. We'll evaluate it and get back to you with our equipment recommendation. If you will note with your sample the size pellets you prefer and the volume you wish to handle, we can give you an estimate of the cost involved.

From this point on, we can do an exploratory pelletizing test, a full day's test, or we will rent you a production machine with an option to purchase. You can see for yourself how efficiently it works and how easy it is to use. Of course, the equipment can be purchased outright, too.

Thanks again for your interest. We'll be happy to answer any questions for you. Simply phone or write.

Very truly yours,

MARS MINERAL CORPORATION

All five elements—envelope, literature, reply element, dealer list, and cover letter—work together to create a cohesive sales tool. The best way to put the package together is to mail the literature and letter flat in a 9-by-12-inch (or larger) envelope. The letter is the first thing the reader should see upon pulling your materials out of the envelope. Underneath the letter is the literature, followed by the reply element. You may want to clip the materials to a piece of stiff cardboard to prevent the package from being folded, bent, or mutilated in the mail.

Inquiry fulfillment and management systems

An inquiry fulfillment and management system is simply a method of keeping track of inquiries and sales leads. The system should allow you to track the following information:

- The number of inquiries generated by each ad, mailer, press release, or other promotion
- The source of each individual inquiry
- The name, address, organization, and phone number of each prospect
- The specific literature sent to the prospect and the date the materials were sent
- The nature and date of follow-up contacts—mailings, phone calls, sales visits
- Facts about the prospect, such as budget, level of interest, specific application, and intent to buy
- Whether the inquiry resulted in a sale, is still pending, or can be considered inactive (because the prospect lost interest or bought from somebody else)

You can devise any inquiry tracking system that suits you. In my own free-lance copywriting business, I use two notebooks to track inquiries. The first notebook is a record of the various ads and promotions I've tried along with the results. For each promotion, it lists the date, a general description, the number of responses, and the amount of business generated (if any).

The second notebook uses a standard form to keep track of individual leads. I keep a separate sheet on each prospect, and the book is divided into sections for "prospects ready to buy," "hot leads," "follow-up required," "cold leads," "inactive prospects," and "past customers."

Here is the form I use for tracking leads. You can easily adapt it to your own requirements.

Date_____ Source of inquiry:_____

Method of response:_____

Name_____ **Title**_____

Company_____ **Phone**_____

Address_____

City_____ **State**_____ **Zip**_____

Type of business:_____

Services required:_____

Status:

☐ Sent literature on (date):_____

☐ Enclosed these materials:_____

_____

☐ The next step is to:_____

☐ Probability of closing the sale:_____

☐ Date of next contact:_____

☐ Comments:_____

_____

Contact Record:

Date: *Summary of conversation:*

_____   _____

_____   _____

_____   _____

_____   _____

_____   _____

Using a detailed form such as this one allows you to track the status of each lead precisely. By doing so, you have a better chance of converting more leads into sales. Of course, the more inquiries you receive, the more difficult it is to keep track of them all. That's why many organizations have computerized their inquiry management systems.

The computerized system uses software and a personal computer to take the place of paper forms and notebooks. The advantage of computerization is that the computer is far more flexible and versatile than paper systems. You can, for example, instruct the computer to print out an alphabetical list of prospects who requested "bulletin X" within the past six months or to erase from the files all leads received more than three years ago. The computer can print reports, customized cover letters, and self-stick mailing labels. By tapping a few keys, you can call up any one of a thousand or more customer files in less than a minute. And you can easily change or update a file at any time.

How can you obtain a computerized inquiry management system? You can have a staff or independent computer programmer create one for you, or you can buy one of a number of packaged systems that come complete and ready to go. Some of these consist of hardware and software installed in your office; others are computerized inquiry fulfillment services that are performed for you off the premises. Here is a list of some of the best-known.

Automated Sales Support System
Epsilon Data Management, Inc.
24 New England Executive Park
Burlington, MA 01803
(617)273-0250; (800)225-1919

DCS
Dynatron Computer Systems, Inc.
127 West 30th Street
New York, NY 10001
(212)947-1212

ISA
Inquiry Systems Analysis
35 Morrissey Boulevard
Boston, MA 02125
(617)482-6256

LCS Lead Conversion System
LCS Industries
120 Brighton Road
Clifton, NJ 07012
(201)778-5588

The Order Prospector
Marketing Applications Software Company
5963 Tulane Street
San Diego, CA 92122
(619)453-8758

Pending Business Reporting System
SMS Sales Management Systems
50 Church Street
Cambridge, MA 02138
(617)492-1571

Prospecting
Key Systems, Inc.
512 Executive Park
Louisville, KY 40207
(502)897-3332

Qualified Lead System
McGraw-Hill
1221 Avenue of the Americas
New York, NY 10020
(212)512-2000

Quantum
Computer Marketing Services
1895 Mt. Hope Avenue
P.O. Box 1011
Rochester, NY 14603
(716)271-2500

The Sales Manager
Market Power Computer Innovations
11780 Rough & Ready Road
Rough & Ready, CA 95975
(916)432-1200

Setting up your literature center

When an organization begins a literature program, an unlucky administrative assistant is usually selected to handle the mailing, stocking, and reordering of brochures. As your literature program grows, one employee working on inquiry fulfillments part time can't hope to keep up with the leads. At some point, you realize that you need to set up a separate area to handle the task.

This *literature center* can be a separate room or the corner of an office. It can require the services of a single worker or, depending on your volume, a team working full-time stuffing envelopes and entering leads into the computer. The important thing is to make the distribution and management of literature a separate function, not something your secretary or clerk does when he or she has some extra time.

Here are ten things to keep in mind when setting up your literature center.

- Have a completely separate room or area set aside for the task. Don't ask a secretary or group of secretaries to do the job in their normal work space. They will quickly run out of room and become overwhelmed. Handling and mailing multiple pieces of literature take space.
- Equip the literature center with shelves for stocking an ample supply of brochures. The best shelves are the metal type found in warehouses. Shelving allows workers to quickly find and pull the material they need. Do not store your working supply of literature in boxes; this makes the material hard to get at.
- Shelves, of course, hold a limited supply and have to be restocked at intervals. The bulk of your inventory is best stored in the original cardboard boxes in which it arrived from the printers. Be sure the literature center has enough room to stock these boxes. Stacking boxes against a wall in a large, open room is best because it allows easy access. A cramped closet makes it difficult to find and open the boxes you need.
- How big should your literature center be? Estimate the space you need to handle your current volume and multiply this number by three. That's the minimum area you'll need to handle your current and future volume. When estimating space requirements, consider all the things you'll need for your literature center. These things may include shelving, space for boxes, desks and chairs, a cabinet for storing office supplies, a computer (if you use a computerized inquiry management system), a postage meter, and a place to keep outgoing mail until the mail carrier arrives.

- The room should be dry, well lit, and kept at normal room temperature. Excess humidity and extreme temperature changes can cause printed material to wrinkle and fade.
- Determine how many people will work in the literature center at the same time. Then put in at least one additional desk. Promotional activities vary seasonally, and you should have space for temporary help when things get busy.
- Set up the literature center as a pleasant, efficient workplace. Workers should have everything they need within easy reach. If, for example, literature is to be bound into spiral or hard-spine notebooks, keep the binding machine in the literature center. Make sure the people can do their work with the least amount of movement and travel.
- Stock the literature center with an ample supply of all essential items. In addition to an inventory of promotional literature, this can include envelopes, stamps, postage meters, cardboard backings, paper clips, rubber bands, mail bags, address labels, form letters, notebooks, forms, pencils, pens, and computer supplies.
- Since there will be a steady flow of mail into and out of the literature center, try to locate the center near your mail room or some other point convenient to the post office or assigned mail pickup spot. Don't force employees to drag or cart heavy bundles of outgoing literature to a distant location for sorting and mailing.
- Ideally, one or more employees should work in the literature center full time. If workers complain that this is boring, you could rotate assignment to the literature center among available clerical personnel.

The main idea behind all this is to process leads and get the literature into the mail quickly and efficiently. Hot leads can cool off fast, and the longer you sit on your inquiries, the more business you lose. Speed is of the essence when it comes to turning leads into sales.

Expanding your literature program

As your organization grows, so will your need for literature. Many large companies have dozens of different publications on all facets of their business. Even small organizations can have multiple brochures or booklets.

There are two basic reasons to create and publish additional bulletins. The first is to explain something that isn't covered in current publications.

The second is because you feel the new brochure or booklet can help you promote your product, program, or cause more effectively than a single booklet can.

The Caterpillar Company, a maker of lift trucks, has an extensive sales literature program. Among its publications are the following:

- *Lift Truck Selection Guide.* A comprehensive overview of the entire line of Caterpillar lift trucks. The guide includes product specifications and guidelines for selection.
- *OSHA Requirements for Lift Trucks.* Explains the Occupational Safety and Health Act of 1970 as it relates to lift trucks and materials handling.
- *You Should See Us Now.* A publication that takes a look at Caterpillar lift truck manufacturing plants, personnel, and quality control.
- *Lift Truck Operator's Guide.* Covers lift truck fundamentals, operating conditions, and procedures. Includes a glossary of terms.
- *Lift Truck Mechanic's Guide.* Covers inspection, troubleshooting, preventive maintenance, components, and attachments.
- *Lift Truck Information Library.* A series of article reprints dealing with various aspects of lift trucks.
- *A Management Guide to Lift Trucks.* Lift truck purchasing guide aimed at upper management.
- *When You're Looking for a Used Lift Truck.* Tips on buying a used lift truck.
- *Lease Plan Selection Guide.* An overview of Caterpillar's various lease plans, plus tips on evaluating whether to lease or to purchase.
- *Why Some Lift Trucks Are Worth More Than Others.* A checklist of forty-nine items to look for when shopping for a lift truck.

Caterpillar, of course, has had many years in which to build and refine its literature program. Although it has many different brochures and booklets, it does not create new literature on a whim. Rather, each piece is designed to fill a specific niche in the company's marketing program.

You, too, should create new literature only when it is needed to fill a gap in your marketing program. Here are some situations that may warrant publication of a new piece.

New products. Your prospects need to be informed of new products, services, accessories, options, and models. Sales literature is often the best medium for bringing your prospects information about your firm's latest developments.

New applications. If you uncover a new application for an existing product, you may want to create a new brochure showing how the product can be used in this application.

New market. The best way to reach a group of prospects is to talk about their problems in their own language. If you uncover a new potential market for your product, you may need a new piece of literature specifically aimed at them.

Targeted communications. Maybe your brochure doesn't address the needs and interests of various buyers as strongly as it should. The solution might be to create separate pieces of literature aimed at specific audiences (top management, purchasing agents, wholesalers, retailers, consumers).

New message. Perhaps you want to say something new about your business. Old literature must be revamped, or new literature created, to get this message across to your audience.

Case histories. Every product success story is another piece of ammunition in your arsenal of sales and marketing weapons. You can publish new bulletins on case histories you feel are noteworthy or of special interest to your customers.

New information. Have you come up with a better way to use, select, size, fix, or maintain your product? Has your organization or someone in it done something that is especially newsworthy or exciting? You may need to publish new literature regularly to provide your audience with a steady stream of information, ideas, advice, and news. A newsletter is often the best vehicle for accomplishing this.

How to decide which projects are worthwhile

If your organization is typical, you won't have to go searching for opportunities to produce more literature. Rather, once your people see how useful your first brochure is, they'll come begging for more. You'll be bombarded with requests to produce all sorts of materials for a wide variety of top executives, salespeople, managers, divisions, branch offices, dealers, and departments.

Sounds great—until you stop to consider that each new brochure takes time and money to produce. Because both those resources have their limits, you must be selective in taking on new projects. You can produce some of those new brochures this year, but not all of them.

The merits of each proposed project must be evaluated, and you and your management team must come to a decision on which to proceed with and which to put on hold. Here are some of the questions you should ask when evaluating whether a suggested project is really worth pursuing.

➤ **Is it covered elsewhere?**
Check to see what you've already published on the subject. You may find that the topic is already covered adequately in your current literature. Perhaps you can even reprint a page from your current brochure or catalog as a separate flier instead of going through the expense and effort of creating a new piece from scratch.

➤ **Does it need its own vehicle?**
Does the topic really need its own piece of literature, or can it be absorbed into, or combined with, another publication? For example, a number of minor case histories can be featured in the company newsletter instead of being published as stand-alone bulletins. A product accessory can be marketed adequately by including it in the product brochure or catalog instead of creating a separate flier for it.

➤ **Is there enough interest in it?**
When someone comes to you with a request to create a new piece of literature, ask how many copies he or she will need. The answer will tell you whether the audience is large enough to justify the cost and expense. Any literature more elaborate than a one-page flier probably cannot be printed economically in a press run of under 1,000.

➤ **Is it important enough?**
A product with annual sales of $450 doesn't justify the cost of a $25,000 color brochure. The bulk of your promotional dollars should go to backing your winners, not your losers. It is not worth your while to produce literature on products that don't sell.

➤ **Is the request serious enough?**
Many managers don't think twice about putting in a request for a new brochure. They do not realize the time and money that it takes to produce quality literature. If they did, they wouldn't make their requests so lightly. Educate your management about the cost, time, and effort involved in each new project. This will cause them to be more selective in their requests for new literature.

➤ **Do you have the budget?**

Your printer, artist, or ad agency can quickly give you a rough estimate of the cost of the proposed literature. Do you have enough money in the budget to pay for it? Assuming you do, are you willing to spend that much? Also, remember that money is a limited resource; the launching of one project means some other project will have to be put on hold. Consider the relative importance of each proposed piece, and then set priorities.

➤ **Do you have the time?**

The person responsible for supervising the literature program has limited time. So does his or her staff, and there is a limit to the number of projects that can be tackled in a year. Again, consider the importance of each project, and set priorities. Do not take on more work than time allows. If you don't have time to complete essential projects, make greater use of outside vendors, and consider hiring more inside help.

➤ **Can it fit in?**

Is there a niche in your literature program into which you can fit the new project? Or does it encroach on the territory of existing literature? If there is conflict, perhaps the new piece is not needed because it deals with subjects already covered elsewhere, or perhaps the subject matter of the new piece must be redefined to give it a clearer direction.

➤ **Is there a more effective alternative?**

Promotional literature isn't always the answer to a marketing problem. Perhaps some other type of communication—a print ad, a press release, a speech, a sales letter, a videotape—can solve the problem more effectively. Don't rush into a brochure project. Take the time to consider the alternatives.

Measuring the effectiveness of your promotional literature

In direct mail, you can measure a mailing's success scientifically by counting the number of orders or leads it generates. But measuring the effectiveness of literature is more difficult because literature is only part of the sales and marketing effort. Therefore, its contribution to a sale is harder to isolate. Still, it is helpful to have some measure of a brochure's success or failure in the marketplace. Here are a few ways of making such measurements.

- Ask selected customers and salespeople to write short letters giving their opinions of your new literature program. Then carefully review what they've written. Although their comments are not a scientific measure of effectiveness, they can give you a lot of insight into how your literature is being received in the marketplace.
- Keep track of the number of brochures you distribute each year. This gives you a rough measure of whether people are interested in obtaining it.
- Survey brochure recipients. Develop a questionnaire, and survey a random sampling of prospects and customers by mail or phone. Ask if they received the literature, if they read it, if they remember it. Quiz them on specific facts to determine how well they remember what they have read. Ask their opinion of its format, usefulness, readability, and appearance. Tally the results, and see what conclusions you can draw.
- Build in a reply element and measure the returns. For example, let's say that the next step the reader should take after reading the brochure is to phone for an appointment with a salesperson. You can put a special code in the copy ("Ask for Department 16") so that you can determine how many incoming phone calls are a direct result of the brochure. The same technique can work for mail inquiries. Have the reader write to "Department 16" or some other key address so that you can measure which inquiries are a direct result of the brochure. If you bind reply cards into literature, code the cards so you know which piece of literature a particular card came from. This device gives you a crude tool for measuring the response to your literature. It is not a perfect tool; brochures do much more than just generate leads. But at least it gives you some idea of how many people have been moved to action by your literature.

Merchandising your literature program

One of my first successes as a fledgling publicity manager was getting a local paper to write a story about my company. The president of the firm was ecstatic. "Let's merchandise this article," he suggested to me. I didn't have the slightest idea of what he meant by that.

Now, of course, I do. I quickly learned that to *merchandise* a promotion means to get maximum exposure out of it by using it again and again, in many shapes and forms.

Let me clear this up with an example. When a newspaper or magazine publishes an article about a company, the article gives the company free—and, we'd hope, favorable—publicity. But unless you merchandise the article, the publicity is over once it is printed.

How can you merchandise an article? Well, the first step is to get reprints. The reprints could be handed to customers by salespeople and made available as reading material in the company's reception area. By circulating reprints, you gain a wider audience for the article than just the readers of the magazine in which it was published.

But don't stop there. You could create a direct-mail package consisting of the article reprint and a cover letter. The article could also serve as the basis for an advertisement. Perhaps it could be reprinted in the annual report. You can begin to see how, with merchandising, a single promotion does double and triple duty and more.

You can also merchandise the elements of your printed promotions (copy, artwork, illustrations, photos). This is a great way to stretch your literature budget. Let's say you are producing a new brochure on product X. You want to take new photographs of product X for the brochure but are shocked to discover that the cost of hiring a first-rate photographer for the day is $500.

Perhaps $500 is excessive for one brochure. But stop to consider how much mileage you can get out of this photo session. You can use the photos in so many other promotions, including slide presentations, press releases, trade show panels, the company newsletter, the annual report. When the cost is spread over all these projects, it seems much more reasonable.

Copy, too, can be merchandised. You may, for example, pay a top copywriter $1,000 to write a corporate ad campaign. But his or her copy, with minor modifications, can be used as the introduction to the annual brochure or as corporate *boiler plate* (a standard, approved written description of the company used in all printed literature). If you run the ad copy in ten different bulletins, the cost is only $100 per bulletin.

Look for ways to merchandise existing artwork, illustrations, photography, and copy. You'll save a bundle.

Here's one additional tip: You can also save money by using rejected art and copy for other projects. For example, your copywriter may submit five headlines for your new advertisement before you find one you like. Save those other headlines; maybe they can be used in other ads, on the cover of a brochure, or as the opening of a direct-mail piece.

In the same way, if you hire a photographer for a day, be sure the fee entitles you to keep the negatives for the entire day's work. Photos that you rejected for your new color brochure may be perfectly suitable for a quickie flier, a press release, or a newsletter.

Storing artwork and mechanicals

Artwork, mechanicals, films, and printing plates must be stored safely. Careless handling can ruin months of costly work.

The best place to keep your printing plates is with the printer. The printer has the space and facilities to store them safely and can fill orders for reprints faster because your plates are on the premises. Also, the printer will guarantee the condition of plates he or she stores but relinquishes responsibility once you take the plates with you.

Mechanicals and artwork should be stored flat on shelves or, better yet, in special cabinets designed for storing artwork. Do not pile mechanicals too high or the weight will bend the boards. Also, high stacks are likely to fall over, and mechanicals can be damaged in the fall. Make sure the surface of the board is protected with tissue overlays. If the overlays are missing or frayed, your artist can put on new ones. You might also wrap each board in a manila envelope for added protection.

Photo prints and negatives can be stored in ordinary manila file folders. Photo files should be arranged alphabetically by subject.

Slides can be stored in special plastic sheets. These sheets clip into three-ring binders. Special slide cabinets provide an even better solution. The slides are stored on a series of vertical metal racks that pull out for easy access. Many cabinets also have a pullout lighted panel to illuminate the slides. Be sure to mark on the frame of the slide which slides are originals and which are duplicates. For security, you may want to keep originals locked up in a separate place.

Numbers and codes

A special code, printed in tiny type on the back page of your literature, can be a great help in managing your literature program. To begin with, the code clearly identifies each separate piece. Let's say your company is called Clarkson Industries, and you manufacture power tools. The first brochure on your new power drill might be coded "CPD-B1," for "Clarkson Power Drill, Brochure no. 1." If you print a new version, it would be coded "CPD-B2," for Brochure no. 2.

You can also use codes to indicate publication date. The code "0181" tells you that the brochure was published in January (the first month) of 1981. But the customer, not knowing your code, won't be able to figure out the publication date. And that's a good thing; after all, you don't want readers to think your brochure is dated.

If some of your brochures have similar titles, there may be confusion about which brochure a prospect has requested. A coding system eliminates this confusion; when the customer requests "bulletin KS-9," you know precisely which piece of literature is wanted.

Is promotional literature obsolete?

Computers, arcade games, and music video aside, print isn't dead yet—and won't be for some time. Book sales are up, magazine circulation increases every year, and more newspapers are published today than at any time since World War II. Microprocessors, optical disks, and micrographics haven't changed the fact that the printed page is still the most powerful medium for disseminating information about products, services, programs, causes, ideas, and organizations.

This is not to say that high technology hasn't made an impact on the advertising world. Many new types of promotion are being tested every day. Here are some examples.

Electronic catalogs. Thanks to the combination of two-way interactive television and videotext, advertisers can now create electronic catalogs that are displayed on TV screens. The electronic pages contain graphics and text and can blink, move, change color, and be combined with sound. The customer uses a control box or keypad to flip through the catalog. The keypad can also be used to order a product or request more information electronically.

Video brochures. Industrial manufacturers have been using films to supplement printed brochures for years. Now consumer companies are getting into the act. Many companies are putting their sales pitches on videotape and sending these tapes to consumers as readily as they send printed brochures. Exercise equipment and other products that are easily demonstrated are ideal for this approach. And as VCR sales skyrocket, the use of the video brochure will increase.

Talking fliers. This technique has also been around for a while but now is becoming more widespread. The advertiser puts the sales message on a small plastic record or a cassette tape, then mails it to the customer or binds the record into a magazine opposite a print ad for the product.

Electronic mail. Reports, letters, and memos are now being sent over modems and telephone lines from one computer to another. Why not send price lists, product specifications, even computer-graphic drawings and promotional copy the same way? Advertisers may soon buy space on various *electronic bulletin boards* and data base services to transmit promotional messages in electronic form. These same messages could also be put onto floppy diskettes and mailed to customers or bound into the pages of a magazine.

New techniques and technologies should be tried, tested, and if they work, adopted. But keep in mind that 99.9 percent of the promotional material in circulation today is made of ink and paper. The printed word still chronicles the history of the world, moves people to action, and sells billions of dollars worth of goods, services, and ideas. If you can master the skills required to produce great promotional literature, both you and your organization will prosper for years to come.

Index

➢ **About the Author**

Robert W. Bly is an independent copywriter and consultant specializing in industrial and high-tech advertising. He has written copy for more than 50 advertising agencies and corporations, including Brooklyn Union Gas, Chemical Bank, J. Walter Thompson, Doremus & Company, Westinghouse, and RCA.

Mr. Bly is the author of eleven books, including *How to Promote Your Own Business* (New American Library) and *The Copywriter's Handbook* (Dodd, Mead). He has been published in such magazines as *Amtrak Express, Cosmopolitan, Writer's Digest, Computer Decisions, Direct Marketing,* and *Business Marketing.*

Bob Bly currently writes a column on catalog marketing for *The Business-to-Business Catalog Marketer,* a newsletter published by Maxwell Sroge. He also teaches copywriting at the New York University School of Continuing Education.